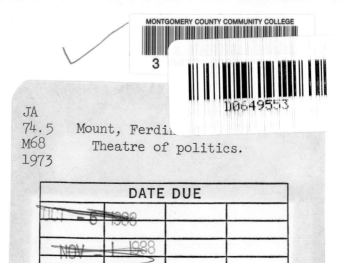
DATE DUE			
OCT - 6 1988			
NOV - 1 1988			
NOV - 1 1988			

THE
THEATRE OF
POLITICS

THE
THEATRE OF
POLITICS

FERDINAND MOUNT

Introduction by Max Lerner

SCHOCKEN BOOKS · NEW YORK

In Memory of Francis

First SCHOCKEN edition 1973

Copyright © 1972 by Ferdinand Mount
Introduction Copyright © 1973 by Schocken Books Inc.

Library of Congress Catalog No. 73-78297
Manufactured in the United States of America

Contents

Introduction:
Political Theater in America

by Max Lerner

It is natural for a British writer to hit on the central insight of this book—that modern politics is shot through with the theatric, and can be understood best only if we view the exchange between political actor and political audience as theater. For British politics has carried rhetoric, eloquence, and the sheer use of language very far. Even more, the actual British theater has developed a brand of acting which combines subtlety, tradition, and showmanship to a degree that Americans must envy. Thus Ferdinand Mount writes as the heir to a double heritage, of actual and political theater in British history.

In embracing the metaphor that politics is theater the author rejects three others—that it is a battle, a pilgrimage (progress toward an ideal goal), and a science. Americans are obsessed with still two others. One is that it is a game, as witness "the great game of politics," and the use of "game plan" and "game theory" to encompass a whole range of rivalries, from football tactics to the intricacies of nuclear strategy. The other is that it is a transaction in the acquisitive market of psychic and power satisfactions (see Harold Lasswell's *Politics: Who Gets What, When, How*).

Yet for the author the theater of politics is a good deal more than a literary metaphor. The "theatrical element running through all politics," he writes, "is central and ubiquitous," and "those who assert the contrary do so largely out of mistrust of the judgment of the masses."

Thus the book aims at a "new theory of politics," a basic set of assumptions about how men arrange power, achieve order, and oversee change through the running dialogue of political communication seen as theater. If you don't think a real dialogue is possible (the author is saying throughout) it must be because you don't have faith that the audience (the people) can hold up their end of it, be changed by it, and bring about changes also in the actor-leaders. Totalitarian politics lacks that faith in the people, so that it may offer spectacle but no real theater, rehearsed scripts but no communication.

This is not a book which is constructed massively and logically of tier on tier of building blocks. It grows by a succession of elaborations and embroideries of the central insight. To change the figure, we go off on a number of scents, getting an alluring whiff each time—of the "theater of embarrassment," the "theater of novelty," the "theater of sentiment," the uses of rhetoric and eloquence, the use and abuse of the language of politics. With each sortie the argument takes on an added richness, so that one ends with the sense not of having completed a set of geometrical proofs but of having been on an exhilarating exploration, whose aim was less to review the old answers than to put new questions.

As one would expect, the author is centrally involved with the British political scene, using Harold Macmillan or Harold Wilson to point a moral or adorn a tale, much as an American writer would use John Kennedy or Richard Nixon. From his own position as a moderate or liberal Conservative he carries on a running intellectual battle with the Marxists on the Labor Left and with the extreme Right of the Conservatives.

But luckily he also has the whole European tradition to roam through in picking his illustrations. Thus while he gives us shrewd portraits of Disraeli and Churchill we also get glimpses into that master theatrical figure, Charles de Gaulle. While he quotes tellingly from Walter Bagehot and Edmund Burke, he also keeps coming back to Alexis de Tocqueville. (Although I count myself anything but a conservative, I must confess that these three European political thinkers have a feel for the continuities of the political organism which most American liberal writers could benefit from.) But the *tour de force* of the book for me is in the pages that light up Moliere's *The Misanthrope* as a drama of true believers against realists in the politics of today.

An American, watching the theater of politics on his own Continent, will be aware that it is brasher, louder, noisier, flashier, more exhibitionistic than in Britain. To get a kaleidoscope of its theatrical enactments, start with the Roosevelt days of the bank holiday, the New Deal, the court-packing plan, the twilight meeting at Yalta, and the President's death at Warm Springs in the setting of a romantic liaison. Go on to the bombs at Los Alamos and Hiroshima, the Hiss trials, and the firing of General MacArthur under Truman. Then, under Eisenhower, to the tortured dominance of McCarthyism, the McCarthy-Army hearings that ended it, the Little Rock confrontation, the ►

aborted summit at Paris. The Kennedy tenure is of course bounded by the Bay of Pigs, the Berlin wall, the Cuban missile crisis, and the assassination. The Johnson tenure vies with it in theater, starting with the oath of office administered in the bloodied setting of Air Force One out of Dallas, continuing with the assassinations of Malcolm X, Martin Luther King, and Robert Kennedy, the bloody street riots and burnings of the cities, and ending with the withdrawal of LBJ from the political arena and with the encounter between demonstrators and police at the Chicago convention.

Surely no Administration that followed could parallel these as political theater. Yet the Nixon years proved anything but anticlimax. Consider the My Lai revelations and the Calley trial, the Cambodian decision, the Kent State shootings, the publication of the Pentagon Papers, the Presidential trips to Peking and Moscow, the astounding Nixon-Kissinger partnership, the mining of Haiphong and the saturation bombing of North Vietnam, and—to top them all—the Watergate scandals and the whole train of consequences they brought in their wake.

Political theater is a form of dialogue between rulers and demos, as the author insists throughout this book. But when the drama becomes as intense, paradoxical, and *theatrical* as it has been in America, the whole dialogue is heightened and takes place in a context at once emotion-laden and distorted.

An observer who has, like myself, sought to be a civilization watcher, cannot help feeling that the element of theater on the American scene has gone beyond politics and pervaded the entire society. It has become history-as-theater. That may be why this book's basic theme came to me with a ring of the inevitable. I had felt for some time, in studying the deep thrusts of evolutionary social change in American society in the 1960s, that these changes were a form of theater, and that we who have lived through such times have been compelled to re-examine our own role, the role of our leaders, and the image of our society.

Hence the concept of "role playing," used widely among American sociologists and psychologists, all the way from Charles Horton Cooley's concept of the "self" in relation to society, through Erik Erikson's dramatic sequence of "identity crises" in the life history of each of us, to Eric Berne's charting of the explicit little interpersonal dramas in "the games people play." These are all individual psychodramas. Ferdinand Mount's concept of political theater broadens it into an interplay between the leaders and the public—the leaders as chief actors, caught between their personal visions of society and their professional need to satisfy the voters, and the public functioning at once as audience and a kind of critical Greek chorus.

Viewing the enactments of our time as theater, we are often puzzled to find the right name for the genre. What kind of theater, for example, were the Watergate scandals in President Nixon's second Administration? It wasn't hard to type the political theater of the Teapot Dome scandals of the Harding Administration: they were straight cowboys-and-Indians frontier drama, with some bedroom farce on the margin, in the form of Nan Britton and the "President's daughter." But Watergate was more difficult.

It was too painfully real to be good suspense make-believe. While there were farcical elements in the cops-and-robbers charade at the Democratic campaign headquarters, it was too tragic to be farce. Yet it was too farcical to be tragedy. Besides, there was a grotesque disproportion between the immensity of events and their consequences, and the blinkered, huckstering, empty men who took the active leads. This made it for many, ultimately, the theater of the absurd.

One might also settle on Watergate being a peculiar American version of a Greek tragedy, with much of the tragic march of inevitability as the story unfolded. If this was the genre, then Richard Nixon was the tragic protagonist—the only one in the cast with anything like the stature for it—with his flawed character and his threatened vision of a new grand strategy in foreign policy.

The trouble about political theater, compared with other forms of theater, lies in the line between illusion and reality. In other forms you have to imagine that the fiction is real, and the admission price you pay to play the game is the suspension of disbelief. Paying that price you have to pinch yourself to remember that the action is made up. In the American political theater of the past decade—given events like the assassinations, the burnings of the cities, the confrontations on street or campus, the Chicago convention clubbings, the Kent State shootings, the Watergate corruptions—the reality is so awesome that it seems either dream or nightmare, and you have to pinch yourself to remember it is *not* a contrived fiction, *not* made up.

The author quotes Tocqueville on the 1848 Revolution in France: "a vile tragedy played by a provincial troupe." It could have been a mordant commentary, more than a century early, on Watergate. Obviously there are degrees of the tragic in politics and diverse angles of vision from which it is viewed. To Edmund Burke, in whose writings the author is soaked and whom he quotes with striking effect, the

French Revolution was high tragedy, but not to Robespierre and Marat. To us Abraham Lincoln's death was tragic; to his actor-assassin Lincoln was a mountebank and tyrant, and the tragedy lay in Lincoln's betrayal of the chivalry of the South to the cause of the blacks.

The author's central concept of political drama is that of the free and lively dialogue between leaders and people. At times this doesn't go much beyond what we call by the already vapid term of "communication." But to him it is far from vapid. It carries with it the whole political process. It is for lack of such free communication that he sees totalitarian regimes as poisoned at the source.

Mount is conservative, in the Burkean sense, in refusing to make a cult of social change and in stressing the long continuities of history which have left a deposit in the minds of the majorities. "The cattle," he remarks drily, "outnumber the grasshoppers, both in number and in substance." He is also conservative in a corollary belief: that it is better to go by what people actually think is good for them than by what they ought to think according to some *a priori* dogma; and that "whether or not people do know what is good for them, they will sooner or later get their own way unless prevented by force." And there is a radical note in his belief that, right or wrong, they have a right to have their own way.

It is in the more dramatic crisis leaders that political theater carries with it the liveliest dialogue. Since America today has a more massive power base than any European nation, its crisis leaders—like the first Roosevelt, Wilson, the second Roosevelt, Truman, Eisenhower, Kennedy, Johnson, and Nixon—have played theatrical roles freighted with high consequence, not only for America but for the world.

"Teddy" Roosevelt had a high-charged crackling energy, and a belief in himself, which turned every political battle into an Armageddon. He was, someone remarked, a cross between St. George and St. Vitus. His theater was the heroic frontier drama. Woodrow Wilson, outwardly the scholar in politics, was inwardly a messianic crusader who was so sure of his pipeline to God that the line between the Almighty and himself became blurred. His political theater was always a morality play. Franklin Roosevelt was a patrician Gracchus who placed himself at the head of the antibourgeois mass, yet in retrospect—despite his rhetoric about the "money-changers in the Temple"—his measures saved the business power-structure against which he inveighed, just as America's role in World War II kept a world power-structure viable against the threat of the "thousand-year Reich." His theater was realism peppered with racy dialogue.

Harry Truman was the ordinary man in the Presidency, but an

extraordinary ordinary man. He raised common sense to the language of high politics, and his plays at their climactic moments always used the plain speech of the people. Both Truman and Eisenhower embodied the morality of the frontier: Truman the homely virtue of self-reliance, Eisenhower the homely virtue of trust. As "Ike" he was the personification of trust, and he exploited to the full his self-assumed role "above politics," which placed him (with a skill equal to that of the political pro's) right in the center of politics. His political theater was high corn, part of what the author calls the "theater of sentiment."

If the second Roosevelt and Eisenhower both played father roles, John Kennedy played the young son who had become head of the family after the death of the father. His theater was breezy, vigorous, muscular—a kind of brittle melodrama that turned into tragedy when he was cut down. Lyndon Johnson's was pistol-packing cowboy drama, in which he tried to combine the roles of the wheeling-dealing cardsharp at home and the intervening sheriff abroad—and it didn't work. Richard Nixon played the corner-cutting heavy in most of his career, then tried to switch roles to that of the high-minded hero with a Grand Design for world politics, but his earlier role caught up with his later one at Watergate.

In a civilization as complex, pluralistic, and fragmented as the American, political theater is essential for effective leadership. "Let us reason together," Adlai Stevenson used to say, and Lyndon Johnson borrowed the phrase from him. But political communication isn't all reasoning, just as it isn't all theater. Some of it—not much—is logic, and here a lawyer like Richard Nixon (the first lawyer in the Presidency since Franklin Roosevelt, who wasn't much of a lawyer) found scope for his talent in turning legal briefs into speeches.

Much of it, as the author points out, is rhetoric, and some of it is oratory. Both are forms of play-acting where each side agrees to puff up the reality into hyperbole. Adlai Stevenson was a good rhetorician, as Woodrow Wilson and Franklin Roosevelt were. All three were fine speakers, although not first-rate orators. Among Presidential candidates the last great orators were Robert La Follette and William Jennings Bryan. Americans lost the art of great oratory after the Civil War, and never recaptured the impassioned rhythms and the ecstacy of argument of Clay, Calhoun, and Webster. The British kept the art longer, as witness Lloyd George, Churchill, and Aneurin Bevan. Whatever the reasons for the erosion, television—which demands a "cool" profile—has completed the process.

There remain myth and myth-making, which the author treats brilliantly. Myth becomes necessary when the reality is so strong or difficult that only the imagination, working with the symbolic, can grasp or define it. The Communists tend to turn their politics largely into myth so that it will not be subject to cold analysis. In America the tragic has become mythic, as with Lincoln's life and death. But except for their wars and assassinations, Americans have proved uneasy with politics as myth. They are unlikely to have the kind of relation to a leader-myth that the French had with De Gaulle or the Chinese with Mao. The time of heroes is past in America, perhaps in France and Great Britain too, and while it means that the audience will no longer be so credulous about its overweening actors, I can't help feeling that something will have been lost in the process.

Robespierre could live saying, 'The republic
of Virtue without la terreur *is disaster,'*
saying, 'Loot the châteaux, *spare Saint Antoine,'*
saying to Danton, 'I'll love you till I die,'
Clean prisons! They learned the guillotine is painless –
La Révolution, *her old Jacobin saying:*
'The theater must remain and remain theater,
play for the traditional, barren audience orgy,
play back the Revolution . . .' Ask the true voyeur
what blue movie is worth a seat at the keyhole . . .
Even the prompted Louis Seize was living theater,
sternly but lovingly judged by critics, who knew
a Mozart's insolent slash at folk could never
cut the gold thread of the suffocating curtain.

Robert Lowell: Robespierre and
Mozart as Stage, from *Notebook*.

Prologue

La commedia è finita. With the words usually given to the clown in Pagliacci, Harold Macmillan took his leave of the political stage in 1963. Vicky, the sharpest cartoonist of the age, had portrayed Macmillan not as a clown but rather as the ageing variety artist, the entertainer of John Osborne's play. Yet both artist and subject agreed in seeing this man, who had a longer spell in power than any British prime minister for forty years, as a showman, deft, resilient and patter-perfect.

During the presidency of John Kennedy, the musical *Camelot* was all the rage. It is not surprising that a parallel should have been drawn between King Arthur and his court and the Washington of this young war hero and his lovely wife. But one might have expected this parallel to be confined to women's magazines and the more feather-headed supporters of the regime. But not at all. The metaphor was widely used by serious columnists. And those inside the White House itself, not excluding the Kennedys, lost no opportunity to illuminate and embellish the picture; the visits of famous savants, Nobel prize-winners and their ilk, the musical *soirées*, even the redecoration of the White House in exquisite taste, all combined into an image of

> . . . the island-valley of Avilion;
> Where falls not hail, or rain, or any snow,
> Nor ever winds blows loudly.

So patent and so costly were the efforts required to weave this glowing tapestry that even those who were enthralled by the effect could not pretend ignorance of the techniques employed to weave it by the nimble fingers of Madison Avenue.

Or again, picture the newsmen squeezed into little gilt chairs in the frosty elegance of the Elysée Palace. In the deep midwinter, once a year, the general would speak. The very rarity of the performance deepened the hush. How carefully the questions were planted and how carefully the general answered them! His syntax was a little richer and his phrasing a little cloudier than in his appeals to the nation on television; for this was a *tour d'horizon*, the grandeur of which must not be impaired by any bathetic detail. For years this performance was repeated; the words followed the same pattern, but the newsman's ear strove to catch the fresh nuances, the differences in tone and emphasis, like a playgoer who never misses a new Hamlet. And when this Hamlet finally departed what hastened his departure but another drama? A performance of a different sort, this one; Raymond Aron[1] called it a psycho-drama. It may not have been 'les événements de Mai–Juin 1968' which finally finished de Gaulle, but it was these events which made his style begin to seem faded and no longer relevant or responsive to the age. Even those who considered the goings-on in the courtyards of the Sorbonne self-indulgent, childish and ultimately destructive could not deny their theatrical impact. How irresistible the promise of endless free-flowing dialogue – witty, sincere and warm! How dazzling the contrast between the stuffy lecture rooms and the fresh faces who had captured them! How crass and brutish the riot police! Above all, how overwhelming to see those theories of liberty *acted out* on a small, enclosed and theatrically perfect stage instead of being obscured by academic jargon on the printed page!

Aron says:

I do not use the term 'psychodrame' without modification. But nevertheless, we have all been acting a part during this period. I took on the role of de Tocqueville; this has its ridiculous side, but others were playing Saint-Just, Robespierre or Lenin, which all in all was even more ridiculous.[2]

Tocqueville himself writes of the 1848 Revolution:

The whole time I had the feeling that we had staged a play about the French Revolution, rather than that we were continuing it. . . . Though I foresaw the terrible end to the piece well enough, I could not take the actors very seriously; the whole thing seemed a vile tragedy played by a provincial troupe.[3]

Melodramatic political events suggest analogies with the theatre; equally, the theatre suggests political lines of attack. Robert Brustein, dean of the Yale Drama School, gives a good account of how the Living Theatre group 'spontaneously' employed storm-trooper tactics to break up a meeting organised to discuss their own aims.[4] To glory in such a conscious fusing of politics and the theatre is increasingly common. 'The play's the thing', says Abbie Hoffman, the leader of the 'Yippies'. When Roel van Duyn, the inventor of the Dutch Gnomes/Pixies, was elected to the Amsterdam City Council, he treated council procedure as pure theatre:

> After all it *was* a theatre. Everyone had a fixed role; all decisions were taken in advance; there was no real debate; and nobody listened to anybody else. So I decided to do consciously what the others did unconsciously. I acted a part – my own little role.[5]

The Radicals believe that their staged confrontations with authority are the only authentic gestures possible in face of a universally repressive society, that theatrical daring is the only way to break up the conventional moulds of political structures and attitudes. The Tocquevilles and Brusteins say that this is all mere play-acting. For them the Radicals appear to be children taking refuge in fantasy from a world with which they are too weak to cope. Brustein says:

> What this violent talk signifies is that American revolutionaries are impotent to act, and that they lack an ideology entirely, though they are hardly lacking in passions – thus, the weakness for rhetoric and gestures rather than programs and organization. The result is not revolution but rather theatre – a product of histrionic personalities and staged events.[6]

Yet surely the same might have been said of 'real' revolutionaries and 'real' revolutions. Might not Tocqueville have found 1789 an equally vile tragedy played by an equally provincial troupe?

It is hard to recall or imagine a successful revolution which has not contained a strong theatrical element. Nor indeed is this element confined to revolutionary situations. This present study starts from a viewpoint opposed both to the Tocquevilles and Brusteins and to the gnomes, panthers and yippies. We do not accept either the view that the theatrical gesture is the only way to break out of the set moulds of conventional politics or the view that the theatrical gesture is a sign of bad politics, a sure indication that the art of government is being botched and its ends perverted. Our aim here, by contrast, is to study the theatrical element running through *all* political activity; to elaborate its implications for politicians and the public; and to enquire what this theatricality tells us about the nature of politics.

Many political scientists are very reluctant to accept the notion that there is such a theatrical element running through all politics. They are inclined to dismiss the idea as superficial, indeed as little better than the case of the parliamentary sketch-writer who, hard up for a metaphor, describes the Palace of Westminster as 'the Palace of

Varieties' or the government as 'the Whitehall follies'. Certainly, it may be said, a politician has to woo the electorate on the public stage; but that is only a small part of politics. The real business is decision-taking. And decisions are taken in smoke-filled rooms, in secret cabinets, in party committees, in meetings between politicians and vested interest groups. It is from these encounters – and the diaries, memoranda and letters which record them – that we must draw our analysis of the structure of party and government, of the process of history and of the nature of politics. We must use the hard evidence too – the voting records and the sociological statistics which summarise the intentions and the condition of the people. But for the political scientist, public rituals and speeches are usually either empty or misleading. There is little useful information to be gained from them unless we can cross-check with more reliable documentary evidence.

To attach any greater importance to them is on this view to make the mistake of imagining that, in Bagehot's terms, the 'dignified' aspect of the political process is more important than the 'efficient'. Bagehot himself says:

It is very natural, therefore, that the most useful parts of the structure of government should by no means be those which excite the most easy reverence. The elements which excite the most easy reverence will be the *theatrical* elements – those which appeal to the senses, which claim to be embodiments of the greatest human ideas, which boast in some cases of far more than human origin. That which is mystic in its claims; that which is occult in its mode of action; that which is brilliant to the eye; that which is seen vividly for a moment, and then is seen no more; that which is hidden and unhidden; that which is specious, and yet interesting, palpable in its seeming, and yet professing to be more than palpable in its results; this, howsoever its form may change, or however we may define it or describe it, is the sort of thing – the only sort – which yet comes home to the mass of men.[7]

Though elsewhere he steers an uneasy course between distaste for the theatrical and recognition of its necessity in some sense for the authority and hence stability and continuity of government, at bottom his Victorian practicality revolts against mumbo-jumbo. Bagehot would be amused by but reproving of 'the selling of the president' as practised today. Both the *suppressio veri* and the *suggestio falsi* of political selling do, of course, deserve moral reproof; yet the reproof both of Bagehot and of Joe McGinniss[8] is given not on these grounds but because 'this . . . is the sort of thing – the only sort – which yet comes home to the mass of men'. The lowest orders are 'likely to care least and judge worst about what *is* useful'. Or, as Halifax puts it, even more condescendingly: 'Monarchy is liked by the People, for the Bells and the Tinsel, the outward Pomp and Gilding, and there must be milk for babes, since the greatest part of Mankind are, and ever will be included in that List.'[9] In other words, the political confidence trick, whether monarchic or presidential, oligarchic or democratic, whether necessary or unnecessary, is at any rate effective, because most people are foolish and gullible. This belief is to be encountered throughout the political spectrum, from Halifax to Stalin. But is it true? Is political history the record of a mass of mugs being taken for a series of rides?

The flaw in the argument of McGinniss and those commentators who have adopted the same easy cynicism is that President Nixon, for example, has remained unlikeable; the most expensive political cosmetics have failed to beautify him; he has never gained any of the charisma that appears to come so easily to such diverse political leaders as the Kennedys, Peron, Soekarno, Kenyatta, and so on. His image remains as it was before the face-lift – that of a dogged, diligent politician, acutely sensitive to currents of opinion, adept in party management, 'flexible', 'unprincipled' or 'tricky Dicky' according to the viewpoint of the observer. Why should such an image not mirror the reality? Naturally the publicist's aim is to make his candidate conform as closely as possible to a Platonic ideal of warmth and eloquence, as well as moral and physical beauty. But even if the subject himself does not prove recalcitrant, the reality shows through; witness the failure of attempts to 'humanise' Edward Heath through his sailing activities and Dr Adenauer through his family games of *boule*; their gifts of public humanity have remained obstinately inferior to those of Harold Wilson and Herr Brandt. This showing through of reality might be supposed to depend upon a vigorous free press and a mature tradition of political debate; no doubt these are assets, but the absence of any rivals to the government propaganda channels did not succeed in making such dictators as Novotny and Ulbricht universally popular. It seems perverse to assume the inevitable success of deceptive propaganda when there are plenty of more pedestrian explanations available for a given political event – rising prices, unemployment, and so on. President Nixon's victory in 1968, narrow and unspectacular as it was, rested on a combination of straightforward political factors – the Democrats' failure to win or end the war in Vietnam; the unpopularity of President Johnson and by association of Mr Humphrey; inflation; a hint of recession; the feeling that Nixon had matured somewhat; and so on. Of course, Nixon's camp used every art to highlight these factors. No politician abjures for long the use of convenient means of putting himself across; witness the speedy conversion of the Nonconformist British Labour Party to the use of professional though unpaid admen in election campaigns. To say this is not to accuse politicians of resorting to unfair or illegal tricks; there is clearly a great difference between, say, the impersonation of voters, or the propagation of libellous personal statements which cannot be refuted until after the votes have been cast, and the powdering out of President Nixon's blue jowl. No, all that this amounts to is that the mechanic does not refuse a more convenient type of spanner when it comes on the market.

At the same time there would be nothing wrong in confusing the hyperbole of the hustings with deep-laid villainous plots if such a confusion did not tend to produce a misleading picture of what politicians are and should be about. For the idea that there is a *real* (efficient, useful) politics which is masked by an *unreal* (superficial) sham show is one of the most potent delusions of our time. This is the delusion which is reflected palely in Bagehot's distinction between 'dignified' and 'efficient', luridly and violently in Marx's distinction between what we (bourgeois parliamentarians) think is happening and what is really happening, and palely again in the modern journalist's distinction between the 'real' politician with his 'real' policies and the politician and policies as presented through the mass media.

Our intention here is to examine not merely the theatrical element running through all politics, but to show that this element is not something which is, so to speak, tacked on afterwards, but something which is both central and ubiquitous. Moreover, it will be a constant theme that those who assert the contrary do so largely out of a distrust of the judgment of 'the masses'. If one believes that people on the whole do know what is good for them, then playing to the gallery is an honourable and essential part of the politician's task; if people do not in general know what is good for them, then the satisfaction of their wishes cannot be a sufficient criterion of political success, although it may be a necessary condition of staying in power.

If pleasing the electorate is an activity distinct from and subsequent to political debate about what is right and possible and from subsequent decision, then it becomes an activity which is also inferior to such debate and discussion; it is 'mere public relations' or 'playing politics'. Such an association of ideas is inevitable; for if the theatrical element is central and ubiquitous, then a major role on the political stage must be conceded to the actual opinions of the public.

The myths and rituals which a regime has allowed or, more usually, encouraged to grow up around itself often reveal something very significant about the real nature of that regime – the essentially populist, good-humoured, consensual nature of Macmillan's Toryism, the aristocratic, activist liberalism of the Kennedys, the autocracy of de Gaulle, which retained its power by a minimal display of that power, by a careful husbanding of political resources. This is not to say that 'the medium is the message' – a woefully vague proposition. But the *implicit* content of a public political event, its style, is extremely important. Indeed, it would be odd if the style were not important when so much trouble has been taken to produce exactly this style, and not another.

But what of the explicit content of the event, that is to say the actual words and deeds of the protagonist? Here again a great deal of trouble has been taken to do or say exactly this and not that. In the case of de Gaulle, we saw a great deal of precision and forethought in the way he formulated his attitude and developed it in public over the years. At each point we knew exactly as much of his mind as he wished us to know; but (to anticipate the cynic's objection) that portion of his thinking which was revealed was truthfully revealed. Every British politician, for example, should have known how de Gaulle's mind was working on the question of Britain's entry into the Common Market before the veto of January 1963. It may be said that de Gaulle was a special case; his clarity of mind and speech were exceptional. Well, then, let us take another case: the inaugural speeches of some recent American presidents, distinguished by clarity neither of thought nor of expression. From each of these speeches one or two sentences are seized on immediately and engraved as the motto of that presidency both during its life and for posterity. This is no accident. Such phrases do express the essence of the presidency they introduce – and deliberately so. They express in verbal form the collision between the temperament and intention

9

of the new president (and his friends and advisers) on the one side, and the mood and circumstances of the times on the other.

President Nixon said in his inaugural speech:

> To lower our voices would be a simple thing. In these difficult years, America has suffered from a fever of words: from inflated rhetoric that promises more than it can possibly deliver . . . we cannot learn from one another until we stop shouting at one another – until we speak quietly enough so that our words can be heard as well as our voices . . . we cannot expect to make everyone our friend, but we can try to make no one our enemy.

What a sharp and deliberate contrast this low-key, soothing, attentive approach makes with President Kennedy eight years earlier:

> Let every nation know, whether it wish us well or ill, that we shall pay any price, bear any burden, meet any hardship, support any friend or oppose any foe in order to assure the survival and success of liberty . . . ask not what your country will do for you. Ask what you can do for your country.

These famous phrases accurately summarise the conscious reaction of Kennedy Democrats against what they regarded as the inertia of the Eisenhower years. An active foreign policy and an energetic interventionism at home resulted from this general predisposition. Nor is the contrast between Kennedy and Nixon an isolated example of a public event epitomising a political era. The whole tone of the Johnson administration was laid down by what was virtually his inaugural, his speech to both Houses of Congress just after President Kennedy's murder; the key phrase in that speech was 'Let us continue'. President Truman's inaugural had one obsessive theme, the threat of Communism. And of course Roosevelt's first inaugural set the *tone* of the New Deal and explained it far more precisely than any summary of its achievements: 'Let me assert my firm belief that the only thing we have to fear is fear itself.' That is to say, the New Deal years were not characterised by a great improvement in the economic situation or the condition of the people; it took the second world war to bring back full employment and economic growth. But a certain feeling of returning confidence did run through those years. Roosevelt's public works and welfare programmes were not so much important in themselves as they were tokens of a feeling that the existing political system might yet prove capable of responding to crisis. And it is clear that this particular tone had to be established from the outset. If Roosevelt had disappointed hopes in his first inaugural, he would have found it much harder to establish his peculiar presidential profile of ebullience and intimacy. He might not indeed have had a second inaugural.

And how close and sturdy is the link between the event and the mood of the times! A speech delivered at one time may strike us as relevant, even inspiring; at another, the same speech would seem flat, irrelevant, inappropriate. And this is not because the physical social realities (the distribution of wealth, the standards of legal justice or administrative equity, the degree of universal opportunity, etc.) have changed, but simply because the concerns, expectation, hopes and fears of the people have shifted, whether subtly or violently, into a new pattern. We are accustomed to talk, for example, of the great changes that came over America between 1960 and 1968. Yet the economic and political structure of the United States had not greatly changed; nor had the profile of income distribution. The crucial changes were in the public mood. And the contrasting responses of Kennedy and Nixon were nicely calculated. Similarly, take President Truman's words of 1949:

> The United States and other like-minded nations find themselves directly opposed by a regime with contrary aims and a totally different concept of life. That regime adheres to a false philosophy which purports to offer freedom, security, and greater opportunity to mankind. Misled by this philosophy, many peoples have sacrificed their liberties only to learn to their sorrow that deceit and mockery, poverty and tyranny are their reward. That false philosophy is Communism.

Such an *explicit* denunciation would sound crude if delivered today. The mood has changed, but have the physical social realities changed so very much? How different is the nature of the Soviet regime and of Soviet foreign policy under Brezhnev from what it was under Stalin in 1948–9? And is there much difference between then and now in the proportion of her wealth which America devotes to defence against the Soviet threat? Nor have the vast majority of Americans ceased to believe in the threat of Communism, or in the superiority of their own 'way of life' to the Soviet way of life; they have merely heard enough discussion of these themes, and ceased to listen. It is a fallacy to imagine that a politician's first necessity is power. Certainly he strives for power with all his might. But his first need is *to gain the attention of his audience;* and his continuing need is to hold that attention. A playwright whose plays are never performed has failed. Academic dramaturges who stage dramas (often in verse) which were never performed in the author's lifetime usually prove only the good sense of the author's contemporaries.

In the same way, a politician who cannot gain or keep an audience is no politician at all. Without an audience there is no play. President Nixon is by temperament and the accidents of his political history a man far more caught up in and interested by the philosophical differences between the American and the Soviet systems than Truman was. And while the circumstances of his inauguration may not have been as stormy as those of 1949, we should recall that he was speaking only a few months after the invasion of Czechoslovakia and the enunciation of the Brezhnev doctrine. Yet all Nixon had to say on this general topic was:

After a period of confrontation, we are entering an era of negotiation. Let all nations know that during this administration our lines of communication will be open. We seek an open world – open to ideas, open to the exchange of goods and people, a world in which no people, great or small, will live in angry isolation.

We do not need to predicate 'a new Nixon', as American commentators are fond of doing. We simply need to understand the importance of the public event. We have to realise that in assessing such an event we are freezing a whole scene, as the Victorian *tableau vivant* used to do, or as a still from a film does. But there is a difference. Here the audience is frozen too. We are seizing not just the actors and scenery but the whole theatre in an instant of political time. And this single moment in a continuing drama may catch people in unfamiliar, untypical attitudes as the camera does – the half-smile on the curmudgeon's face, a confident nation in a mood of self-doubt, the veteran of the Hiss case in conciliatory mood.

The public event is not isolated from its context. More often than not, it is a response to pressure. For example, both before and after taking office, Harold Wilson repeatedly pledged himself in public to maintain the parity of sterling. If he had not done so there would have been an immediate run on the pound. The doctrines of the Labour Party contain no commitment to fixed parities: rather the reverse – Socialist economists of the school of Lord Balogh and Professor Kaldor tend on the whole to favour flexible rates of exchange. Yet the public pledge, given by political necessity, eventually came to form the central theme of the economic policy of the Wilson government; 'selling sterling short' was denounced as the worst crime in the book. When finally devaluation was forced upon the government in November 1967, it could not be represented as a mere technical adjustment; it was a political failure, almost a betrayal. In an effort to put a better face upon this setback, Wilson made his famous broadcast in which he claimed that devaluation did not mean that 'the pound in your pocket' had been devalued.* This second public event had two consequences; it was a gift to the Tory campaign to discredit Harold Wilson as a trickster, for the statement was in one sense plainly untrue; but also, in order to sustain the thesis that Britain had not suffered a disaster, Wilson had to soften the measures of internal deflation which should classically accompany devaluation. This helped to delay the beneficial results of devaluation which would have done much to give him victory in a general election in 1970 or 1971. It is possible to dispute the emphasis in this chain of circumstance. But there is no doubt that these two public events – the pledge to defend sterling, and the 'pound in your pocket' broadcast – are of crucial significance for any discussion of how Labour lost power.

Now note the difference between Harold Wilson's two statements. In the first case, he made a pledge which he honestly intended to keep; in the second, he gave an interpretation of the situation which was generally thought to be intellectually dishonest. After the events, commentators agreed that he should have been dishonest in the first case (he had to promise to defend the parity, but he should have been ready to break the promise without hesitation when circumstances demanded it) but that in the second case it would have been more politic to place the facts honestly before the public. In other words, there was no simple moral rule to guide his conduct in the two situations. Nor do the experts generally contend that either event was inevitable; Harold Wilson was well able politically to choose the way in which he faced the two practical necessities – to reassure foreign holders of sterling and to explain devaluation to the public.

The speech in which President Nixon announced the virtual devaluation of the dollar (15 August 1971) makes an instructive comparison. The words used were not dissimilar to those of Harold

---

* The actual words were: 'From now the pound is worth 14 per cent or so less in terms of other currencies. It does not mean, of course, that the pound here in Britain, in your pocket or your purse, or in your bank, has been devalued.' (20 November 1967.)

Wilson: 'Let me lay to rest the bugaboo of devaluation. What does this action mean for you? If you want to buy a foreign car, or take a trip abroad, market conditions may cause your dollar to buy slightly less. But if you are among the overwhelming majority who buy American-made products in America, your dollar will be worth just as much tomorrow as it is today.' But the context was totally different. Foreign trade is far less important to the United States than it is to Britain. The balance of payments had not become an occasion of public debate and therefore of anxiety to ordinary families; the attention of the American public was concentrated upon President Nixon's domestic measures – the reductions in taxation and public expenditure, the freezes on prices and wages. These measures were generally well received. Naturally the Nixon administration had previously promised not to devalue the dollar, but the public had paid equally little attention to that routine disclaimer. So the phrase about 'the dollar in your pocket' was shrugged off as the usual politician's effort to make things look a little better than they are. It was not treated as a major betrayal of the truth because the virtual devaluation was a minor element in a popular set of measures, not a major event which the public had been told to dread as a national disaster. And it was equally defensible on the grounds that 'simple folk' had to be reassured that the same amount of money would not buy a lesser quantity of groceries on the morrow.

We do not judge the political career of President Nixon or Harold Wilson – and the utterances which make up those careers – as the recording angel must judge a man's private life. Moral criteria are certainly relevant, but they are subordinate. We see the politician rather as an actor who takes on a part; and we judge him according to whether he plays it well or badly. We do not examine his fidelity to the text with the scientific detachment of an archaeologist sifting a handful of earth. What counts is the total effect of the actor's performance within the context of the play. Our criteria are theatrical: does his rendering 'go over' well? Does he 'put it across'? Does his rendering contribute to the success of the play? And, taking a more general view, is the play good or bad?

Certainly, within this theatrical language we may attempt moral inflections: was it an honest rendering, an honest play? Or was there something false, something phoney about it? Were we perhaps taken in by 'the bells and the tinsel'? Or were the bells and tinsel really a symbol, a vulgar adumbration of something genuine, important? But dominating all this is the main question: did it work, did the play go over well?

There is a strange disjunction between the way we all – liberals, Marxists, conservatives, even 'apolitical' spectators – review a particular public event and the theories that most of us adopt to explain politics in general. We actually judge the event in the way described above, in the light of its practical consequences for us; yet we constantly search for, or indeed pretend, that we have found some hidden principle that guides the whole drama. We stoutly maintain that we do not believe in fairies; but there are few of us who do not believe in some form of 'the figure in the carpet', the hidden hand of history.

We are dimly, uneasily conscious of this disjunction. For we cannot help seeing from our own experience how important are public events. We see how those slips of tongue, those hasty reactions, those missed trains, those sudden failures of nerve on the big occasion, those equally sudden spurts of courage or sympathy, bring consequences vast out of all proportion to the human scale of the comedy on stage. As Burke says in discussing the interaction between social laws and individuals: 'The death of a man at a critical juncture, his disgust, his retreat, his disgrace, have brought innumerable calamities on a whole nation. A common soldier, a child, a girl at the door of an inn, have changed the face of fortune, and almost of nature.'[10] And we also see how little all this has to do with our grand theories of progress or dialectical struggle or the national destiny or the historical process. Hence we often try to overcome this disjunction by arguing that public events are merely anomalous interruptions of the pattern, isolated stains on the carpet.

For example, the 'apolitical' cynic will see political speeches as mere advertising for a product which has already been manufactured by cabals in smoke-filled rooms, 'a PR job' as the current slang has it. Even the metaphor betrays the weakness of this view. For is not advertising/marketing/selling an integral part of the business of an industry? Does not the need to sell a product shape it? And does not the consumer's refusal to buy a product (equivalent to nationwide protest about some government measure) compel the producer to redesign that product – or abandon it?

Even those who believe in public debate are liable to underrate its value because of an overriding belief in some figure in the carpet. Parliaments, public meetings and demonstrations, they will say, are healthy safety valves, but the real business is done elsewhere. They will draw an analogy with the legal axiom that 'justice must not only be done – it must be seen to be done'. In reality the two cases are quite different. It is perfectly possible for a man to have a fair trial in secret; the administration of justice is governed by fixed rules which do not depend on the presence or absence of the public. We demand public trials to make sure that these rules are being observed. Only in the judge's *obiter dicta* is there a need to communicate with the public; for there is little point in him issuing a warning against a repetition of such-and-such a crime, or informing the public of a growing problem in the enforcement of the law, or laying down 'public policy', if the public cannot hear him.

All this is a minute fraction of legal business. But it is the greater part of the politician's life. What point would there be in him making a patriotic speech in the solitude of his bedroom? And yet patriotic speeches, no less than the discovery of oil or the distribution of national income, shape our history. The public political act is not just a political act which happens to be performed in public; it is not merely justice-being-done plus justice-being-seen-to-be-done. It is something quite different, an organic event of which the public aspect is the germ and crux. And to refuse to accept this fact is to refuse the evidence of our own eyes; it shows a lack of respect for reality.

Nevertheless, we shall need briefly to examine the fashionable figures in the carpet, the prevailing theories about politics; we shall need to see why the theorists have adopted such an extraordinarily oblique attitude towards the evidence of their own eyes. Only thus may we learn to look at politics in a clearer and more straightforward way.

These prevailing theories about politics have themselves had a great influence, not always for good, upon the way that politics is actually conducted. Political science has the peculiarity of being *reflexive* to a more marked degree than any other of the 'human' or 'social' sciences. We are not all biochemists; but we all have political views or anti-views which themselves amount to views. Even statements such as 'I don't give a damn about politics – politicians are all crooks' carry with them implied opinions about the importance and nature of political activity. Thus all of us are both political scientists and the political scientist's field of research.

In this film we are not only actors but directors and cameramen at the same time. This awkward but inevitable arrangement leads to much joggling of the hand-held camera and hence a wearying succession of blurred, partial and fleeting images; a *cinéma vérité* which conceals and distorts as much of the truth as it reveals. To make any sense of the film, we shall first have to consider what leads people to play around with movie cameras; how and why do people form theories about politics?

ACT I

ACT I

I

Towards a New Theory

We tire easily these days. Our attention span is limited. Even if somewhat guiltily, we tend to reject the nagging problem as being 'dead', *passé*, irrelevant. So with political theory. The spectacular crash of this century's ideologies has tempted us to proclaim, in Daniel Bell's phrase, 'the end of ideology'. This phrase is an evasion. We may well accept that an all-embracing, fully articulated theory covering each minutest facet of our lives no longer seems to meet the case. A vast and complex structure of doctrine, such as Thomas Aquinas laid down for the medieval church, may not have the flexibility, the built-in adaptation to change – in our modern jargon, the feedback capability – that modern life demands. But that is very different from saying that we no longer approach politics armed with a general theory of what politics is or should be about. And that is just what the lazy proclamation of 'the end of ideology' means to imply. We are, it is said, all pragmatists nowadays; theory is dead.

There is something strange about this assertion. How can it be possible to practise a craft without any idea of what we intend to do? 'The pragmatic politician does what is expedient.' There is a measure of tautology about this statement; it means no more than that he does what 'has to be done'. Even if we inject into the notion of expediency some implication of short-sightedness, of taking the short-term action suggested by the immediate circumstances rather than the more beneficial long view, we are thereby involved in defining that long view. We must ask the question: 'Expedient to what end? Is it to the maintenance of power or of political stability? Is the criterion of expediency the nature and strength of public feeling, or the needs of progress, or the rationalisation of political institutions, or what?'

This disenchantment with political theory is nothing new. It is liable to happen whenever one particular theory has failed its devotees in the same way as the doom of capitalism is always prophesied when a great company crashes. Tocqueville found something of the same disenchantment in 1852, four months after Louis Napoleon had seized power. He was to give a stern rebuke to the disenchanted:

You deny the existence and the power of the political sciences? Look around you, and see these monuments and these ruins. What raised the former and brought the latter down? What is it that has changed the face of the world today so that, if your grandfather came back, he would recognise neither the laws, nor the mores, nor the ideas, clothes, customs that he used to know, and scarcely even the language he used to speak? What caused that French Revolution, in a word, one of the greatest events in history? I say the greatest and not the most useful, for this revolution is still in progress, and I await its final effect to be able to characterise it by such a word. But what did cause it? Was it all the politicians, princes, ministers and great lords of the eighteenth century? They do not need our blessing or our curses, but only our pity, for they almost always did otherwise than they intended, and in the end arrived at a result they detested. The great shapers of this formidable revolution were every one of them men who did not take the smallest part in public affairs: they were, as everyone knows, authors. It was political science, and often that science at its most abstract, which put into our fathers' heads the germs of those new ideas which have since suddenly blossomed into political institutions and civil laws unknown to their forebears.

And we must note that what the political sciences did here with such brilliance, is continually done everywhere, although more secretly and slowly. Among all civilised peoples the political sciences create, or at the least give shape to, general ideas; and from these general ideas are formed the problems in the midst of which politicians must struggle, and also the laws which they imagine they create. The political sciences form a sort of intellectual atmosphere breathed by both governors and governed in society, and both unwittingly derive from it the principles of their action. Only among barbarians is practice alone recognised in politics.[1]

This formidable argument considers only the *effect* of political theories; it does not consider whether they are true, or morally right, or suited to their times. Tocqueville simply points out that it is theories put forward by those mere scribblers which have changed our lives and attitudes out of all recognition. Keynes, of course, was making the same point when he remarked that so-called practical men were merely the slaves of some long-dead economist.

Acton makes the point in terms of the study of history when he argues that it is 'the living thoughts of men' which should concern us more than the 'dead letters of edicts and of statutes'. 'It would be easy to point out a paragraph in St Augustine, or a sentence of Grotius that outweighs in influence the Acts of fifty Parliaments, and our cause owes more to Cicero and Seneca, to Vinet and Tocqueville, than to the laws of Lycurgus or the five Codes of France.'[2]

This brings us to an important inconsistency in the way we talk about theories, whether they be political, scientific or even artistic. At the time, the proponents and to a great extent the supporters of a theory will describe it as 'true' or 'correct'. Posterity and the historian are more likely to talk about whether the theory was 'fruitful'. The outsider, whether in time or space, is struck more by the effects of the theory than by the justification of it. And not without reason. The advances which resulted from Newtonian dynamics, the pictures which the Impressionists painted, are more important to us than the actual arguments Newton used or what the Impressionists thought about light. This is not to say that the Impressionists' ideas were without meaning in a positive sense, or that Newton's arguments, even if superseded by Einstein's, are not worth analysing. We are merely discussing the usefulness of each theory as a *tool*.

Men doing practical work use language for practical purposes. The carpenter says 'this is the right way to do this' or 'this is the right tool for the job'. He may even say 'this is the only way' or 'the only tool'. He does not bother to state carefully: 'In the present state of my craft, this is the way/tool that gets the best results.' He wants to get on with his work. He also needs to have confidence in his tools. When we consider a whole field of work, this psychological need becomes even stronger. If the rules of the game are constantly questioned, the game is held up. Simplicity and elegance of operation are much to be desired. Both in philosophy and in the natural sciences we notice that researchers are delighted to come upon a theory possessing these qualities. This delight is in part aesthetic; but it is an aestheticism of function. The better a tool serves its purpose, the more time and trouble it should save.

When we come to look at politics, it is only natural that we should be the more pleased with a theory the more it purports to explain. When James Mill says that 'the man who subjects the largest province of human knowledge to the fewest principles is universally esteemed the most successful philosopher',[3] he is stating no more than a fact. Whether a man deserves esteem for such a feat is a different matter.

But there is no doubt that what is so appealing about Marxism, for example, is its thoroughgoingness. If Marx had claimed merely that the economic structure of a society was one of the principal factors determining its nature, his influence would have been far less; similarly with Freud, the Manchester economists, or the behaviourists. It is precisely the 'nothing but' reductionism which is so attractive about the great theories. Yet this comprehensiveness entails a more binding commitment; when we back a great theory of this kind, we back it with all our resources of time and energy. When we tackle a matchbox puzzle, we try the pieces first one way, then another, until we find a way that fits. Each unsuccessful arrangement is rejected without hesitation; there are no 'hard feelings'. But in adopting a *great theory*, we are more like a man who has invested all his capital in vast and cumbrous machinery. He wants to get his money's worth out of his investment. He will use the machinery as long as he possibly can make a profit out of it – and probably much longer. Only when he has failed to make a profit for a considerable time will he junk the machinery. Similarly, it is possible to refute, say, the labour theory of value in various particular instances; but that will not persuade the true devotee to abandon it if the general tenor of the theory still helps him to understand the world. Even if, as Popper convincingly argues,[4] there is nothing which the labour theory of value explains which the theory of supply and demand does not also explain and there are many phenomena which only the latter explains, the devotee will still cling to the Marxist notion of value because it is such an important element in the Marxist view of the world. Theory is prior to observation in political discourse, and a great theory is prior to its subsidiary theories.

Well, this may be so; but should it be so? Should we not first observe what happens and then try to build from this a coherent explanation of how politics works and thence a serviceable theory, if needed, of how it could be made to work better? Isn't this the true scientific method – experimental, empirical? And even if, as present-day philosophers of science contend, that is not how natural scientists work, would they not make more progress if they did?

We have already referred to the practical and psychological reasons for sticking to a tried method until it becomes hopelessly unworkable. But there are other reasons why the student of politics is enmeshed in theory at the very beginning of his career. He cannot begin to work without selecting some facts for study and rejecting others or at the very least deciding their relative importance. And by such selection and rejection he has already defined his field of study; he has implicitly or explicitly decided what is significant and what is not.

We may in addition suggest three practical reasons why theory precedes study for the political student. First, he is not an all-seeing god. He is limited by time and therefore must limit his field of study in order to achieve any useful results. Second, he is not first in the field. He has to take account of a vast mass of theories and of pre-selected evidence accumulated by previous students. Third, unlike, say, the physicist, he is not dealing with an inanimate world. His field of study is peopled with self-conscious beings, to wit politicians and voters. These beings themselves express a variety of theories about politics. For the student of politics the evidence, so to speak, answers back.

That theory comes before study is today a widely recognised phenomenon. In perception, for example, we have moved away from the old idea of sense-data as being in some sense raw and unmediated facts. We realise that the eye is not an impartial, all-inclusive organ. It selects, highlights certain things and rejects others. We *see* what interests us, or what we are trained to see, or what we want to see. And similarly with the natural and social sciences. The young natural scientist is indeed even more theory-bound than the student of politics. For he is trained exclusively in the prevailing theory, for example Newtonian or Einsteinian physics, but not both; even now he is given very little information about discarded or unfashionable theories, that is, the history of his speciality. And his subsequent work after training is based on that same theory which he learnt as a student; his work is to solve the puzzles which that theory presents, to make it more precise and more fully articulated and to deal with any new anomalies which his researches produce. Thomas Kuhn[5] calls this work 'normal science' because it forms the vast bulk of scientific work done; only when the anomalies begin to sprout in profusion will there be any question of re-examining the basic assumptions of the theory, let alone of attempting to form a new theory.

In the social sciences the situation is somewhat less constricted, *not* because social scientists proceed on more empirical lines but because an unfashionable theory can survive alongside the theory which has taken its place. The pedagogic process may, for example, concentrate on instilling Keynesian economics into the students and practitioners of political economy; but pre-Keynesian or anti-Keynesian theories will still be in currency and may even make a comeback. This of course is also the case with political science. It is not our intention here to discuss in detail the reasons for the difference between the natural and social sciences. But we will just suggest one line of thought. In natural sciences like physics and chemistry we may presume nature to be constant; what do change are the preconceptions of scientists, their instruments, methods of procedure and use of evidence. If the scientific establishment has total and absolute control of scientific education, it can not only decree that a theory is obsolete but also make it extremely difficult for it to be revived, in the same way that a Soviet encyclopaedia can declare that a disgraced comrade no longer exists. But in the social sciences 'nature' is constantly changing. Time confirms some assumptions and falsifies others. Of course, the Kremlin for example will attempt to train its subjects' eyes so that they can 'see' the world only in the light of the approved inflection of Marxism. But there is a limit to how far perception can be programmed to deal in the approved manner with the world of ten years hence.

We are in no sense complaining about 'the primacy of the abstract' (the phrase F. A. Hayek uses in his essay in *Beyond Reductionism*).[6] Theory comes first, for the very good and practical reason that this is the only way to make progress. The abstract, the theory, the pattern, the system, the paradigm (Kuhn's preferred and illuminating term) are all simply ways of describing man's attempts to make sense of the world. This fact, which is really little more than a fact of definition, is much obscured by the attempts of philosophers to apply a dichotomic true-or-false test to each and every theory, with little or no regard to what the theory is trying to do. In the natural sciences, for example, the theory's aim is to illuminate and explain the workings of nature. To the extent that the theory does or does not *fit* nature, we may call it true or untrue. Yet the basic reason for framing a scientific theory is not to make an indisputably true statement; it is to make progress. An Einsteinian may describe Newton's theory as incorrect or false. Yet he cannot deny that Newton's theory was extraordinarily *fruitful*, that over a great part of the field which it covers it does work and can be and has been elaborated with dramatic results.

This is clearer in other fields where the purpose of framing a theory is different. In painting, for example, we would not say that the calligraphic tradition of the east is less true than the plastic tradition of the European Renaissance, nor that the latter is less true than the attempts of the Impressionists to render light. We would be more inclined to say that any effort by an individual painter within a tradition is more or less successful in terms of what he is trying to do. Again, in economics we are conscious that most theories are both descriptive and normative. We usually want to ask at least three questions about any economic theory: does its description of how the economy works agree with the evidence? Would the concrete measures suggested by the theory have the desired effect? And how desirable is the effect?

We can certainly give some true-or-false answer to the first question by empirical methods. We can also do empirical research into the likelihood of the measures suggested having the desired effect, though we could not give a true or false answer until we had actually tried out the measures. But to the third question we could give no true-or-false answer at all except one of the form 'Yes/No, it is/is not the case that I desire this particular effect.' A similarly confused picture will result from any attempt to apply true-or-false tests to political theory. For the only test that we can usefully apply is quite different: namely, does this theory help me to make sense of the political scene? When I look down from the Stranger's Gallery of the House of Commons, does it help me to *see* what is going on?

What then is the nature of politics? How does the political world work? What do its workings suggest to us by way of future action? And finally what results do I desire, and would the suggested actions have these results? Now it is perfectly possible to ask these questions more or less in the reverse order, starting with my desires and ending up with the way the world works and the problem of how to impose my desires upon the world. This tradition starts by asking such questions as What is Liberty? or, What is Good? And it is a tradition with a very long history, from Plato and Aristotle going through Locke and Rousseau down to Marx as revolutionary and the neo-Marxists. It has certainly had a very great effect upon the course of history: for it has a power to move hearts and minds because its driving force is basically derived from a moral norm rather than from a sociological description. The other tradition was founded by Aristotle. It continues with Machiavelli and proceeds through Montesquieu, Burke, Tocqueville, Bagehot, Marx as a sociologist, down to the prevailing political science of the present day. Clearly the practitioners in this latter tradition produce very varied conclusions. But they share a starting-point; they all begin by attempting to enquire how societies actually work. This is certainly a more 'scientific' approach in that its theories are to be tested against the world as it is; but it is no less theoretical or paradigmatic for that. Nor, it may be added, has this approach been less influential when viewed as a whole. If we may schematise a little colourfully, it produces not physical but intellectual revolutions. Consciously or unconsciously, millions of non-Conservatives now use a quasi-Marxian view of class interest as a handy tool; equally, millions of non-Conservatives are saturated with a Burkean understanding of the importance of settled institutions and customs, the importance of tradition. We must not exaggerate this distinction. Locke clearly influenced Montesquieu, and Montesquieu, Rousseau. Yet there is a distinction and its functional result is this: the moralistic political scientists have an effect upon the general way we look at the world, in particular upon the moral relation between the individual and the world; while the sociological political thinkers affect the way we look at the political structure and process. Naturally the moral aspect has implications for the political structure; but it does not in itself shed any light upon the nature of politics.

In this essay it is the nature of politics with which we are concerned. We shall therefore want to assess the paradigms put forward by the sociologists more than those of the moralists. Western political sociology seems to me to have produced three main paradigms to describe the way in which men 'attend to their political arrangements', in Professor Oakeshott's superb low-key phrase. I shall call the three:

Politics as battle
Politics as pilgrimage
Politics as science.

Let us attempt very briefly to summarise these three notions.

THE OLD PARADIGMS

Politics as battle
The notion of politics as a continuous struggle is the oldest of the three principal paradigms of political thought. We may take Machia-

28

velli as its originator, at least in its scientific form. For clearly many millions before and since his day have experienced life as a brute struggle for survival and have concluded that this is the nature of life. But Machiavelli was the first man to analyse the political structure on the assumption that government rests on force alone. Certainly, if possible the ruler should acquire or maintain his power by other less violent, less costly means; economy of effort is always to be praised, for it leaves resources free for use in future emergencies. But where the use of force cannot be avoided, the ruler should not hesitate to use as much as is required to attain his object. And he is to eschew the use of force where possible, not for moral reasons but only because its use may diminish his strength, for example by alienating his subjects; even in such a case, Machiavelli is less than wholehearted in recommending conciliation as the more politic course.[7] He does not deny, particularly in the *Discourses,* that this is an unattractive paradigm. He acknowledges the existence of higher moral dictates. But he asserts that force is the only effective basis of power, for he presumes that the ruler's power is perpetually threatened; there is always trouble brewing, a rival plotting to overthrow him, or a rebellious force gathering strength. The natural tendency of a governing community is dissolution; force is the only effective method of holding things together. The link with Hobbes' view of society is plain. Indeed, their work is really complementary. Hobbes puts 'for a general inclination of all mankind, a perpetual and restless desire of power after power that endeth only in death'; he outlines a psychology of egoism which accounts for the perpetual insecurity of power observed by Machiavelli. Hobbes then deduces from this that the only way for the citizen to achieve at least some security is for him and all his fellows to submit to a single sovereign authority. Machiavelli for his part discusses the methods by which the ruler may improve his own security. Between them the two men elaborate a politics of egoism.

The assumptions of this general attitude survive in many modern attitudes towards politics. The Communist's dictatorship of the proletariat contains Machiavelli's major premises: that anarchy is the natural tendency of unregenerate society, that there is always a rival waiting in the wings to take advantage of this tendency, and that force is the only protection. Revanchist/revisionist/imperialist elements are merely different ways of describing the rival prince. These assumptions are also to be found in milder form among loyalists

29

in all political parties. For keen party workers and for the party leaders themselves there is always an enemy waiting in the wings to take advantage of weakness; witness the suspicion of plots and the attribution of tireless cunning to the enemy. In part we may explain this belief as a psychological need. A certain degree of paranoia may be a necessary spur to activity. Yet there is certainly more to it. The all-pervasive use of battle metaphors in the tamest municipal election argues a deep commitment to the notion of politics-as-struggle: for example, 'We shall fight to the end', 'The battle will be long and hard', 'We shall march our troops towards the sound of gunfire', and so on. Nor is this commitment weakened by the acceptance of certain rules of political conduct on both sides; a war is not any less a war if both sides abide by the Geneva Convention. We do not expect our opponents when in power to pass a law extending their period of office indefinitely; but we expect them to use all means to maintain their power short of such a measure. And if they were ever to pass such a measure, we in turn would no longer consider ourselves bound by the rules of the game. We would take to the hills or the streets as so many disenfranchised activists have done in the past.

Such rules of war do constitute a refinement of the notion of politics-as-battle – but only a refinement. The same may be said of two aspects in which the Marxist view of politics-as-battle differs from Machiavelli's. First, Marx is determinist and historicist whereas Machiavelli is open-ended. That is to say, for Marx the battle is bound to go a particular way – his way – in the long run; history is on his side. A great deal of ink has been expended on historicism, even more perhaps than has been expended on Calvin's determinism. And yet, as with Calvinism, the practical consequences of historicism are virtually confined to cheering up the troops. For the Marxist and the Calvinist both have to act as if the outcome were not historically or divinely predetermined, in other words as if they were in an open-ended situation. To that extent, historicism is, as we said above, only a refinement of politics-as-struggle. So is the second Marxist variation from Machiavelli's paradigm. The Marxist believes that in the long run the struggle will have an end; conflict will be abolished, thus allowing the state as the defender against anarchy-and-the-alternative-prince to wither away. Again, this has the effect of cheering up the troops, but in terms of practical action its consequences are little different from Machiavelli's notion of an unending struggle. It does not, for example, lead to any softening in the quantity or frequency of the use of force *now*. Nor does the fact that the proletariat may be presumed to be on the side of its own dictatorship lead to any relaxation of vigilance; after all, the fact that Caesar Borgia might on occasion be popular with his subjects would certainly not have been regarded either by him or by Machiavelli as any justification for slackening his guard. The smallest germ can infect the body politic. The enemy is always within or at the gates.

Politics as pilgrimage

The second notion of politics is more usually referred to as the idea of progress. And indeed there is an obvious disadvantage in my use of the term 'pilgrimage'; for this implies a shrine at the end of the road and many people who believe in progress would deny that they believe in the existence of a goal, a utopia. Yet 'pilgrimage' seems to me an apt term all the same; for the idea of progress implies more than moving forward in the right direction. It contains within it a certain feeling of a consecrated journey. It is the only one of our three paradigms which has about it a certain moral elevation. This may become clearer as we examine the whole idea more closely.

The idea of progress is closely associated with the rise of secular humanism. Yet the humanists of the Renaissance are only partially its authors. Certainly they redeveloped the notion that man is responsible for his own destiny. And they accepted the idea of the voluntarist *movement* of a society, but more in the sense of reviving the cultural values of antiquity than of a continuous movement *forward*. In this sense they are more akin to the reforming clerics of the Middle Ages who wished to revive an earlier, purer expression of Christianity than to the progressives of the eighteenth century onwards. The true progressive idea of continuous movement forward takes its starting point from the scientific revolution of the later seventeenth century and the technological revolution which this prompted. Its rationale has indeed a strong technological flavour although it may be couched in moral or, more rarely, religious terms. For it is impossible to see a new machine or the more precise measurement of a natural phenomenon as other than an improvement. The sudden, continuous and seemingly endless spate of such improvements gives a thrilling feeling of forward momentum to intellectuals in a society, at least in one where there is little or no divorce between 'science' and the 'humanities'.

Parallel with this humanist sense of confidence go a decline of interest in the past and, often, a revulsion against religion. The progressive finds his loyalty increasingly to the future and to the cause of progress; he also finds himself under attack from the guardians of the past and the guardians of the eternal verities (which come to much the same thing, for what is eternal cannot also be progressive). So he then finds himself with a holy war on his hands. And to fight it, he must project his own cause as the holier of the two. Even when and if he wins the war, that is to say when the guardians of tradition at least partially embrace the new faith, he remains committed to a necessary pilgrimage unless he himself loses his faith. That is to say, as long as he believes in the possibility of progress he is committed to work for it.

Again, the Marxists' belief in the inevitability of progress is no more than a refinement. It does not excuse the believer from working for progress now. Nor does the belief of many in a shrine at the end of the road, belief in a utopia, have much practical consequence for the present. It may impart a greater fervour; witness, for example, the difference between the impassioned revolutionary and the milder progressive. But it does not affect the practical paradigm. Progress is both possible and desirable; it is also the guiding principle of history. For both the Whig historian and the Marxist the significant aspects of history are those which show forward movement. The rest must be explained away either as a congeries of anomalies and anachronisms soon due to disappear or as inevitable reactions to the forward movement. Liberals, radicals and the extreme Left are all much given to elaborating sub-theories to explain apparent movement backwards; these sub-theories usually boil down to some version of 'two steps forward, one step back'. Bertrand Russell was indeed willing to describe a world which had already experienced Hitler and Stalin in these terms. Lenin expected severer temporary retreats in the overall progress: 'One step forward, two steps back . . . it happens in the lives of individuals, and it happens in the history of nations and in the development of parties.'[8] Even in the first blooming of the pilgrimage paradigm, its supporters were already explaining away unpalatable events as part of such a dialectical advance. Turgot, for example, says in his celebrated second lecture at the Sorbonne:

Thus the human race seen from its origin appears to the eye of a philosopher as one vast whole which itself, like each individual composing it, has had its infancy and its development.

We see societies establishing themselves, nations forming themselves, which in turn dominate over other nations or become subject to them. Empires rise and fall; laws, forms of government, one succeeding another; the arts, the sciences, are discovered and are cultivated, sometimes retarded and sometimes accelerated in their progress, they pass from one region to another. Self-interest, ambition, vainglory, perpetually change the scene of the world, inundate the earth with blood. Yet in the midst of their ravages manners are gradually softened, the human mind takes enlightenment, separate nations draw nearer to each other, commerce and policy connect at last all parts of the globe, and the total mass of the human race, by the alternations of calm and agitation, of good conditions and of bad, marches always, although slowly, towards still higher perfection.[9]

The idea that man is only just beginning to grow up (as opposed to having reached maturity in the age of Pericles or Augustus and having declined ever since) is an essential inflection of the pilgrimage paradigm, most confidently enunciated by Bacon. The proposition that even 'the dwarf sees farther than the giant, when he has the giant's shoulder to mount on' is a great support to the paradigm. For we can, so to speak, allow the dwarf to possess the same moral and intellectual shortcomings as the giant and still be confident that in the end he will improve on ᵢhe giant's performance.

Thus in just the same way as the existence of certain rules of war does not really affect the battle paradigm, so the notion of 'halting progress' (even to the extent of history resembling a game of grandmother's footsteps) is not really a weakening of the pilgrimage paradigm. For the time-scale and the elegance or clumsiness of the progress are of little account to the pilgrims: what count are the sense of movement, its direction and its necessity.

Politics as science
In describing the third paradigm we must be wary. By politics as science, I am not referring to activities such as the following:

– Research into social conditions, characterised by the use of statistics.
– Research into the state of public opinion through opinion polls and various psephological techniques.

- Pilot programmes for social projects.
- Research into techniques of economic management.

Such activities are more properly to be described as 'science *in* politics', and no sensible man could or would oppose their use where appropriate. I refer rather to a more general theory, a paradigm covering the whole field; namely, the belief that politics *is* a science just as biochemistry is a science. On this view, it is possible by rational enquiry to discover the *correct* structure for a political community; and, furthermore, because what is correct must surely also be realisable, to establish such a structure.

This belief would seem to have very close affinities with politics as pilgrimage. And indeed the two paradigms are frequently simultaneously accepted. Certainly they spring from the same historical roots. If nature and even the structure of human society yield up so many of their secrets to the scientific method, why should not also the political aspect of human society? If even political economy is a science, why not politics itself?

Yet there is a clear distinction to be drawn between the pilgrimage and the science paradigms. Both look forward to improvements in the state of society as opposed to the battle paradigm's attitude that 'holding one's own' is about the best that can be expected. And in terms of practical policy the two frequently coincide; yet the basic beliefs are very different. The pilgrim sees morality, or conscience, or religion, as the impetus to reform; Turgot, in his earlier Sorbonne lecture, says:

How is it that this humanity, this love of mankind which our religion has consecrated under the name of charity, did not even have a name in the ancient world? Is sensitivity to the misfortunes of others not then engraved in every heart? If the insights of that sensitivity were sharp enough to grasp the holiness of revealed religion, why were they not sharp enough to make that revelation unnecessary? After four thousand years then Christ came to teach men to love one another! His teaching, by reviving those qualities of sensitivity which each man finds in his heart, must in some way have unveiled nature to herself.

Would it be possible here not to mingle the evidence of moral progress among men with the evidence of the increase in their happiness? No, the two things are too closely linked; it would be futile for the rules of rhetoric to try to separate in speech that which is so nearly integrated in reality. What motive other than that of religion has ever committed a host of persons to abandon their families to concentrate exclusively upon the interests of the poor?[10]

The scientist, by contrast, sees the scientific method as the motor of all progress. Condorcet, originally Turgot's disciple, also visualises mankind as growing up; his *Esquisse d'Un Tableau Historique des Progrès de l'Esprit Humain* is really a *curriculum humanae vitae.* But the guiding principle of this development is the scientific method:

All the errors in politics and in morals are founded upon philosophical mistakes, which, themselves, are connected with physical errors. There does not exist any religious system, or supernatural extravagance, which is not founded on an ignorance of the laws of nature. The inventors and defenders of these absurdities could not foresee the successive progress of the human mind. . . . Man's moral goodness is as infinitely perfectible as his other faculties and nature links in an indissoluble chain truth, happiness and virtue.[11]

Condorcet believed that a universal language, akin to the languages of science, such as algebra,

. . . would be the means of giving to every object that comes within the reach of human intelligence, a vigour, and precision, that would facilitate the knowledge of truth, and render error almost impossible. Then would the march of every science be as infallible as that of the mathematics, and the propositions of every system acquire, as far as nature will admit, geometrical demonstration and certainty.[12]

The *certainty* of mathematics; progress under such conditions is the production not of human love made manifest but of man's stumbling upon scientific truths which are immutably valid. For the pilgrim, it is man who creates the progress or is given the power to do so through divine grace. For the scientist the potentiality of progress has always existed in the physical universe; if only man, poor sap that he is, had not been too ignorant and superstitious to realise that potential! For the scientist, too, the precise direction and nature of progress are also immutable, being derived from scientific laws. Once science has 'found the answer', there can be no argument. This continual reference to an external and unchallengeable standard in dealing with our hopes and fears can be cold and even frightening. If we may anticipate a little, it is not just the progressive flavour of revolutionary or military regimes which is responsible for their extreme harshness and rigidity; it is the scientific element. For if the rightness of some political structure or decision is 'scientifically proven', any deviation by an individual or a group can be the result only of madness or criminality and must be stamped out and punished.

Andrei Amalrik, in a secret television film smuggled into the west, says of the use of mental hospitals as a means of disposing of opponents of the Soviet regime:

> I think it's the most disgusting thing this regime does. At the same time it seems to me that this is a clear indication of the complete ideological capitulation of the regime in the face of its opponents, if they can find nothing else to do with them but declare them to be out of their minds.[13]

On the contrary, what else could they do with them? If they accepted the legitimacy of opposition, that in their own eyes would be the ideological capitulation. For it would be an admission that what the regime had claimed to be scientifically proven was in fact still open to argument. Well, and why not, we might say? Is not the perpetually attempted refutation the basis of the scientific mode of discourse? Not according to the Soviet notion of science. That notion, so brutally and hilariously epitomised in the Lysenko affair, is one of the oddest constructs of the human mind. It would have seemed odd to most scientists at most times, but never more so than today when philosophers of science tend to stress the provisional, hypothetical nature of scientific theories rather than the solid contributions they make to our understanding of nature. And it is clear that Lenin, for example, uses the idea of science in a very unscientific way. Indeed, there are few metaphysical and epistemological lengths to which he will not stretch the idea of science in his quest for certainty and, above all, authority. For the idea of science will not help to bring about the revolution if any hint of the provisional creeps in. And it does not make matters much better if the philosopher of science pleads that, despite their provisional nature, scientific theories are the best, if not the only, way of coming to understand and even 'master' nature. The revolutionary, that is to say the prophet of a new religion, will not be satisfied with the best. He must be able to offer *perfection* if he is to move the masses.

To us the confusion between science-in-politics and politics-as-science seems to be an elementary confusion between 'is' and 'ought'. We can see that, say, plotting a demand curve and analysing the structure of a molecule are the same sort of activity, that is investigation of the world as it is. A discussion of how income should be distributed in a society seems to us a totally different sort of activity: it is basically a discussion about values. We do not need to take a logical positivist line that discussion about values is ultimately meaningless; we can only say that such a discussion bears little or no relation to the methods of science. We can argue about the merits of statements made about liberty, equality, justice, order, and so on; we can discuss how far such qualities will contribute to our notions of a good society. But we cannot test the validity of such statements in the same way as we can test the validity of a statement about economics or chemistry.

But this well-known confusion between 'is' and 'ought' is really irrelevant to our discussion of politics-as-science as a sociological phenomenon (though highly relevant if we wish to discuss whether politics-as-science is sense or nonsense). For the truth is that this paradigm is employed for *practical* reasons, not because its users want to describe the world, but because they want to change it; hence all Marx's attacks on bourgeois logic. And, the users may ask, why shouldn't we? We shouldn't for the simple reason that it is a false use of the notion of science – not merely false but dishonest. The desire to lend certainty and authority to his cause pushes the advertiser into using the most potent form of appeal; sexual stimulation, for example, is widely regarded as an effective aid in selling the most unlikely products. In the last couple of centuries science has occupied in the more elevated parts of the brain the place that sex occupies in the baser spheres. It may be used to sell anything: not merely political ideologies, but religion via Teilhard de Chardin and various forms of witch-doctoring and myth-making from Freud onwards. We do not claim here that there is no merit in these formidable effusions – merely that there is no merit in their claims to scientific method.

THE INADEQUACY OF THE OLD PARADIGMS

Indeed, when we look at the three old paradigms as a whole, we see that they share this same common feature: that their real aim is not to describe the world but to act upon it. This applies equally to the various possible combinations of paradigms which, when set as hard as concrete, are usually termed *ideologies*. For example, Marxism may be seen as a battle plus pilgrimage plus science; in a much thinner and milder form Bagehot's work also shows traces of all three paradigms – battle from his study of practical politics, pilgrimage from the unreflecting way in which he shared the general social optimism of his time, and science from his dabblings in Darwinism. Both Machiavelli's method and the counter-revolutionary conservatism of American thinkers such as James Burnham are based mainly on the battle paradigm, though they naturally also claim to be elaborating a science of conducting battle, but this science is induced from the world, not deduced from the world as it ought to be. It therefore corresponds more closely to our idea of science-in-politics rather than to our idea of politics-as-science. Utopian social engineering, on the other hand, of the kind denounced by Sir Karl Popper in *The Open Society*, is based equally on the pilgrimage and on the science paradigms. Piecemeal social engineering of the kind applauded by Popper is a straightforward pilgrimage in which the right road towards a humane society is found by trial and error (which is admittedly how Popper believes progress is also made in the natural sciences, though the most recent historians of science disagree, but it is sufficient here to keep to our distinction between politics-as-science and science-in-politics). Statements such as Harold Wilson's 'the Labour Party is a moral crusade or it is nothing' indicate that the speaker sees politics as both a battle and a pilgrimage. Sometimes the mixture of elements within a particular ideology or personal political view cause fierce conflicts: for example, the conflict between the battle paradigm and the pilgrimage paradigm within Marxism, a conflict to which the dialectic provides an answer which only raises new problems. Similarly, the overlap between science and pilgrimage is confusing. Beatrice Webb asks in the introduction to the first volume of her memoirs:

Can there be a science of social organisation in the sense in which we have a science of mechanics or a science of chemistry, enabling us to forecast what will happen, and perhaps to alter the event by taking appropriate action or persuading others to take it? And secondly, assuming that there be, or will be, such a science of society, is man's capacity for scientific discovery the only faculty required for the reorganisation of society according to an ideal? Or do we need religion as well as science, emotional faith as well as intellectual curiosity?[14]

Well, if there is already an 'ideal' in existence, then 'emotional faith' must already be directing the scientist, who then becomes only a technician, a social engineer whose job it is to reach the ideal as quickly as possible. But if 'man's capacity for scientific discovery' can tell us not only how society works but also how it should work, if 'a science of social organisation' can not only analyse but prescribe, then what need have we of ideals? In fact ideals might be positively harmful if, being false, they conflicted with the verdict of science. Beatrice Webb's difficulty is in deciding just what kind of science a science of social organisation is or would be. If it is like 'pure' mechanics or chemistry, it must be purely descriptive; it would be absurd to talk about what the chemical composition of water *ought* to be. No, clearly, this science must be an applied science; it must act upon the world, not just describe it.

And why not? What is the use of a theory about a practical sphere of activity which has no practical implications? Very little perhaps. In fact, it is hard to imagine a theory of this kind which does not have practical implications. All the same, Marx's celebrated antithesis between describing the world and changing it is a false one; how can philosophers change a world of whose nature they are ignorant? Is not a philosopher's duty to give an adequate account of the world and its shortcomings before announcing why and how he proposes to change it? Otherwise his prescriptions are mere slogans without any rational backing.

All political theorists, from Machiavelli to Marx, do in fact accept a duty to describe the world before changing it. Indeed it is an agreed convention of political discussion that the philosophers' proposals for a better world should take account and lead out of the world as it is. That, to take a famous example, is the method of procedure adopted in *Das Kapital*; it is only when the philosopher has patently failed to take account of the world as it is, particularly when his account is refuted by the course of history, that he resorts to the theory of the clean and total break with the past (as witness some thinkers on the New Left).

Moreover, we should not forget that these paradigms openly profess to describe the world as it is. We must take them at their word and not accept the debased standards of the propaganda bureau. Further, even in propaganda work it is a sound principle that, wherever possible, it is best 'to tell the truth', or something close to it. If a much-publicised doctrine is repeatedly disappointed by events, such a doctrine will survive neither as an acceptable theory of how human society works, nor as a guide to conduct, nor as a morale booster to the citizens; the repeated failures of the Soviet economic system, for example, have brought about a collapse in both intellectual conviction and popular morale, a collapse over a far wider area than that of the material shortcomings which may be the direct result. Whatever action may be suggested by a paradigm, and whatever view one may take of the primary use of political paradigms (whether they are propounded as rallying cries, as guides to action, or as theories about the nature of human society), clearly any paradigm must take full account of the field with which it proposes to deal and also help us to understand that field.

Yet none of the three old paradigms takes full account of the political field or gives us any general understanding of that field.

Take what is called in political debate 'law-and-order'. The maintenance of law and order is a continuing, practical and immediate task of government, some would say the primary task of government. No government in history has been able to dispense with the traditional armoury of laws and judges, troops and/or policemen, the notion of crime and the reality of punishment. In fact, those very regimes which have professed the intention of minimising or renouncing this armoury in the name of liberty have often in fact strengthened that armoury. This is indeed characteristic of revolutionary regimes. One of Lenin's first acts on achieving power was to set up a new secret police. The ever-increasing power of that body, the growth in size and influence of the army, the intense discipline exerted by the regime at all levels and in all spheres of Russian society, are well known. Indeed, the Soviet citizen may be said to *experience* his government almost exclusively in the role of policeman. He does not find or expect to find the politician in other roles which are familiar to citizens of other nations: for example, the politician as beggar, appealing for our votes and our affections, the politician as rhetorical gladiator against another politician, the politician as our spokesman against other politicians or the government. For the Soviet citizen, many if not most of the vital questions affecting his life are to be asked of the politician-as-policeman; may I move to another town? May I say what I think or consort with whom I wish? May I go on strike? May I leave the country?

The Marxist-Leninist's defence to this is twofold: first, it would have been possible to found the Soviet state on brotherhood alone, had it not been for the existence of a dissident minority, inspired by ignorance and/or malice, which made the severe enforcement of law and order necessary; second, this enforcement is only a temporary means to a permanent end – the withering away of the state. To the hypothesis about the past, one can reply only with the historical fact: the dissidents existed, the severities took place. One may also ask whether if a state can be based exclusively on brotherhood some signs of progress in that direction ought not to have become evident over the half-century since the Russian Revolution. No, replies the Leninist, not until the final struggle is won, not until the Capitalists have raised their siege and admitted defeat. This reply is weakened by the tendency of Soviet leaders to give differing assessments of how far the Soviet Union has progressed on the road leading through Socialism to Communism. Thoroughgoing Leninists are in their own terms right to object to the 'revisionism' associated with Khrushchev (although Stalin himself was on occasion subject to the same failing), which by boasting of a high degree of progress already achieved weakened the contrast between the present temporary struggle and the future lasting brotherhood. Revisionism thus comes dangerously close, however unintentionally, to accepting the present relation between the state and the citizen and hence accepting a permanent need for the enforcement of law and order. But even the thoroughgoing Leninist still faces a dilemma: brotherhood, when it comes, will have been attained in part at least by the stern enforcement of law and order; is not the brotherhood-state (or, strictly, non-state) then in one sense based upon law and order? Further, if that brotherhood is menaced by dissidence or revanchism, will it not have to be defended by the traditional means of law and order? Surely brotherhood is a condition to be enjoyed, not a means of defence. For even if the overwhelming majority band together as brothers to 're-educate' a minority of dissidents in the gentlest, most well-meaning fashion possible, the majority's power to do so derives from their possession both of authority as the embodiment of right-thinking society and of force to carry out society's will – the characteristic properties of law enforcement in all societies.

The Leninist's way out is to posit a sharp and total discontinuity: at one moment, society still requires the strictest possible enforcement of law and order to control dissidence; at the next, there are no dissidents to be controlled. Yet this is merely to posit a society whose laws are always obeyed, not a society without laws. If in our present society nobody had for years broken the law forbidding incest, we would not assume in consequence that any future offender would not be punished or that the law should necessarily be repealed because it was not invoked. Even if the brotherhood-state at one stroke did repeal the entire penal code of the preceding law-and-order state, we would not then imagine that, for example, it was open season for murder. The prohibition on murder would presumably continue to be a social or moral convention, no longer reinforced by statute but none the less endorsed by society's disapproval and society's readiness to take action against any offender.

The Leninist therefore envisions a *successful* society, one which has completely succeeded in fulfilling this task of maintaining law and order by means of establishing a perfect social harmony; he does not envision a society which lacks either laws (written or unwritten, statute-reinforced or purely social/moral) or the *readiness* to enforce them. We would no doubt all agree that such a perfect social harmony is to be desired, as is a country without crime, criminals or prisoners, though we might disagree with the Leninist about the correct method of attaining this harmony. But this desirability does not mean that we do not believe in the necessity of laws and of enforcing them. Whether the structure of our society, our laws, and our methods of enforcing those laws are the right ones and suited to each other – these are different questions. Law and order remains a basic necessity of any society.

How then do the old paradigms take account of this basic necessity? At first sight it might seem that politics-as-battle would be appropriate here. Are not the authorities engaged in a constant and unremitting struggle against criminals on the one hand and political dissidents on the other? Do we not talk of 'the fight against crime'? And is not the news of any politically inspired breach of the law greeted, at least by those who are on the side of the authorities, as 'the threat of anarchy'? Finally, do not most of us, whether rulers or ruled, see society as a fragile structure liable to dissolution unless force is applied to cement it together? Whatever our party labels or professed political convictions, are we not all Machiavellians under the skin?

Such a general view is indeed common; and it is of great interest to the student of human desires. For it shows how strong is most people's loathing of anarchy; the fear of chaos is never far from our minds; we search eagerly for the swiftest and most infallible remedy against the disease, to wit, force. And yet I believe this view to be mistaken, though not because human societies are not fragile; they are and we do right to worry about them if we hold them in affection.

But this does not mean that force is a necessary or sufficient cement. Certainly force can help to hold a society together; this is obvious. Yet even in the extreme case of a tyranny, the hated tyrant has to rely upon consent as well. If his palace guards will not obey him, how is he to stay alive? If his soldiers and secret policemen will not obey, how is he to make his writ run? The ruler has to establish his authority; he may do so by frightening his subjects, though this method is always subject to the risk of some bold popular leader rising up to say 'this is only a man like any other'; he may do so by charm and glamour; or he may do so by establishing a relationship of trust with his subjects through an exchange of services, or as we would say today, by establishing a dialogue. However large the element of force involved in the acquisition of power by, for example, a guerilla leader toppling a rotten regime, some measure of consent must precede, accompany and follow each act of force. And to the extent that consent is given, even if sullenly and reluctantly, the element of force diminishes; indeed one of the problems facing the Bolshevik or the Castroite after achieving power is that he has no longer the continuous drama of battle to seize the popular imagination.

But if the relationship between force and consent is complex in the case of the bandit who is an avowed Machiavellian, that is who believes that force is the only basis of effective power, how much more complex is the relationship in our subtler, more highly articulated societies.

It may be legitimate to talk of war between the authorities and the professional criminal or revolutionary. But criminals and revolutionaries are in normal times a tiny minority, and their activities do not threaten the established order unless they are joined by large numbers of new recruits; they will gain such recruits only because of some breakdown in the political harmony of the community, not because of some failure in the enforcement of law and order. This is the true danger; in extreme terms that is the point of the famous dialogue:

Louis XVI: C'est une révolte?
La Rochefoucauld-Liancourt: Non, Sire, c'est une révolution.

A revolt can be crushed by force, though whether it should be is another matter; a revolution cannot be crushed, the word implying that a change in the balance of power has already taken place. The scales have already tipped. Revolutions are therefore to be avoided, not by force but by the maintenance of political harmony (which will of course include the maintenance of law and order in the regular sense–it would be a strange citizenry, one hitherto unknown to history, which called with one voice for more burglars and more political assassins). Even within this harmony, law and order is not synonymous with force. There are many laws which we do not break not because we are frightened of punishment but because breaking them would be morally repugnant, or have no point, or expose us to public ridicule, or hurt others or ourselves, or do violence to our loyalties, or offend our common sense. The advent of some laws is welcomed, if not demanded, by almost everybody; for example, most road safety regulations are applauded even by those who may later be charged with breaking them in a moment of inattention or intoxication. And even when we call for the use of force, it is not necessarily in our own defence; a full-grown man may consider that he is well able to look after himself, but he may still favour police patrols at night for the protection of unaccompanied women.

There is indeed a constantly shifting frontier between the law-abiders and the law-breakers. Most of us play many roles in relation to the law: traffic violator, penal reformer, opponent of new laws, advocate or opponent of capital punishment for child murderers, ignoramus about some new bureaucratic edict, and so on. In a reasonably harmonious society there is no universally accepted view of the law; some laws we support, others we do not, sometimes we feel the law is on our side, sometimes on the side of Them. Only a small minority who feel themselves to be entirely outside the society will claim that the law is always hostile; only a very blinkered policeman or judge would imagine that the law is always a sure shield against injustice and anarchy.

Compare this wide spread of viewpoints with the single-minded way we look at the enemy in wartime or the way one boxer looks at another: that is, as an opponent, not necessarily with hatred or contempt, but as a force to be defeated. Looking at the law, on the other hand, we are looking at a whole living context of which we ourselves are part, a many-levelled political structure. The rules of a team game are not designed to ensure that one particular side should defeat the other; nor is their primary object even to protect the referee from assault by the players (though we would expect such a rule to be included). Their aim is simply to make as good a game as we know how out of the available material. We shall do this often by trial and error over a long period; new rules will emerge, others will be dropped if they are frustrated by developments in tactics or by the wish of players and spectators for a somewhat different kind of game. The enactment of strict rules, enforced by a strict referee, does not ensure a good game. In fact, very often the reverse. On the whole, experience would seem to indicate that the fewer rules the better.

At this point the Machiavellian will object that, whatever the intention of having rules, in order to be effective these rules must be enforced. In the same way, he will argue, relations between nation-states may have many varied purposes, such as political unity, cultural exchange, and the increase of trade, but a nation-state cannot be sure of survival let alone independence and security unless it vigilantly maintains its military defences.

This argument is either circular or based on a false premise. Of course, laws have to be enforced; that is in the nature of what we mean by a law. If a prevailing moral code or mere advice from the authorities is able to prevent people from doing something harmful then no law is required. The law merely lists those harmful actions which, it is thought, can be deterred only by the prospect of punishment. In the same way, if a nation is attacked or threatened with attack by a rival, it can survive or retain its independence only by being so strongly defended that it would not be worth the rival's while to attack. This much is obvious. A law is a law. Strength defeats weakness. The Machiavellian's argument really depends on a more extreme proposition: that at all times men can be 'kept in order' *only* by the threat of punishment; that the rival nation-state is ever present and can be kept at bay *only* by the prospect of military defeat or at any rate the inflicting of unacceptable casualties.

Yet consider the vast area of action possible within civil society which is not prohibited by the law; consider also those actions which are prohibited by the law but which clearly the law alone could not prevent. Is it really only the prospect of jail which prevents every quarrel ending in murder? Or the dread of being caught that prevents us from shooting every traffic light, stripping the shelves of public libraries, and robbing blind men in dark alleys? It is surely more likely that enforceable laws derive from and reinforce social and moral conventions and taboos, rather than that they are the basis of civil society. Similarly, the Machiavellian view of international relations accounts nicely for the cold war, colonialism and imperialism. But it does not account for peaceful decolonisation or the survival and prosperity for long periods of nations without large standing armies. It is as arbitrary to posit the ubiquity of a warlike expansionist rival as it is to refuse to see such a rival when he is glaring you in the face. Expansionism, like other political tendencies, is the product of contingent forces. In Machiavelli's Italy, or in postwar Europe, expansionism may seem a permanent feature of life. But to select for examination in history only those tendencies which express the desire of one man or group to dominate others is like writing a history of the Royal Academy which deals solely with power struggles within the hierarchy and omits all mention of the pictures painted. Such a history would give only a mechanical, bloodless account of reality. Not only is the purpose of an enterprise at least as important as the means used to pursue it, but there is a constant interaction between the two. For example, in a two-party system the Machiavellian cannot explain such simple political phenomena as the following:

– A government piloting through a measure which is unpopular and which may therefore weaken its hold on power.

– An opposition supporting such a measure.

– An opposition refusing to cash in on a popular sentiment (for example, dislike of people of another colour) although fully aware of the damage that could thus be done to the government.

Such things can only be explained by a full examination of the relationship between the intentions and inclinations of political leaders, the pressure of opinion-formers and the degree of strength and stability of public opinion.

The arbitrary idea of a universal will to power helps us to understand only one aspect of this relationship; and indeed it is of no more and no less value in discussing politics than in any other field of social enquiry. In other words, politics-as-battle tells us only that in politics, as in other kinds of life, some people fight by fair means and foul to get to the top and others do not, and that the fighters will usually trample on the others. A banal observation, though a useful reminder to those who imagine that politics is or could be based solely on mutual endeavour, that we possess some special faculty of cooperation in public life of which we can see few signs in our private lives. But as soon as the battle paradigm goes beyond this banal observation and claims that politics is *nothing but* a struggle for power, then it becomes quite plainly false. And the failure of this wider claim strips the paradigm of much of its glamour for the self-styled realist.

The claims of the pilgrimage and science paradigms may be more speedily dismissed. Certainly, liberals have claimed to discern a pattern of progress in the maintenance of law and order over the past two centuries: we no longer hang sheep-stealers; it is safe to walk about the streets of London even at night; we may note also the growing sophistication of the penal system, with its dedication to the rehabilitation of the criminal through a careful gradation of method – the probation service, borstals, open prisons, maximum-security prisons; we may note also the greater training and the higher educational level of the police force and its use of modern technology. Such progress, it will be claimed, is both humane (pilgrimage paradigm) and based on rational methods (science paradigm).

Yet it is clear that, whether or not we regard these changes as 'progress', they are only piecemeal changes within a vast and complex structure of circumstance. Yes, of course there is progress within this structure; if a policeman can be taught to read and write, his son following his father's profession can be taught to use a typewriter. Yes, of course the use of the scientific method will prove fruitful; we can find out by scientific trial and error which prisoners respond to open-prison treatment and which must be kept under close guard for the protection of the public. Yet the whole history is not a progress; law and order is not a science.

The contrary evidence is well known: while capital punishment is on the way out in the western world, jail sentences are becoming longer and longer; London may be safe at night, but New York and Washington very definitely are not; not only have the penal reformers failed to deal with recidivists but the number of young offenders (who do respond to humane treatment) also increases, despite higher living standards and greater educational and career opportunities; the police may be becoming more skilled but so are the criminals and their lawyers, with the result that rates of detection and conviction in the western world are at best static; above all, the incidence of crime increases at a rate which cannot be explained away by the more comprehensive reporting of crimes to the police. And we have not begun to take account of the increase in criminal acts inspired by political dissidence – bombs, riots, burnings and so on.

Why is this so? Why do the best efforts of honourable and intelligent men fail to achieve a steady and uniform progress? One revealing answer is that dishonourable intelligent men are also doing their best. The criminals are as quick to apply technological advances as the police. In a curious way the Progressive fails to realise the significance of time; he imagines himself to be acting upon a world that stands still, a passive, fixed context. For example, he assumed that the coming of affluence and opportunity would satisfy and tame the children of the poor, not realising that affluence and opportunity would so alter their outlook that what had previously seemed so much to be desired would come to be taken for granted. Each action calls forth a reaction which creates a new world, posing new problems, demanding new solutions and a new jargon in which to phrase them. We might be able to describe this process as 'progress' if it were clear that each new problem to be tackled was smaller than its predecessor, that is to say if we were gradually working towards a fault-free system. How often does this happen? In the reduction of infant mortality and the elimination of malnutrition, in the provision of free access to legal advice and the impartiality of the courts – there are examples like these, but not nearly enough to provide support for a working paradigm. Just as often we find that 'one step forward' is followed by one if not two steps backward.

And this is so for the very simple reason that in politics, as we said earlier, 'the material answers back'. For human beings are not like a stable chemical substance which may be refined and refined to the nth degree of purity. The reformer sketches out his plan for the perfecting of this or that institution. But the reaction of the human material is unpredictable, as volatile as any explosive. This is not a sentimental statement to the effect that 'we cannot fathom human nature', but a mere fact of observation. For example: the executive council of a trade union votes 11–10 for a strike. There follows a sequence of unpredictable events: the strike may trigger off violence at the picket line, it may plunge the industry concerned into bankruptcy, it may merely clear the air, it may lead to other strikes. If only 'the eleventh man' had voted the other way! Could anyone have predicted this margin precisely (and precisely it would have to be; an error of one vote may be a total error, a miss as good as a mile)? No, not even those who had spent a lifetime studying the affairs of that particular union. For the eleventh man himself may not have decided until the final moment. Had he not had indigestion after a large lunch, he might have voted for a peaceful settlement. This element of unpredictability is familiar to us from classical times and has never been lost to view: *'Le nez de Cléopâtre; s'il eût été plus court, toute la face de la terre aurait changé.'*[15]

We understand how the eleventh man can nullify our best supported forecasts; and we have begun to understand how radically such forecasts differ from scientific hypotheses.[16] Yet we have not perhaps appreciated what a shadow the eleventh man casts on the whole theory of progress. His unpredictability does not of course affect our duty to aim for progress or, in an old-fashioned phrase, to do our best'. But if the eleventh man may upset the apple cart at any time, what becomes of the image of the steady and sure progress of the cart to the storehouse? And if the eleventh man is liable to have indigestion, why not the twelfth, thirteenth and fourteenth as well? In other words, are human affairs at crucial moments liable not only to marginal but also to violent swings?

This unpredictability is such a striking fact of history that all progressive theorists of any stature have had to take account of it. And they have all chosen the same method – the silencing of the human material. Rousseau's legislator, the Benthamite tradition of the social engineer, the Communist tradition of the dictatorship of the proletariat, all work on the assumption that the mob must not be allowed into the planning office. For if the common people are allowed to participate, they will exercise their human freedom to make mistakes. And once that freedom is permitted, progress will be neither sure nor necessary; we are liable to see the errors of our parents repeated. Of course the common people are not to be neglected; they are to be taught to understand and appreciate the true way so that at the last they may participate fully. But the first necessity for progress is silence in the classroom.

Thus gradually the ideal area of dialogue and decision is pushed backwards from the market place, through the council chamber to the dictator's study; from the earthy interplay of natural forces, to the rule of transient popular majorities, to the rule of permanent unpopular minorities. At each stage the regression is justified by a search for scientific exactitude and an ideal model of progress. Even within the oligarchy the regression continues and with increased ferocity; for the losing faction inside a *politburo* does not live to fight another day; it is condemned to physical, intellectual and moral Siberia. Science acknowledges only one correct theory at a time. In the end the only way of putting into practice an irrefutable scientific theory of progress is to leave its elaboration entirely to a single ruler and for the society to work on the simple premise that this ruler's words and actions do in fact form a coherent, complete and flawless picture of the world and of the correct method of dealing with it. Stalinism is the logical culmination of the search for an internally coherent theory of progress. But such a theory has to be as shut off from reality as the innermost sanctum of the Kremlin. It has and can have no firm footing in the world. Yet only by grounding our theories in the everyday conditions, desires and affections of men can we begin to understand politics, let alone suggest political remedies and improvements.

WHY THE THEATRE?

Our task, then, is to study the transaction of public business: to understand how men act for, against, with, and upon each other; how we protest, bargain, persuade and decide; how we translate feeling into argument and argument into action; how we alternately mould and yield to circumstance. The street-seller's trade is to buy and sell; the nutritive quality of his fruit and vegetables is another matter. Naturally the quality has a great effect upon the demand for his wares; that aspect would certainly interest the economist because it impinges upon buying and selling. In the same way we are profoundly interested in the notions of politics discussed above, not because they are full descriptions of politics – they are not – but because they have exercised such influence upon the minds and actions of men. We are familiar with the way in which the battle paradigm lures parliamentary or congressional oppositions to oppose even measures which are beneficial and popular. We are familiar too with the way in which the science paradigm leads administrators to try and impose tidy, 'rational' reforms upon untidy situations and irrational citizens. And, increasingly, we have begun to study the way in which the pilgrimage paradigm has increased the demands made by the public upon the government: the 'revolution of rising expectations'. The psychological effects of the three paradigms are enormous and still growing. Never has political theory exercised a deeper influence upon the minds of people who profess no interest in 'ideology' or even in politics itself, indeed in most parts of the world upon people who cannot read or write. All the same, these theories are still no more than elements in the political universe. They do not explain to us how that universe works; and hence, according both to common sense and to the practice of scientific enquiry, they do not explain how we could make that universe function better.

The observer who approaches public politics in such a spirit of common sense and scientific enquiry is immediately struck by the strongly *theatrical* flavour of political events. The man in the Stranger's Gallery sees below him a succession of events which are meant to be *seen;* seen by the colleagues and opponents of the politician holding the floor in the first instance, of course. But the ripple of theatrical intention immediately widens to reach his constituents, in particular his own party activists, to his party in general and to the public as a whole.

In each case he is speaking to an audience. And the expectations of that audience greatly influence the manner and content of his speech. In talking, say, about an economic slump, he will quite properly refer:

– To unemployment among his constituents, although the situation may be far worse in other areas.
– To the need for the revival of the principles of free enterprise/ Socialism, although there may be little scope for ideological action in the circumstances, which are entirely brought about by, say, a decline in world trade.
– To his confidence in the nation's ability to climb out of the depression and achieve a rate of growth second to none, although he is well aware that in reality the prospects are gloomy.

Now all these references would be irrelevant or actually misleading if made in the course of an impartial analysis of the situation; the editor would cut them out of any journalist's copy, the tutor would censure the student for straying from the standards of scholarship. And even in the case of the politician, the moralist would attack him for 'hypocrisy'; yet the moralist would be mistaken, for he has failed to understand the politician's trade.

There is no question of any direct falsehood. Some of his constituents are unemployed; it is quite possible that the doctrinaire application of political principle might reinvigorate an economy rendered sluggish by compromise; and if the prospects are gloomy, what is a politician for but to transform prospects? It is in fact the *purpose* of the politician's speech that the moralist misses.

The politician was elected by his constituents. Is it suggested that he should minimise or ignore their hardships? His task is surely to speak up for them and to let them know he is speaking up for them (otherwise how can they judge his performance fairly?).

The politician was elected by his party. He must let it know that he clings to the principles which he professed when he was chosen.

The politician owes a duty to the country, for he has put himself forward as a national leader by the fact of having stood for election. Are we to suppose that his leadership should spread despondency?

In each case the politician's reference is a practical act of communication. He is not a critical philosopher whose task is to deal in the truth or falsehood of propositions. The politician always has a practical aim before him, even when he seems to be engaging in speculative discussion. In the three references above he is pitching an appeal to specific sectors of the public. And what matters to him is the success or failure of that appeal. Of course, such an appeal may contain statements to which we can assign a truth-value as well as those to which we cannot; and it is of great importance to know whether the former statements are true or false.

For example, the politician may say: 'The enemy has fifteen tank divisions on our border; we must prepare to fight now before it is too late.' The first half of the statement is factual; we can argue only about whether it is wholly or partially true; there may be ten divisions, or they may not have moved up to the border, or the whole thing may be a fabrication. The second half of the statement by contrast concerns policy; we can argue about whether it is advisable to fight now, or to fight later when our army is stronger, or to sue for peace, or simply to wait and see what the enemy intends. These are questions of wisdom or folly, not of truth or falsehood. Moreover, in conjoining these two statements, the politician has an overarching *intention*; by stating a threat and following it with a policy he intends to stir the public to action. This is his aim; his reporting of the threat and the formulation of his policy are only elements in his effort to achieve that aim.

His speech is a political act. And it rests upon the assumption that he shares with his audience certain common aims and beliefs: in this case the defence of national territory, the conviction that it is better to risk loss of life than loss of independence. Aneurin Bevan writes:

The first function of a political leader is advocacy. It is he who must make articulate the wants, the frustrations, and the aspiration of the masses. Their hearts must be moved by his words, and so his words must be attuned to their realities. If he speaks in the old false categories they listen at first and nod their heads, for they hear a familiar echo from the past. But, if he persists, they begin to appreciate that he is no longer with them. He is not their representative any longer in the true meaning of that much-abused term.[17]

The actor wishes to work a particular effect upon his audience. He invents little pieces of 'business' which he knows will please; or he goes for nobler effects. But the whole performance is always directed at the audience upon whose reaction its success depends. A performance without an audience is only a rehearsal. And, conversely, a man sitting alone in a room does not usually applaud or boo a play on the television. A 'live show' implies an actor and an audience reacting upon one another. We shall discuss this relationship in greater detail in the next chapter. For the moment it is enough to point out that while the expectations of the audience influence the actor, the actor also influences the audience.

The actor cannot spring upon a totally unprepared public an entirely new style; but equally he will not, or at least should not, rest content indefinitely to churn out the same old stuff which has gone down so well in the past. The relationship between actors and audience is, despite the circumstances of the medium (the proscenium arch), a relationship of equals; for on both sides of the footlights there are human beings with an equal right or at least an equal determination to make up their own minds. Such a relationship is eternally unpredictable – which is only another way of saying 'alive'; the eleventh man sways the meeting, the man who laughs at the first joke in the play sets others laughing and makes the comedy a hit, the man who coughs or giggles in the deathbed scene spoils the atmosphere, the marginal voter decides the election.

The historian, by which we mean a man who is in a position to take a longer view of the consequences of an event simply through the passing of time, can enlarge on this simple calculus of success or failure. He can ask whether the object was a wise one and whether the methods used to achieve it were apposite, economical and fair. Even the most superficial history is able to distinguish a foul method in a fair cause from a fair method in a foul cause. In the heat of political battle, or in instant analysis when the field is still obscured by smoke, it is not so easy to lay out the elements of a political event for examination. We are therefore tempted to adopt some quick universal rule of thumb, such as 'true or false', 'right or wrong'. The historian's analysis is not necessarily better than any of these but he does have the advantage of having at least limited access to the full chain of cause-event-consequence.

The historian can take a broader as well as a longer view. For his distance from the event allows him a wider perspective. He is not confined to the view from the gallery or the stalls or the insider's view from behind the scenes. He can see that the audience's role is not confined to applauding or jeering the actors, to the running commentary of its representatives, the critics, and to the ultimate choice of paying its money or not. There is also a political theatre in which the roles are reversed. The political leaders become the audience, and the public the actors. We see this happening in trade union demonstrations, in peace marches or civil rights marches, in meetings of local political activists, in the press, and, as yet to a lesser extent, on television: the aim may be to frighten a section of the political leadership, or to animate it, to demand a change of programme or of personalities, to evoke sympathy, to stir up trouble or to quieten things down. But in all cases it is the quality of the *performance* which decides the outcome, not the quality of the message – which may be some very simple slogan as 'Smith out – Brown in' or 'Ban the Bomb'.

By the quality of performance we mean the timing, style, appearance and numbers of the demonstrators, the lengths to which they are prepared to go, the determination with which they make their demands. When dockers marched in support of Enoch Powell's policies, the event administered a severe electric shock to the political elite; and similarly when American construction workers, 'the hard-hats', staged patriotic marches in support of the war in Vietnam. The conventional interpretation of such events is that feelings on these lines must have been bubbling up from the collective subconscious and that the events themselves are merely their final open expression. And yet surmise about such feelings is a long way from political fact. Theories about the intensity of the bubbling 'below the surface' are not much help to the politician. The real interest and importance of the events lies in the interaction between the demonstrators and the political leaders. The 'hard hats' altered President Nixon's conduct of the mid-term elections of

1970 to a marked extent, but, it is important to note, to no particular advantage; in fact, it would be reasonable to say that he over-reacted very largely because he himself wished to believe in the hard-hats' marches as a sign of the times. This interaction is thus not an irresistible pressure; that is to say, it is not that the hard-hats' marches give President Nixon a piece of political information which dictates a precise course of action to him. He still has to make his own decisions. The public event is more in the nature of a shower of rain; it shocks the system, but it is up to our own judgement whether we take action by sheltering in a doorway, or going home for a rain-coat, or whether we stride on saying 'it will pass'. It is in this sense a theatrical process. The audience is conscious only of the play and of its own reaction to it; we need to know nothing of the rehearsals, the producer's struggles to lick the play into shape and, further back, the impresario's struggles with the 'angels' and the author's struggle with the blank sheet of paper. It is significant that to describe a successful interaction we say 'that was good theatre' – using the name of the place for the process which goes on inside it. 'Good theatre' (as distinct from a good play) thrives on shock/novelty and sentiment. Peace marches become effective when they are led by solid citizens rather than bearded bohemians. Militant Socialist dockers are more unexpected antagonists of coloured immigrants than middle-class house-holders who fear that property values will go down if a black family comes to live next door. A procession of mothers and children are more stirring advocates for a new school than an official's report to the city council.

Such is the way in which important public business is transacted. When we come to think of it, they are odd shows, these awkwardly staged public acts, these artificial shocks so crudely administered to the body politic. How did they come about? Is it in the nature of relations between men that politics should be a theatre? Or is it a historical accident? What kinds of distortion does it introduce into our lives? And could we manage things better without the micro-phone and the grease paint?

II

The Theatre of Embarrassment

'It is a part
That I shall blush in acting.'
(*Coriolanus*, Act 2, scene 2)

The flesh being weak, formality has its limits. Even in the best-run gatherings, emotion breaks through. The trembling hand, the stifled yawn, the voice suddenly dropping its polite modulation, the vain attempt to conceal the curling of the lip in contempt or laughter – these are the familiar signs that beneath the calm surface of social intercourse the inner life is heaving. And the greater the depth of the inner seething, the greater the pressure on the crust of convention. Where our most vital desires and passions are concerned, the eventual explosion at surface level may be seismic. This contrast between the inner and the outer life is a mainstay of comedy and tragedy alike. How could it be otherwise? We crave society. Society demands restraints on our passions. Our passions demand gratification. The friction is the dilemma of being human.

It is out of the crack in the mask of convention that great dramatic art explodes. The dramatist, social seismologist, entertains us by charting the progress of that crack; either it is eventually closed up and the ground smoothed over, the characters are regenerate and we have a comedy; or the crack widens until it fills the screen, the characters are engulfed in the abyss and we have a tragedy. We are delighted or appalled by the *dénouement*; we sympathise or, on occasion, identify with the leading characters. But the characters of great drama do not converse with us directly and intimately. They are sealed off in the world that the author has created for them. They are distanced from us.

This is true whether the actors throw themselves into their parts (the Method School, and in the milder sense old-fashioned naturalism) or whether they present the drama as a parable of which they themselves are the narrators rather than the characters (the concept of Bertolt Brecht). In the first case, the actors are super-puppets;

in the second, lecturers. Neither species breathes the same air as the rest of us.

In inferior art that distance is abolished. No longer is the drama acted out for us by a group of persons who are clearly set apart from us by the proscenium arch. The whole theatre becomes a stage. Not merely does the audience join in the choruses. The audience is the chorus. This inferior art has recently been systematised in the concept of the 'happening' – a more or less organised sequence of unconnected shocks administered to the audience to jolt their consciousness. A still more recent example is that of the Living Theatre, a troupe which assaults the audience both physically and emotionally. The old Theatre of Embarrassment (Francis Wyndham's excellent term) made the audience *feel* it was participating in or overhearing the extremely painful scene taking place on the stage – for example, Dame Peggy Ashcroft in *The Deep Blue Sea* as a cultured lady physically attracted to a common young man. In the new Theatre of Embarrassment the audience *is* participating in a painful scene in which, for example, a naked actor may be badgering an elderly businessman into burning his money and throwing off his pin-stripe suit. This is an unashamed attempt to embarrass, paralleled in the old theatre only by what Wyndham calls 'the embarrassment of threatened disaster'; that is to say, the fear/hope that the show will not go on, that John Barrymore will be drunk, that Judy Garland will forget her lines and turn up late or not at all. That is drama indeed.

But why do we call this an inferior art? Its supporters point out that it is at least immediate and therefore alive; it is happening *now*. A businessman being insulted is a unique and spontaneous event; a third-rate production of *Hamlet* is a stale and worthless repetition. This line of reasoning is attractive but false. First, no happening of this kind is spontaneous, least of all one in which a large number of people have paid money to congregate in a given place at a given time. Secondly, the further the performers flee from 'art', the more artistic their performance becomes. Dislike it as they may, they find themselves choosing between techniques of embarrassment, how best they may shock, titillate or bore the audience. A technique which achieves a desired effect on one night is likely to be re-employed the next; snd if that technique is consciously *not* used in order to avoid staleness, the decision to do so is itself an artistic decision of some sophistication. Nor can this sophistication be avoided by avoiding repetition. For even a one-night stand has this character of *intention* about it – it is the special performance of the guest star for one night only, it is saturnalia, it is the one night of the year on which we do this, etc. For the trouble is that the mere fact of performance creates an artefact, and moreover, an embarrassing artefact. The one merit which was claimed for the 'free' theatre, namely spontaneity, is nonexistent. Ann Halprin, whose Dancers' Workshop in San Francisco is one of the longest established of the 'free-expression' theatres, admits or claims that the 'situations' which she creates are in fact well controlled; the situations are initiated and directed by her 'captains' or group leaders. A typical situation may involve the audience being instructed to drop on all fours and imitate lions and tigers, the aim apparently being for them to lose their inhibitions and gain the sense of being part of a herd or tribe, 'to merge their individual personalities'. A more political example is that of Ariane Mnouchkine's production of *1789, The French Revolution, Year One.* The actors playing 'the people' mingle with the audience, who join in their laughter and celebrations at the fall of the Bastille, their boos at La Fayette's calls for order. What would be the leading parts in a conventional drama – La Fayette, the king, Marat – are played in ritual, puppet fashion; the people (actors plus audience) are the protagonists, the flesh and blood of the piece. The parallel with modern political events is explicit. Michael Kustow reports:

The night I went the audience booed La Fayette and drowned his threats by chanting and stamping the most durable slogan of May 1968, *Ce n'est qu'un début, continuons le combat.* . . . On the night of 14 July this year, they gave a free performance. Five thousand people crammed into the Cartoucherie. ('We felt we could take them with us to storm the Bastille all over again', said an actress.) When they reached the episode of the Bastille, they stopped the performance and the evening became one huge *bal musette*, the multifarious crowd singing and dancing through the night. . . .[1]

The theatre is transformed into the political convention hall. The immersion of the audience in the dramatic process may not be complete; the actors are still distinguished by their costumes and their speaking of lines. Yet it is the degree to which the audience feels immersed which is the production's avowed criterion of success. In so far as the audience retains its detachment and its freedom to criticise either the technique of the production or the ideas propounded in it, the production has failed.

Such events correspond both in purpose and technique to the party game which is intended by the hostess 'to break the ice'; and they are equally artificial, equally lacking in spontaneity.

They are also equally inferior as art – inferior in the same sense that a man leading a cup final sing-song is producing inferior art to a man conducting the Brandenburg concertos. His material is inferior and his attempt to excuse that inferiority on the grounds that he is presiding over a spontaneous uprising of song is patently ludicrous: a hundred thousand people have bought tickets for the occasion, song sheets have been printed, and some of the audience are singing comic words to the tune of 'Abide with me', words which have become almost as well-worn and traditional on these occasions as those they parody.

The Theatre of Embarrassment then is inferior; and it is to the Theatre of Embarrassment that our subject, the political drama, belongs. This may be admitted without shame. Some may feel that politics would be more inspiring if it was conducted on a heroic, distanced level. Many indeed have tried to do so. Yet the intimate, local scale of our concerns gives an earthy asymmetry to our reactions. It is only when we are all suffering in the same way at the same time (famine or the threat of invasion) that the drama takes on a heroic, monumental aspect. If we examine our feelings about history, we shall note that only in such times (Britain in 1588 or 1940, Ireland in the Potato Famine) does rhetoric invoking the collective soul ('this great nation', 'the people of this country') have power to move us. At other times appeals to the collective soul ring cheap or positively fraudulent. No doubt in the long run a statistical mean reaction is observable. But it is not merely that in the long run we are all dead but that the long run is a succession of short hops. The business of politics is the managing of these short hops. It is not necessarily the *aim* of political activity; the short hops may be stages on some greater journey or they may be ends in themselves. A stockbroker may justify his activity on the grounds that it rationalises the investment of national resources. It may indeed be that the *effect* of his activity is to direct capital where it is of most benefit to the community. But his activity actually consists in dealing in stocks and shares and thereby earning his living. A devout clergyman aims to serve God, but in order to do so effectively he must cajole people to come to church. To keep his congregation he must develop the techniques of oratory, flower arrangement, choir management, which enhance the message that he has to deliver. Much of his time may indeed be spent in these tasks. It would not be inappropriate for him to include them under the heading of 'serving God'; but we should not forget that we are thereby defining the activity not in terms of its own nature but in terms of the motive which lies behind it. We would find it less appropriate to describe the arranging of flowers for a gangsters' convention or rhetoric lessons for Hitler as 'the service of God'.

Similarly we may describe the aim of politics in such phrases as the 'liberation of mankind' or the 'building of democracy'. But these are of little help in discussing what actually happens in political situations, what politicians have done, and by contrast or extension what they could or should do. In reality, as opposed to the diagram or the vision, we have to deal with the short run, the local, the intimate and above all the embarrassing.

For while great art at its distance can touch us deeply, it cannot embarrass us. It is too generalised, too abstracted to give us that feeling of being unpleasantly close to a painful situation. We see the face distorted in misery, the tears coursing down the cheeks, but we do not smell the breath of the woman so racked by grief that she has not brushed her teeth. Only bad art produces the unfiltered 'slices of life', dumped raw and fetid in our laps.

We have devised many sophisticated rituals to sift and filter the expression of strong feeling in politics: the rules of procedure at public meetings, or the procedure of Parliament itself. But the voice from the back of the hall is not to be silenced. The filter is not a baffle; its function is merely to screen out the ugliest aspects of the emotion, to give room for the calm and, we hope, sensible consideration of the problems involved. Yet the emotion never loses the roughness of its origin. The poetic transformation of grief or indignation by orators such as Lloyd George, Aneurin Bevan and John L. Lewis retains in its fluent cadences the initial force of these emotions; that is what makes a great orator – the combination of technical skill with a willingness to share in popular emotion without reservations about 'good taste' or 'intellectual honesty'.

Consider the emotion of national or racial pride, the patriotism of tribe or territory or both. Harold Macmillan describes the march past of the British army in the victory parade in Tunis on 20 May 1943.

In a long file they came, formation after formation, regiment after regiment, unit after unit.

The Theatre of Embarrassment

Unlike the French and Americans the British were in drill, not battle, order – shorts, stockings and boots, battle blouses or shirts with short sleeves – no helmets (forage caps and berets). The helmet gives a soldier the look of a robot. . . . With the forage cap or beret you can see his face – his jolly, honest, sunburnt, smiling English, Scottish or Irish face – relaxed now, not worn or harassed as men look in battle – and confident and proud. All these brown faces, these brown bare arms and knees, these swinging striding outstepping men – all marched magnificently.

Just before the saluting base (a very old parade trick) there was stationed a band. This of course got all the men marching at their best before they reached the saluting point.

My mind went back to Kitchener's Army and the Battle of the Somme. I had always thought that these were the finest British formations that had ever taken the field. But now I had to admit that the First and Eighth Armies were just as good. These men seemed on that day masters of the world and heirs of the future.[2]

Eldridge Cleaver describes a black power meeting:

I thought the cops were invading the meeting, but there was a deep female gleam leaping out of one of the women's eyes that no cop who ever lived could elicit.

I recognised that gleam out of the recesses of my soul, even though I had never seen it before in my life; the total admiration of a black woman for a black man.

I spun around in my seat and saw the most beautiful sight I had ever seen: four black men wearing black berets, powder-blue shirts, black leather jackets, black trousers, shiny black shoes – and each with a gun![3]

The pride in both these passages is simple and unfeigned. Both men are telling us what drives them on, why the pattern of their lives, which may to the rest of us appear a strange compound of hardships and eccentric dealings, is for them a necessity, the only possible life. The interest in these passages lies not in the particular emotion expressed; millions of American blacks or Englishmen would feel the same. We are interested in the proud statement of such plain feelings by such sophisticated men. Macmillan's sophistication is hinted at in the passage itself by his remark on the stage managing of a parade. His view of the world is cool but not indifferent, as his record in the 1930s showed. Cleaver has a considerable grasp of the comic side of racial pride and of the swagger of youth; but this never weakens,

61

perhaps it even enriches, his belief that the black man has psychic scars so gangrenous that they can be healed only by a full and radical expression of black patriotism. The passion is hot; but the eye is cool, the words deliberately chosen. However sincere the intent, what we have is a performance.

And the aim of this performance is the communication of emotion. The new Theatre of Embarrassment attempts to eschew words, regarding them as a sophisticated corrupter of the pure emotion. This is an extremely naïve view both of language and of communication. For it is language that lends form and point to inchoate emotion. The surge of pride which Macmillan and Cleaver feel at the sight of fine young men is not merely a surge of the blood; it is enriched by the complex concepts of tribe, race and nationality, concepts elaborated by philosophers and demagogues (the two not always easy to distinguish), celebrated in song, and consecrated by history. Few emotions, certainly not those which have any application to politics, are without a similar 'literary' content. However minimal the objects presented to our gaze – a bare stage, silent actors in black – our mind immediately drenches them in memories and metaphors, groups them into our preferred categories, draws inferences from the slightest gesture. We are incurable interpreters. By avoiding words, the actors merely concentrate our attention upon movements, lights, music, just as a newly blind man concentrates and develops his sense of hearing, yet draws upon his stock of visual memory to complete his mental world. In this sense the actors cannot hope to communicate to us a 'pure' emotion uncontaminated by our preconceptions. For communication is contamination, modification. The more successfully a politician communicates with his audience, the less his talk will directly reflect his own private opinions and emotions, the more it will respond to, though not necessarily follow exactly, those of his audience. Even the most dedicated theatre of spontaneity comes to be shaped by its audience, its receptivity to certain techniques, its patience, its sympathies. If this does not happen, there is, to quote a Mike Nichols sketch, 'proximity but no relating' – in other words, a flop.

In normal discourse we take it for granted that proper communication should involve modification. Inherent in the idea of 'talking it over' is an understanding that both A and B should be ready to change their previous positions with the aim of coming closer together unless of course A wins B over to his way of thinking during the meeting, or *vice versa*. Some kind of equality between the two parties, a readiness to listen as well as to talk, a spirit of good will which expresses itself in a flexible, amenable manner: these are some of the qualities we might invoke to define the idea of 'dialogue' or 'conversation'. They are rare enough qualities in private life, but necessarily rarer still in public life.

Moreover, a feeling is growing that in recent years the number of effective public 'communicators' has been diminishing; indeed it is significant that in using this now fashionable word we usually refer to journalists and television commentators and not to politicians who should, by nature of their trade, be the communicators *par excellence*.

Throughout western civilisation people are profoundly dissatisfied with the politicians. They are not so dissatisfied with their doctors; the failure to find a cure for cancer is not greeted with derision. When one considers that medicine has discovered no more than three or four important totally new drugs in this century, the western politicians' rate of more or less successful innovation does not show up too badly – the national health service, speed limits, NATO, the Common Market, PAYE, etc. The failures in foreign and economic policy between the wars were spectacular and tragic. But nobody under thirty – the age-group allegedly most disaffected from the political process – can remember these events. Since the second world war almost all western countries have known only rising prosperity and almost unbroken peace. Why should this golden age have brought such discontent with those chosen to preside over it?

There would appear to be a bundle of reasons, all essentially deriving from the embarrassment of political dialogue. All of them may be inherent. We may never be able to remove them totally. But that is no excuse for failing to do what we can.

THEM AND US

The primary reason for our distrust of our governors is the nature of our system of government and hence the nature of our governors. For we – and this includes most of the western world – live under a *representative* system of government. That is, we elect by one means or another a comparatively small number of men to rule over us; there are limits to their powers, principally those laid down by custom (the rule of law, quinquennial elections, etc.) and the situation of the nation (economic, geographic, political, etc.). Within these limits – what we may call the rules of the game – those elected have a reasonably free hand. Occasional efforts are made by disgruntled citizens to remind the governors of what they promised in order to gain election – their manifesto. But the further effort to build upon this the concept of the mandate ('they must carry out their promises and only their promises') stirs but the sleepiest response in the populace of most western countries. Naturally, total failure to carry out promises will make a government unpopular; but as these promises will include such undisputed goods as 'peace' and 'prosperity' this unpopularity is hardly surprising. It does not take the notion of a mandate betrayed in order for us to wish to 'throw the villains out'. No, on the whole we recognise the need for a certain flexibility in the orders we give our masters. We choose the best people we can find, lay down some general rules of conduct for them, sketch out to them the achievements we would most welcome from them and leave them more or less to get on with it.

This system is in sharp contrast to the others that have been and are being tried. There are basically three of the latter.

First, the participatory. Everyone contributes to the making of decisions in tribal conclave. This method is associated with simple societies, whether primitive or newly formed like the town meetings of the Pilgrim Fathers and their early successors. Everyone has his say; typically a consensus emerges, if possible, without a vote; and because everyone identifies himself so closely with the society, he abides by the decision with enthusiasm.

This charming mode of self-government still pops up all the time, but inevitably on a small scale: pressure groups, parent-teacher associations, clubs. For the defect of the participatory system is that it becomes hopelessly unwieldy once the number of participators passes a certain point. We must emphasise that schemes such as those in the cooperative movement or in Yugoslav industry are not participatory, but representative. The worker or the customer has a share in the enterprise just as he has a share in any western government; and he hopes to gain profits from that share. But the only share in the *managing* of the concern which he may hope to have is in the election of managers by workers, rather than by shareholders and/or by fellow managers. But this is not participatory democracy, any more than the House of Commons is participatory democracy. Participatory democracy in industry is, for example, three brothers with equal shares and skills in a carpentry shop – and no underlings.

Second, there is the delegated method of government. We choose men to speak for us as in the representative method, but instead of allowing them some latitude, we dictate precisely what they shall say. This is practised most widely today in the trade unions and some professional bodies. The branch decides how their man should vote at the union's Annual Conference. And that Conference determines how the union's men should vote at the mammoth TUC. This ensures that there can be no mistake. The views of the membership – or that activist fraction thereof which bothered to vote at the original meeting – are resoundingly expressed. The trouble is that by the time they come to be expressed, these views may be out of date. Delegation is an extremely inflexible system. And it is of interest to note that its most zealous partisans tend to use the system only when dealing with topics which are not of immediate daily moment to their doings. In the trade union movement the full process of democracy is observed in discussing whether Britain should leave NATO or whether the banks should be nationalised; but the tactics of a strike will typically be dealt with by an executive of twenty or thirty men or, in certain bodies, by one supremely powerful man.

Such tactics may be later confirmed or overruled by the vote of a mass meeting or in a very few cases (the National Union of Mineworkers is one) by a secret ballot. But in all cases it is the executive which *initiates* new tactics. In fact we may conclude that delegate democracy, like participatory democracy, is in most structures today largely symbolic in value. The day-to-day power rests with representatives. Should we wish radically to alter the way in which that day-to-day power is exercised, we must elect new representatives. Voting for or sending delegates to vote for resolutions which call for a new direction will have little effect if the old directors are allowed to remain, except to remind the latter that their jobs are in danger. To make this clearer, consider the example of the British Labour Party in power. The policy of the Labour Party is in theory decided by the delegates to the Annual Conference. It is in fact decided by the representatives in Parliament, who choose the prime minister, who in turn chooses his cabinet. All recent history has shown that a Labour government makes up its own mind but will respond very quickly to the feeling of the electorate which has the power to eject it and replace it with another (Tory) government. The prime minister himself responds to the feeling of Labour members of parliament who have the power to eject and replace him. He does not pay a great deal of attention (historians differ over how much) to the views of his cabinet in so far as these views are purely personal; where they reflect feelings in the PLP he will pay a great deal of attention to them. When the PLP is happy, the prime minister can hire and fire whom he likes and can introduce the most unexpected new policies. When the PLP is unhappy – which tends to mean that the party is unpopular in the country – the cabinet ceases to be a collection of the prime minister's place-men, it grows into a squad of watchful and hostile representatives of the PLP. At no time, however, in all this are the views of delegates to Annual Conferences of much weight, except in so far as they reveal the feelings of the party in the country, which are in any case more strongly and relevantly reflected in the feelings of the PLP. The question of who exercises the power and who has the overarching power to appoint or dismiss the exerciser is paramount. And no written constitution, no academic doctrine of *'primus inter pares'*, can obscure that. This is the thrust of politics, and it is felt more swiftly and directly in an age which is so impatient with form and ceremony. Both participation and delegation have proved too unwieldy for large, complex societies; both involve too much delay in making decisions. Representation is all.

Yet there is a third system of government, out of fashion in the modern academy, advanced in few textbooks, praised by few sages, yet prevailing over most of the earth's surface: the authoritarian system. Here the only 'act' of the people is to acknowledge the authority – whether priestly, royal or ideological – of some man or group of men. Once that imagined moment has passed, the people may either continue in their assent to that authority or rebel against it.

Many people will regard such a system as bad, for two reasons. First, the choice between assent and rebellion is too crude to permit an unstrained dialogue between ruler and ruled, and hence to permit peaceful change; only the violent shock of revolution can alter the system. Second, the dictator is likely to abuse his power and to do so with impunity; not merely has he time and freedom to build up an apparatus of repression which can be destroyed only by a fully fledged force of rebellion, but also the people will be deterred from the efforts necessary to form such a force. Both these reasons may be valid; but it does not follow that because the authoritarian regime is in these senses bad it will necessarily also be unpopular with its subjects. Similarly, as Professor Plamenatz points out, the contention of the Communists that 'the governors of a capitalistic state so corrupt the minds of the poor that they are thus artificially induced to desire the maintenance of an economic and social system which involves their exploitation' does not mean that 'the poor do not consent to their governors' actions merely because they are not aware of their own best interests'.[4]

Whatever the mode of government, the choice before the citizen is always the same: to consent or not to consent to it. It is the means of expressing this choice, and the degree of influence which this choice will have upon public affairs, that vary with the mode of government. There is no need to posit, as Locke does, the notion of *tacit consent*, given by each citizen by virtue merely of residing within or travelling through the dominions of a given government. Such a notion entails that any government which exercises power effectively must therefore have the consent of all its citizens. It would be absurd to maintain that all black South Africans or all Crimean Tatars consented to the form of government which rules them merely because it does in fact rule them. And yet if we leave the logic of theory for the logic of practice, we must admit that to survive over a long period the authoritarian regime must enjoy the consent of at least some of its subjects. The dictator who fancies himself largely insulated from the pressures of the civilian public still has to secure the loyalty of his armed forces; for, as we said earlier, if his soldiers and his secret police will not obey him, how is he to make his writ run? Moreover, while discontent among the military may sometimes centre upon purely military grievances such as low pay (and can therefore easily be settled by taxing the civilian population to raise the cash), in the end civilian discontents are almost certain to infect the military also. Soldiers too have parents, wives, children; their interests cannot be entirely divorced from those of society as a whole. Some dictators have even attempted to effect such a divorce, for example by the employment of eunuchs and foreigners as bodyguards; such an effort to isolate the power structure from the 'native' population is really an effort to turn the territory into a kind of internal colony, and it runs the same risk that colonists do, that of stirring the excluded natives to arms.

In one way or another, political pressures are likely to make their impact upon the most insensitive authoritarian regime. The survival of such a regime over a long period is not a proof that the majority of its citizens have consented to it; but it is at least an indication (strengthened with the passing of time) that a measure of consent is likely to be present. Aneurin Bevan says:

The answer is not the simple one that the masses were held down by sheer physical force. That is possible for a short time: but it cannot explain the continuity of centuries of the same conditions. The institutions and modes of behaviour of these societies must have, in part at least, commended themselves to ordinary men and women or they would have been undermined by sheer disapproval. Ultimately, rulers, however harsh, must share the same values as the ruled if their empire is to persist. Obedience is rendered in the last resort, and for any considerable length of time, by accepting the moral and intellectual sanctions that lie behind social compulsions.[5]

The question is why even this measure of consent should be granted to the authoritarian regime which acknowledges no duty to carry out our wishes or to cherish our rights. The answer may be given in several different forms: security and stability, the avoidance of anarchy, the promotion of effective government, the pleasures of continuity, the absence of faction. Bevan himself gives an oddly conservative version:

... there must always have been compensations and amenities, pleasures and common rituals, making life seem worth while and forming the cement that bound ancient societies together in a continual reaffirmation of willing consent.[6]

But these answers are at best consequences of a successful authoritarian regime. None is the cause of its success. In a long-lasting dictatorship we may hope to enjoy one or other of these benefits; but the benefit itself is not the reason why the regime is able to provide it. Moreover, none of these benefits is common to all types of authoritarian regime; some dictators are competent administrators, others are hopelessly incompetent; some continue to foster old mores, customs and institutions, others are radical and unpredictable innovators, who deprive the citizen of all certainty and security. The common condition of their survival is the widespread public acceptance of their rule as in some sense *legitimate*.

This kind of acceptance differs from the concept of consent in two important ways. We may accept our form of government and/or our rulers while disliking either or both. In the language of consent this could at most be described as 'reluctant consent' – not a very powerful concept. Secondly, legitimacy springs not from our saying Yes or No to the regime but from some external standard. In deciding problems of legitimacy we must ask such questions as: is this man the true heir of the Dynasty? Are these men the true heirs of the Revolution? Does this man embody the Apostolic Succession? Or the Spirit of the Nation? Or the Consciousness of the Proletariat? Naturally it is we who choose what the standard should be – Monarchist, Communist, Religious, Nationalist. But that choice once made, the question is to be discussed more or less objectively. In that way we hope to lend certainty and continuity to the political structure.

A sense of legitimacy characterises all long-lasting, comparatively stable, authoritarian regimes. And any such regime, on coming to power – which it usually does by violent means – has to make every effort to establish its legitimacy as quickly as possible. Otherwise it will not last long. The establishment of legitimacy is a perennial problem for military regimes in particular. The colonels who overthrew the monarchy and seized power in Greece are a striking modern example. Papadopoulos, the prime minister, who has significantly dropped his military title, stresses that his regime stands in a continuing tradition of 'Hellenistic and/or Christian inspiration': 'Civilisation is the factor establishing cohesion, and it is Greece that gave birth to that civilisation. . . . In war, we were the first to show the world the road to victory, by fighting the war in 1940 with booty captured from our enemies.' This, then, would seem to indicate that the aim is to continue the tradition of parliamentary democracy stretching from Pericles to Churchill. But no, 'the past as a democracy will never return to Greece . . . the Revolution is the reality through which will be born the State of the Constitution of 1968.' The spirit of this constitution is clearly defined: 'Democracy implies the exercise of responsible authority by the mandatories of the people, to satisfy the public interest, regardless of whether satisfaction of the public interest clashes with what would satisfy side A, B, C or D, with regard to the next election, demagogy and vote-hunting.'[7]

Such a conception is far removed from the popular idea of Greek democracy. In fact it stands in total contradiction to exactly those parts of Greek history out of which Papadopoulos chooses to weave his tapestry of civilisation (although he might perhaps find an equivocal ally in Plato). The regime's attempt to place its ideas in this continuing tradition will only remind some people that such very diverse figures of the old regime as Karamanlis and the Papandreous, father and son, do genuinely have a place in that tradition.*

Yet the military regime has no alternative. There being no other politically appealing standard to attach themselves to, the new rulers have to lay claim to legitimacy on the old standard, however inappropriate that claim may seem. For all that a military junta can offer is a promise to clean up the mess left by the old gang; it cannot, unless its leader is of the highest calibre, or has some other claim on public feeling (preferably both – de Gaulle's titanic political strength after 1958 derived both from his great personal qualities and from a historical claim, to have embodied France in 1940), anoint itself with the true holy oil, as can an undoubted sovereign or a priest of the true faith – whether of this world or the next. What then are the characteristics of such a legitimate sovereign?

Nobody disputes the legitimate sovereign's right to the throne. He may therefore be expected to produce stable government. The people trust him, because by definition they could have no better sovereign (any other sovereign would not be legitimate). As his title is undisputed, he has no reason to engage in paranoid acts of repression. He has plenty of time to dispense justice with an even hand. He and his people may speak simply and sweetly to one another. They may speak without embarrassment. Such a happy state of affairs is far from usual. Yet traces of such relationships are to be observed under many authoritarian regimes, many of them by no means benevolent. Even in Soviet Russia where, as we have said, most of the citizen's political dialogue is conducted with the politician-as-policeman, it is recorded that peasants, ignorant of Khrushchev's murky past, could cry without embarrassment and with the unclogged sentiment of Mother Russia, 'give us bread, Nikolai Sergeyevich', or 'let us keep our few poor acres for ourselves, Little Father'.

This concept of legitimacy is a mixture of the observable results of legitimate sovereignty in action, of the beliefs of the people about legitimacy, and of the hopes they place in it. Whether or not these results, beliefs and hopes add up to a defence of legitimacy against radical action in an extreme situation is not our concern at present. We wish to note the point that people can talk to a legitimate sovereign as they cannot to one whose claim is not yet legitimised; this ease of dialogue may still obtain even if the legitimate sovereign's intentions are cold and repulsive while the illegitimate wishes the

* The elements of political tradition are discussed more fully below (pp. 167–91).

people nothing but well. Is the reason similar to that which allows some people to talk frankly and without embarrassment to their family doctor or lawyer when they could not do so to the immediate members of their family? Is there some combination of familiarity and disinterest which always unlocks the heart? The usurper is a warring competitor for affection, like a stranger or a brother; the legitimate sovereign is a familiar figure whose shadow is protective rather than threatening.

Yet the legitimate authoritarian system is not alone in preventing embarrassment either. In the tiny society everyone knows everyone else and everyone is a ruler. Who can be embarrassed in giving instructions to himself? There may be violent quarrels with fellow-rulers, but the intimacy and sense of community are inevitable. And here we notice a similarity with the delegated system. Delegates are and were from the beginning messengers: each brings tidings from his own community. He is always part of that community. There can be no stiffness in handing the message over to the messenger; in fact we may expect (in the trade unions for example) that the messenger himself will have played a leading part in the formulation of the message. For the κηρυξ is no mere Buttons, prey to alienation and the other ills of a society ruined by the division of labour; he is a dignified and mature ambassador or jury foreman. He is himself a trusted elder of the kirk.

So we see that in the legitimate authoritarian, the participatory and the delegated systems, political dialogue flows freely and intimately between rulers and ruled. And yet for the largely educated electorates of modern industrial societies, the authoritarian mode has proved intolerable, the participatory has proved unwieldy, and the delegated inflexible. The representative mode has alone proved able to satisfy the needs of the machinery of government and industry. What provision does the representative mode make for easy and intimate political dialogue between rulers and ruled? The answer is that it makes few provisions. And most of the channels that it used to keep open are long since dried up.

The reasons for the drying up of the dialogue are also the reasons for the success of the representative system. We are discussing the defects of the system's virtues. For modern government requires the close and continual attention of the rulers to the business of governing. To say that a society is 'complex' is to say in large part that the disparate claims of its citizens and bodies of citizens have increased and are increasing in number. For example, the division of labour means that each stage of manufacture develops into a separate interest. Where a man chops down his own tree and turns it into a table he has no quarrel with his neighbour who does the same unless the tree lies on the boundary between their two properties. Where the wood is imported by a shipping company on behalf of a merchant, who then sells the wood to a furniture company which then distributes finished tables to retailers, which then sell them to consumers, a variety of conflicts may arise. Such conflicts may involve international law, shipping law, excise law, company law, etc. The complexity increases not only qualitatively, but quantitatively with the growth in the population. We shall not deal here with the way in which the apparatus of regulation in both the executive and legislative branches of government tends to generate its own growth; that is to say, the bewildered rulers in response to a clamour from one section of the public act in a direction which arouses opposition from another section, forcing the rulers to act again; more abstractly, a set of actions designed to correct certain anomalies usually creates new anomalies.

It is enough to say here that ruling the country becomes a full-time job. In the days of Simon de Montfort, counties and cities may have 'sent' knights and burgesses to represent them in Parliament in the sense that a nation will send an eminent representative to a great occasion – a president's funeral, a royal wedding – in another country. On such a mission, the legate embodies the feelings of his native region. If his duty is merely to bow and smile and walk in a procession, it matters little whether we call him a delegate or a representative. If he is to speak at a conference which may last days, weeks or months, his assignment may vary from the strictest delegation to the freest representation. But the crucial point is that he is expected to return home as soon as the assignment is completed. His constituency is his head office and his home. This will naturally make him extremely careful to master the views of his constituency, otherwise this brief assignment will be his only moment of public prominence. If, on the other hand, he is a man without ambition, who simply desires to serve his turn once, he has no reason to try to do other than reflect the views of his constituents. His public duty done, he must after all live among those he has claimed to serve.

There is certainly still nostalgia today for such a relationship between electors and representatives. In the United States, would-be congressmen and senators are almost always required to show a long and intimate connection with the state they propose to represent; once elected, they must maintain a home in that state. Conservative associations in Britain often insist on the second and sometimes on the first of these conditions. Other parties in Britain and in western Europe make similar, if weaker, demands.

But these conditions are face savers, mere lubricants of the friction inherent in modern representation, for the member of parliament has to spend most of the year at Westminster, the congressman in Washington. Even when he goes 'home' for the holidays, his associations with his constituents are mere symbolic acts, they are not part of the business of government. Naturally he will try to assess the strength and direction of local opinion on the issues of the day, but he could do so equally well if he took his holidays in another neighbouring constituency. In the United States this increasing distance between rulers and ruled is still veiled by the informality of the party system and the possibility of doing favours for constituents. In this sense the American political system has managed to remain partly insulated from modern pressures. And yet even in America there is a strong feeling growing up that everything is decided in Washington. And this feeling is largely justified. The bureaucracy of the executive burgeons; party affiliations become more ideological than regional; and party organisation is becoming stronger. These trends all emanate from Washington. It little matters if a senator spends every moment that he is not legislating back in his home town if it is in the legislature that his mind is shaped. Sooner or later he will be spotted as one of Them by the public.

Perhaps the most significant parable of this development is the use of 'the Establishment' as a term of abuse. This ironical usage no doubt originated in left-wing circles (though Henry Fairlie fertilised its most recent flowering) but it is now current almost everywhere. Yet the original meaning of the word was the 'legitimate hierarchy'; that is to say, a class of rulers which was popularly accepted as being preferable to any other. The Church of England could not have been referred to as 'by law established' if there had been strong feeling that its establishment had subsequently become illegitimate, that is to say if there had been sudden public clamour for the nation to pay homage to the pope. In other words, the old criterion was, so to speak, whether we had approved *Their* establishment. But now the Establishment is used to denote those who have established *themselves*, by hook or by crook, and who seem immovable or who if removed would only be replaced by men of the same sort. In its common (nonrevolutionary) use, the term is despairing: that is, we are stuck with them. Naturally, if the despair becomes too bitter, the common use may turn to the revolutionary. A similar but more specific usage is 'the military-industrial complex'. Again, most people feel, 'We must keep these people under our control, what can we do?', to which the answer is, 'You will never do it with your present over-elaborate structure. They have climbed too far up the scaffolding for you to be able to get at them. Your only hope – the only hope of all people at the bottom of the structure at all times in history – is to knock the whole thing down. That you have the power to do.' It is the feeling that They have climbed out of our reach which makes Them alien beings unresponsive to our wishes, however much we liked Them once. We must point out here that one striking aspect of the new *strangeness* of our representatives is that they are now associating with a group of men whom we have never known, who have, so to speak, arrived on the building site overnight, immigrants no doubt from some more primitive culture; to wit, the bureaucrats. Both politicians and bureaucrats are wont to complain that the general public does not understand the difference between legislators and executives, even where, as in America, their separation is stressed. But this is barely surprising, seeing that the two branches are daily intertwined. The monarch receives his subjects' petitions; the delegate his people's instructions; everyone must attend the tribal meeting – in each of these systems, the public is intimately involved in the transaction of public business. But in the representative system, executive and legislature are all jumbled up together, passing problems to each for ratification or administration, negotiating on financial and legislative priorities. In constitutional theory, the distance between the White House and the Capitol, or even between the Treasury and the House of Commons may be enormous; but the public sees it as no more than a geographical expression. There is perhaps one kind of drama in which the separation of powers becomes vivid to the public – the congressional committee.

The clash between the elected representatives and the nominated cabinet ministers or officials there seems real and important. How significant that in the only instance where the hazards of the representative system, a necessary development of complex modern society, are overcome, they should be overcome by the modern development of television. And yet the great impact of, say, the McCarthy or Fulbright hearings should not leave us unconscious of the fact that the televising of these public dramas was not as crucial as it seemed at the time. It so happened that the cameras were switched on as these dramas were nearing some kind of crisis. The Senate would have censured McCarthy without television; public opinion would have moved against American policy in Vietnam without the Fulbright hearings. The gaffes of the former, the cost in lives and money of the latter, were too glaring to allow the situation to continue indefinitely. And naturally the views of the public were an important pressure for action in both cases. But the fleeting feeling of the American public that it was actually participating in the transaction of this business was largely illusory, a good show laid on by a combination of technical innovation, chance and political cunning.

THE ROLE OF THE ELECTIONS

We do not suggest that the prevailing feeling – that They take no notice of our wishes – is justified. If that were so, the system would be patently intolerable. No, our elected rulers are bound to heed our wishes if they want to remain elected. But this prevailing feeling is to a great extent a metonym for the justified feeling that we are left out of the *process* of decision. We feel ourselves to be in the position of a mentally ill person of great wealth. Doctors, lawyers, investment advisers discuss what should be done with our body and our stocks and shares. We are prey to constant fears that these counsellors are dishonest or incompetent or both. We know they are bound by the rules not to commit us to an asylum unless certain criteria of insanity are satisfied. We know that any misconduct on their part will, if detected, make them liable to disbarment from their professional bodies. We know that it is in their interest that our financial, mental and physical state should improve; no funds, no commission – no body, no fees. We know also that unless we are certified as insane first, we retain the ultimate power to dispense with their services. The theory is comforting: they are our hired servants. The practice is humiliating; we are their wayward wards, to be comforted, cajoled, bullied, but never to be treated as equals, never to be told more of the truth than suits their present purposes, and too often to be told off-white lies. Our only sanction is our right to withdraw our custom; but if that threat is to have more than a passing impact, if it is to arouse in them a greater concern than the amused observation that 'the natives are restless tonight', it must on occasion be publicly and finally exercised. We must sack our advisers, dismiss our governments. In both cases, the aftermath is as painful as the event itself. This is probably inevitable. The floating centre of the electorate might have wanted to say to the Conservative government in 1964: 'You have done the state some service. But we feel that your grip is now slackening and that you would benefit from a spell out at grass.' Indeed, many centrist commentators did sketch out such a message, to which R. A. Butler replied at the 1963 Conservative Conference with the argument that 'if you wish to throw us out in favour of this untried alternative, you must have some more powerful reason than mere fashionable fatigue with the *status quo*'. And in fact more powerful reasons were drummed up during the 1964 election campaign. Harold Wilson produced the 'Thirteen Wasted Years' and the 'Technological Revolution'; these were elaborations of the vaguest, least specific feelings in the minds of a minute section of the populace – albeit the fulcrum. In their power and colour these elaborations rival Sir Arthur Evans's reconstructions at Knossos. Both have outlasted the electoral festivities. They still stand, the bright paint only a little peeling, the one as memorial to the disappointments of Tory rule, the other as a monument to the exaggerated hopes of Labour rule. Some commentators have blamed Harold Wilson for thus dramatising what were bound to be at most marginal shifts in government policy and achievement. But if the electors have only the residual power of dismissal, dramatisation is necessary. Indeed, a general election after five years of undisturbed reign by one faction is bound to be a great dramatic event with a vast audience. In such a theatre, language must be simple but vivid, issues crystallised, feeling heightened. Quinquennial confrontation is an artificial convention. It does nothing to reduce the distance between ruler and ruled. Rather the reverse. The actor's homely chat with the audience may set the spine tingling with that unique theatrical embarrassment which at first sight we may mistake for the intimacy of emotion. But once out in the cold night air we realise, not that we have been 'had', but simply that we have been to the theatre. By our applause we may ensure a long run, a short run or no run at all. Indeed, some actors reckon to be able to judge from the enthusiasm of even a specially selected first-night audience how long the play will run. But that is the limit of our powers. We cannot talk to the actors, nor can they to us; indeed the more they attempt to do so, the more embarrassing the experience. Earlier in these pages we saw how even the most serious efforts to overcome this problem (the Living Theatre) are frustrated by the 'one-timeness' of the experience. By contrast, let us imagine a troupe of this nature whose performances were for some reason attended night after night, by exactly the same audience, gluttons for punishment. Would not some fellow-feeling gradually spring up between members of the audience and the actors? At first the badinage would be rough and strained in the traditional music-hall fashion; later it might relax into something approaching pub conversation, and later still the conversation of friends. The theatrical element would diminish with repetition. Of course, one might then ask why one should bother to go to theatre for such an experience which would be obtainable at less expense and inconvenience at home.

Hence a general election, far from narrowing the gap, increases the sense of distance between rulers and ruled. History is seen as a succession of occasional meetings between strangers. And these meetings have a violence about them because the tension has been building for so long and because the prize money is so high. Throughout this part of the argument, we have been discussing the case of Britain, which exhibits the representative system in its purest form. The United States, because of the separation of the powers, the bicameral system and off-year elections, does not show such strong contrasts. Nor do countries such as fourth republic France and present-day Italy, where the drama lies in the forming and re-forming of coalitions rather than in the general elections. But in these countries and in many others the long-term tendency is towards the British system. Five years of doing more or less what one fancies is a devil's wish indeed. It is worth bending the truth a little for that. Hence even periods of comparative calm and prosperity have to be mythologised as intolerable years. It may still be legitimate to stigmatise 'the slump', 'the Thirties', 'appeasement', though the realities may seem more complex, the guilt more divided than they did once. Yet 'austerity' and 'never had it so good' may seem on reflection frail sticks with which to beat opponents; the one a speedy and fairly painless conversion from a war economy to a peace economy in which production increased rapidly, full employment was preserved, and the base of the welfare state expanded. The other, the most dramatic and most generously shared increase in prosperity in British history.

If the needs of our industrial base were neglected during this period, there was a strong case and a widely felt public demand for a spell in the sun after so many years in the shade. Nevertheless, in the one-time drama of a general election, these myths do take root. They undoubtedly have some considerable effect on the policy of subsequent governments; that is not our concern here. But their sum effect is to diminish the public's esteem for the politicians responsible for governing during these years. Naturally the opposition politician does not tell the voters that they themselves were in any way to be blamed for the black side of these years. Appeasement, for example, was according to the myth entirely created by Neville Chamberlain, Baldwin and the Cliveden Set. That the Labour Party voted against the military estimates more often than not, that it was led in the early 1930s by a pacifist, that the public generally wanted, in so far as we may legitimately interpret what the public wanted, peace at any price that could be described as honourable, these facts are largely overlooked. Even the East Fulham by-election is used as evidence not of the pacific mood of the public but of Baldwin's feebleness in pressing the case for rearmament. The 'East Fulham myth' alleges that Baldwin concealed the issue of rearmament at the 1935 general election, and in the House of Commons he later (12 November 1936) confessed that the East Fulham by-election had shown him that 'nothing would have made the loss of the election from my point of view more certain' than to ask for a mandate to rearm. R. Bassett[8] shows clearly that Baldwin was referring not to 1935 but to the period immediately following the East Fulham by-election in 1933, and that in 1935 he did openly seek and obtain a mandate to rearm. Richard Heller[9] further convincingly shows that in fact Baldwin's recollection of the East Fulham by-election was extremely hazy; the by-election was largely fought on domestic issues and the result was not universally hailed as a win for the 'peace vote'. Public opinion in 1933 may have been passionately in favour of disarmament; but the by-election at East Fulham is not sufficient evidence of that mood. This controversy, then, concerns three simple and easily verifiable pieces of evidence: the 1933 by-election campaign (including the contemporary reaction to it), the 1935 general election campaign, and Baldwin's speech in 1936. Yet thirty-five years later the controversy still simmers. And the sum effect remains the general belief that during 'the locust years' Britain was led by men of straw. The mud, when it has been applied with vigour, sticks.

Now it may be healthy that the government itself should take the credit or blame for carrying out what is no more than a nationally accepted policy; if, for example historians come to take a more tender view of Chamberlain's policy, the Chamberlainites will not say, 'But of course, he can't take all the credit. He was just obeying the sound instincts of the public.' But at all events the effect of these myths is further to distance politicians from the public. The myth implies: politicians are a group of people who make the mistakes which land us in war and misery; we, the public, are powerless either to divert them from error or force them to translate our views into action or to replace them with non-politicians. They form a self-perpetuating oligarchy. They are bred by parthenogenesis, the local party or caucus or civil service selection board being unravished by the virile common sense of the public. Even if they have wives and lovers – as their newspaper photographs claim – when they leave home for the office, they become zombies. In the short distance between his home and his office the politician is transformed from a man of flesh and blood into the protagonist of a myth, more often scapegoat than hero.

Students of politics may protest that the myth is not the case. Both the executive and the legislature are not only responsive to but closely supervised by the lay public. When, for example, the Minister of Transport proposes to close a railway line, there is built into the procedure a Transport Users Committee which must be consulted. Local authorities may put their views. And in Parliament the local member may put his view to the minister with the maximum of publicity and effect. All this may be true; those consulted may genuinely speak for the public, and government may really listen to what they say. But that is not what the public believes. The distancing of the representative system overrides any benevolence on the part of the representatives. That is to say, the public feels that consultation – the daily expression of liberty in a representative system – is in that system a licence, not an easement. It is revocable at any time which suits the rulers, not fixed as an ancient right of way granted in perpetuity. The American constitution, for example, might seem to be the greatest of all easements. And yet the mere fact of government by continual representation with only intermittent election means that the rulers can bend and build on to the rules and it will be some time before the public can make its pleasure or displeasure known. Size, distance and time attenuate the sturdiest of our rights.

In an American small town, where decisions are taken on the spot by persons known since childhood, Washington and to a lesser extent the state government are the interfering strangers. We may feel a long-standing personal dislike for our mayor, but we cannot fear him as a zombie over whom we have no control.

POLITICAL CONVERSATION

This then is what has led to the general lack of enchantment with our present politics: the necessary distancing of the representative system, the lack of close and continuous dialogue with our rulers, the lack of control over their actions, all this leading to Marx's concept of 'the ruling class' and 'alienation'; Marx's error was to confuse appalling social conditions with the growth of representative government and with capitalism. The three are distinct phenomena. The growth of representative government has usually tended to improve social conditions; benevolently regulated capitalism has tended to improve social conditions vastly; unregulated capitalism, insufficiently representative government and costly wars made life wretched for millions in the late eighteenth and much of the nineteenth century, but that is no basis for a theory of welfare. Marx, at least in his earlier works, sees well enough that the division of labour in industry, and in government too, makes workshop comrades into strangers. But he makes a crucial mistake in failing to understand what may and what may not be said to strangers. It is his assumption that in existing society neither our physical nor our spiritual needs can be communicated to strangers and/or that the strangers will not listen to us.

This is not of course so. A few adjustments to the mechanism of existing society – wider representation, regulation of conditions in industry, a more charitable and better organised system of welfare, increasing sophistication in the management of supply and demand, all lubricated with risk-capital and technological advance – and our physical needs may be well enough satisfied. And there is no particular reason why this should not be so. To see a shop badly run is no ground for assuming that it is impossible to run a shop well, so that it simultaneously provides profits for the shopkeeper and service to the community. This is a matter of organisation, not an easy one, but soluble. A balance has to be struck. Men must band together in unions to stand up to their employers. The strength and continuity of the executive must be disciplined by the electoral system. Demand and supply must be so managed as to correct each other's excesses. The metaphor of the shopkeeper is carefully chosen here. For all this can be obtained by using plain shopping language: 'I want that.' 'How much is this?' 'Is that included in the price of this?' 'Will this plug into the one I have already got?' 'Can you repair this or is it too far gone?' 'What would you give me for this?' 'Would you take it in part exchange?' This is the brusque question-and-answer of normal, practical talk. We may ask anyone such questions, provided that person is in the appropriate situation, that is behind the counter, ushering us to our seats, telling us the way, etc.

There is, of course, another way of talking to strangers. This way is frequently remarked on. It normally happens on long journeys, in a long-stay hospital bed, in a remote place where there are no other people or none of the same race or language, in quiet hotel bars. In this mode, there need be little question and answer except by way of introduction (Where are you going? Will you be staying long?) This is a discursive mode – A talks of his life, his pleasures, his misfortunes, his loves, his hopes. B merely provides a sympathetic ear. Common ground is found: 'How interesting, that is just how I felt when I. . . .' Then the roles may be reversed; B talks, A listens. The subject-matter resembles that of conversation between old friends; indeed sometimes it may be even more intimate, for seeing that neither has any reason to expect to see the other again, there is no cause for A to omit things which might prove embarrassing to B or the knowledge of which might make their relationship more difficult. Yet the conversation differs from that of old friends in that nothing can be taken for granted, there can be no quick allusion to shared sympathies or experiences. Each must start to block in the background on the blank canvas. Time is therefore essential, which is why such fascinating encounters are rare; only in unusual and artificial circumstances do we spend hours with somebody we do not expect to see again. Indeed we remark on these encounters precisely because they are so rare. They form only a minute part of our encounters with strangers. The pressure of time is such that we must usually unburden ourselves only to close friends and relations. In the official world nobody but the somewhat scatty old lady dares to describe her problem to the bureaucrat in all the riches of her emotional history. That is why she is regarded as a joke; her approach is quite incongruous. Moreover, if her rarity did not make her a

joke, she would become a threat to the efficient workings of government. The policeman could no longer afford to smile at the way she
begins her story of the loss of her pet cat with her feelings on her
wedding day fifty years earlier; he would be forced to throw her out
of the police station.

Within the family or among friends, matters are very different.
There custom dictates that we listen, willingly or unwillingly; to
refuse to do so is to be labelled 'difficult' or 'antisocial', and not
without reason. For by refusing, we deny those most connected with
ourselves the precious pleasure of releasing their pent-up feelings.
And knowing the background as we do, we are peculiarly suited to
afford them this pleasure. Refusal to listen makes life more difficult
for ourselves by creating in them growing resentment; enlightened
self-interest as well as natural sympathy makes the exchange of
feelings the basis of intimacy. Speech more guarded than that prevailing in a society is traditionally taken as a sign of unfriendliness.
The normal degree of self-revelation may well vary enormously
from culture to culture; but even the alleged dourness of the Scot
must seem engagingly warm and frank beside the inevitably
official manner of the income tax inspector. It is not surprising
that people who are not allowed to say what they wish to say about
themselves should tend to become dissatisfied.

What, then, is it that we wish to say but are prevented from saying
by the remoteness of our representatives? Those intimate emotions
which are suitable for political dialogue may be roughly classed as
either affections or aspirations. Affections would include such
sentiments as liking for one's country, one's family, sect, trade
union and/or the dislike of others; also the converse; all loyalties to
people and places; the liking of things the way they are; the respect
for the familiar; the penchant for old methods, fly fishing, handmade
pottery; the tendency to recall with love the way things were; the
belief, whether justified or no, in the existence of ancient truths, laws,
liberties and social harmony – the noble savage, Young England,
Merrie England, the Founding Fathers, the Pilgrim Fathers, the
Golden Age, the world of Hans Sachs, the Nibelungen world, the
Pléiade, the Greek world as seen by Aeneas Sylvius; in a word,
the conservative.

Affections, therefore, are the deposits of the past. Even the immediate affection of an intellectual refugee for the country that
receives him springs from gratitude for a past kindness – his recep-

tion; before he is allowed in, he can feel ṇo gratitude. This gratitude is then deepened by what he may know of the country's tradition of accepting refugees; he follows in the line of Kossuth, Mazzini, Marx, Louis Napoleon, Lenin, and countless others.

In strong contrast to this, we have our aspirations, our hopes and fears for the future: hope of prosperity for ourselves, education for our children, universal brotherhood, an end to war, famine and pestilence, the breaking-down of taboos, the freeing of subject peoples, of domestic serfs whether hired servants or dependent relatives, or the 'liberation' of women; the belief in the perfectibility of man; then the fears: of atomic warfare, of over-population, of total pollution of the planet, of boredom; and the dreams, serious half-mocking but never without a tinge of hope – dreams of Utopia, of Erewhon, of a Brave New World,* of all science fiction, of the withering away of the state, of an empire which would last for a thousand years, Cloud Cuckoo Land, Cockaigne, the Abbey of Thelema (these last three, though imagined in the present, being fantastic are to be conceived of as dreams of the future rather than of the past); in fine the radical, the progressive. In such aspirations we find a free-flowing confidence. The progressive basically despises the conservative as timid; the conservative despises the progressive as a dangerous fool.

These deep and often conflicting prejudices – prejudices in the neutral sense of the word – are not to be confided to strangers. In many cases it is hard indeed to articulate them precisely, even to explain why one feels them to be relevant to the situation in hand. They can be presented only by gruff allusion, easily understood by a friend but easily misunderstood or underestimated by the visiting politician. If the latter is of a down-to-earth temper, he may dismiss the affections as outdated prejudice – in the pejorative sense – or the aspirations as pie in the sky; he will continue on his 'pragmatic' way until he has offended every deep-rooted sentiment. He will then express surprised regret at the resultant explosion which may upset not only his own applecart but the stability of the whole society. If, on the other hand, he is an 'idealist' in the popular sense, then he will fight to the death for his aspirations and affections. And he will not die alone. Again, if he concentrates on the affections which he shares with the bulk of the people he may become blind to those

---

* The souring of youthful dreams is a commonplace; the contrast between Aldous Huxley's *Brave New World* (1932) and his *Island* (1962) is a rare but not unique example of the reverse process – the sweetening of youthful nightmares.

aspirations of a minority which can and should be gratified. While if he goes hell-bent for his aspirations, the offence he will cause to the affections of those people who are securely rooted in the existing society may far outweigh in its unhappy consequences those other offences which it is his aspiration to remove. A politician who observes the public misery caused by either the cloddish insensitivity or the arrogant idealism of his fellow-politicians will naturally resolve – or should resolve – not to repeat those particular errors. But it is our contention that those diverse errors of political conduct spring not from the failings of individuals but from a single general cause: the failure to integrate political emotion into political science. And the reason for this failure is that modern divorce between rulers and ruled which makes the expression of political emotion deeply embarrassing to both sides.

EMBARRASSMENT AND ALIENATION

It is clear that the use here of 'embarrassment' corresponds in some degree to the Marxist's use of 'alienation'. But there is an important difference. The concept of alienation attempts to describe the total human condition in a manner comparable to the Christian doctrine of the Fall; alienation blights everything, from our work to our personal relationships, from our physical well-being to the depths of our souls. According to R. D. Laing:

> We are born into a world where alienation awaits us. We are potentially men, but are in an alienated state, and this state is simply not a natural system. . . . [and] The relevance of Freud to our time is largely his insight and, to a very considerable extent, his *demonstration* that the *ordinary* [that is, sane by the standards of society – a highly questionable interpretation of Freud who was usually careful to stress the clinical, extraordinary nature of his evidence] person is a shrivelled, desiccated fragment of what a person can be.[10]

We are unable to communicate to one another our desires and affections, let alone to love one another 'simply and genuinely'.

This theory is not confined to Laing, nor does it arise empirically from his interesting work on schizophrenia; it is all part of the great Rousseau tradition. '*L'homme est né libre, et partout il est dans les fers*'; from the moment those words entranced the human spirit, all doctrines of original sin, even the milder notion of life as a moral struggle against evil, were doomed. Man is naturally good – he is distorted by society – such has been the message of a vast host of writers, poets, playwrights, scientists, political theorists and heretical clerics. All evidence to the contrary is pushed aside; note Laing's effrontery in turning Freud on his head. For the conclusion of Freud is essentially that we keep sane only by means of the most delicate structure of subconscious controls on conscious feeling and behaviour; his originality consists in his analysis of how these controls break down to produce neurosis and in the mythic paradigm which he elaborates to describe the structure. Laing uses the paradigm, but boldly and wrongly concludes that it is not the failure of the controls but the controls themselves which cause the breakdown, therefore away with the whole structure of learning, all the social training of the child. 'The initial act of brutality against the average child is the mother's first kiss' – which is not what Freud had in mind at all. The truth is, of course, that while in some respects Freud's paradigm is of use to the Rousseauists, his conclusions are not. He does not, for example, believe that going mad is the only sane way to confront an insane society. Even if we claim that undergoing psychoanalysis is in some dim way equivalent to going mad, its purpose is strictly therapeutic and limited. The aim is not to overturn society but to cure the patient – which in large measure means restoring him to some comfortable relationship with the values of society – to make him happy. But modern playwrights like David Mercer and Joe Orton seem unwilling to accept Freud as a doctor rather than as a revolutionary. He is forcibly dragged into the pantheon where Marx and Lenin already lie pickled in cant.

Perhaps the most extreme example of the Rousseauist's attitude towards this uneasy conjunction of Marxist alienation and the Freudian paradigm is to be found in the much admired English playwright, Edward Bond. His plays *Saved* and *Early Morning* have shown an undoubted power to shock even a numb theatrical sensibility. In particular, the scene in *Saved* where a baby is stoned found its way to a still tender public nerve. The extreme violence of his work explodes out of a passionate belief that men are naturally good and are twisted out of shape by society:

Edward Bond: I think being born into the western society is a very uncomfortable thing to have happened to anybody, but I think it is true of probably most societies that I know anything about. The thing is, you see, that our society is not geared towards protecting, preserving, enjoying life. The moment anything is born it must be put into society; it must be codified, it must be taught, it must be trained, it must be disciplined. Now all these things I think are absolutely disastrous. If one lives in a bad society, then one wants to breed a generation of children who are not conditioned to our sort of society, otherwise they can't change it. You see, the thing is this, if you take a dog and you chain it up from the moment it is born, the dog will become vicious. Now this is in fact what we do with human beings. . . .

Irving Wardle (theatre critic of *The Times*): But this doesn't answer my question of where it all starts. I mean, if there is a kind of inborn goodness, where does the canker begin?

Edward Bond: It answers your question completely. I mean the thing is if you won't let the child flourish and grow up in its own way with total freedom, and I really mean total freedom, then the child, all his natural energies and so on get forced in on the child. It can't explore, can't behave in the way it wants to so it becomes devious, it becomes perverted, it becomes difficult. There isn't something called 'evil' which has to come out – by in effect attacking the child – that is, educating him. We create in the child a state of chronic defensiveness, which we call aggression.[11]

Now a theory of this kind can be neither proved nor refuted. For it is predicated upon the existence of a 'potential humanity' which has not yet been actualised. Indeed, only thus can the theory hold together. For as soon as we look at the world and try to get some hint of what this 'potential humanity' would be like, we find some facts which prove rather inconvenient to Rousseau, Laing and Bond. On the whole, the happiest and kindest people seem to be the product of the most intense and continuous 'socialising process'; that is to say, they are the children of united homes. The children of broken, unstable or neglectful homes, on the other hand, often find it very difficult to make themselves at ease with the world, to engage in satisfying and durable relationships with other people, and even to keep on the right side of the law. Child psychiatrists work entirely on the basis that the child's first need is for security and affection; even Bond refers to the child's need for security. Yet a mother can provide these things only by laying down the limits of the child's world: at first protecting him in the cradle of her arms, later preventing him from falling down stairs or crawling into the fire, later still giving the child rules of behaviour. At each stage she denies the child the 'total freedom' which Bond demands; she curbs his 'natural energies'. And if she did not, the child would not survive.

The evidence suggests clearly that alienation can result from 'over-mothering' as well as 'under-mothering'; Laing's own work on schizophrenia[12] shows how the structure of controls can be so over-loaded that the patient, faced with a mass of incomprehensible, conflicting and exhausting instructions and expectations from his family, goes mad. But this does not mean that the controls are useless or even damaging; it shows only that as in all human affairs the golden mean is hard to find; and the mother's task of achieving the right balance between protecting the child and allowing him the freedom to live his own life is as delicate a problem as we are likely to be confronted with.

In other words, the empirical study of alienation presents conclusions which are not at all sympathetic to the Rousseauist alienist. It is why he eventually rejects empirical study. For the happy home and the lessons learnt at mother's knee are precisely the mode of life from which he is struggling to escape. He wishes not to restore the alienated to the bourgeois family circle but, vice versa, to smash the bourgeois family into alienated fragments. And this can only be done by postulating a radical break with existing society; for Marx and for Freudian Marxists like Marcuse a revolution, for social psychologists like Norman O. Brown and Charles Reich a new consciousness. If some people are mad and some people are sane, the obvious answer is for the sane people to try and cure the madmen. A revolution of consciousness must therefore rest on the premise that we are all mad, denatured; such a premise is metaphysical, for its truth cannot be tested by looking at the physical world; indeed, students of the physical world will find difficulty in attaching much meaning to the premise. If we are all mad, what can we mean by sanity? Presumably a state which none of us have achieved and all long for – in short an ideal akin to sanctity. A sane society would be a communion of saints.

Thus the notion of alienation becomes less and less scientific and specific, the more central it is made to become. As a description of a teenager numbed by pop music or of a man spending his working life in somnolent boredom on an assembly line, 'alienation' is a precise and poignant concept. But it cannot stand the weight of an all-embracing theory of society. It crumbles into unmeaning.

Our discussion of 'embarrassment', by contrast, rests upon certain observable dissatisfactions. People are unable to communicate their feelings across the vast distances which now separate rulers from ruled. The actions of the rulers therefore do not harmonise with the desires and affections of the ruled, which causes frustration and discontent; these latter feelings then become more intense when the ruled find that they cannot communicate them to the rulers either. A shouts to B in a public place. B does not hear. A shouts louder. B still does not hear. People turn round to look at A. A, red-faced, shouts loudly and angrily. B hears and retorts testily: 'There's no need to shout. What do you want now?'

There are clearly two solutions. One is to shorten our lines of communication. The other is to improve the existing lines so that they seem shorter. The politician has to do both; to make politics as local, intimate and participatory as the circumstances allow, and where circumstances do not allow for real local participation (for example, in macroeconomic decisions) to maintain the *feeling* of intimacy. It is this double requirement which makes politics a many-levelled dramatic experience. And it is this complexity which demands such skill and sensitivity from its practitioners.

III

The Political Actor

'I will counterfeit the bewitchment of
some popular man.'
(*Coriolanus*, Act 2, scene 3)

Though in many ways credulous beyond previous periods, this age
has developed one new and valuable form of scepticism. We have
come to doubt whether pure objectivity is possible. We see the
relation between observer and object as so intricate that it seems to
us impossible to clarify that relation without boiling away most of
what is useful in the observation. We cannot distinguish between the
proper strands (the facts about the object) and the improper strands
(the distortion of subject by object and vice versa). With the exception of much of the natural sciences, this scepticism poses stiff
problems for almost every branch of knowledge and enquiry. The
anthropologist is or should be worried by the never-ending search
for a method of analysis of other societies which is not in some
degree shot through with the preconceptions of his own society.
The historian cannot forget the fashions in the writing of history in
eras which have preceded his own – Whiggery, Marxism, etc. Impartiality is for him a fading dream. The film director is much puzzled
and yet dimly excited by the idea of the camera as voyeur.

There are two approaches to this problem; not 'solutions' because
in a logical sense there can be no solution. A reporter is a reporter.
But there are two approaches which honestly recognise the problem,
which put it on public display and proceed with a certain amount of
nonchalance under its enervating shadow. The first is the method of
extreme caution, the labelling of impressions and conclusions and
their sorting into degrees of objectivity. The material is first laid out
in its raw state. The observer then recounts the conditions under
which it was collected. At the end of the exhibition he displays a
few choice conclusions. Even these will be conspicuously labelled
'interim only' or 'further study needed'. For example, let us take a
middle-class person investigating the condition of the poor. Some of

his raw material will be straightforward and fairly easy to establish: 'Average family income in this district is £x.' 'There is one w.c. for every y inhabitants', and so on. But as soon as he tries to establish the inhabitants' degree of deprivation, he will be involved in considerations which are relative to his own standard of living and expectations of life. What should family income be as a reasonable minimum? What w.c. ratio is sufficient for the purpose of public health or of minimal comfort? But at least such questions can be answered in a modest, provisional tone. His worst problem is that his questions are also liable to have prejudged the answers; he has involuntarily pre-processed the material before putting it on view. This dilemma is most typically shown in the work of the opinion sampler who finds it almost impossible to avoid loading the questions. 'Do you believe that the steel industry should be nationalised?' and 'Do you believe that the steel industry should be streamlined for the public benefit?' are questions which may evoke very different answers, yet both could be related to the same government action.

The careful sampler will realise that 'nationalised' is for most people a pejorative word, and 'streamlined' a favourable one. He will search for some neutral, colourless word. 'Rationalised'? But that again begs the question; who would wish to have an 'irrationalised' steel industry? 'Taken over by the government'? Here it will be objected that the aim is that the people, not the government should own their own steel industry. 'Taken into public ownership'? Here may be made the counter-objection that, whatever the aim of the take-over, the *effect* is to remove the industry from even the partial public control of the market and place it in the hands of irresponsible bureaucrats.

It may be argued that such influences upon the raw material of research do not come solely from the researcher himself. This is true; they may come from the mere fact that research is being carried out. People may give the answers which they think the researcher would like to hear or which make them appear in a more flattering light. The unexpected question may sting them into overreaction or cow them into insincere acquiescence. The influence may also come from the general context in which the observer-object relation is placed. If this is no more than to say that the relation exists in the world round about us and not in a vacuum, that is just what we are after. We do not claim that the observer's influence is of a different kind from other influences but only that it will necessarily bulk very large.

The second approach to the problem of objectivity fastens on the fact of this colossal size of the observer in the general picture. This approach maintains that it is no use trying to screen out the observer when he permeates every part of the observer-object relation. If we exhaust ourselves trying to excise every trace of him, we shall be left with nothing of value. The only way out is to make the best of it and allow the observer a hero's part. It is argued that we shall thereby at least see what is going on in reality; we shall move out on location and get away from the artificiality of the studio, the smell of glue on the model. The reflection of the object in the observer's eye will give us a richer view of the object than all our attempts to isolate the few sterile aspects of the object which have not been contaminated by passing through the observer's hands. This amounts to the view that a genially admitted subjectivity can be more objective than the most painstaking objectivity. Of course this attitude too contains its own artificiality, as we can see in the superb work of this school by Norman Mailer. The impressions which he conveys of, say, dissent in America or the American political process are indeed rich and telling; but they are in constant danger of being overshadowed by the increasingly stylised figure of Mailer himself.

Our purpose here is not to debate the merit of these two approaches and the impact that they make upon the society to which they are applied when the observer becomes the actor. We may indeed associate the cautious method with Disraeli's picture of the Peel era – 'decent times: frigid, latitudinarian, alarmed, decorous'. In such times political action may be based on sociology and justified by a utilitarian rationale. At other times there may be a general welcome for the view that 'who dares to be good, dares to be great'. We may then expect fireworks, dramatic radical action justified by appeals to an individual or collective daemon.

But in either situation we must never overlook the importance of the protagonist. Instead of the belief that the importance of the individual's actions varies with the historical context in which he is placed, it would be truer to say that the context may vary but the importance of the individual's effect on that context remains constant. The great flaw in most determinist views of human history is their extreme narrowness. That is to say, most of us will be impressed by a well-worked and well-supported argument of the form 'situation A *had* to give way *in the end* to situation B which *sooner or later* was *bound* to lead to situation C'. We are familiar with so many recurring chains of events in our own personal life which we use this sort of language to describe that we are quite ready to use the same words about the movements of nations. In fact we are often struck with parallels between the private and the public worlds to such an extent that the jargon of the one may be used as a metaphor to describe the other. Examples: 'Turkey is the sick man of Europe' and 'I declared war on my wife'. But we accept these parallels in a broader sense. Our notion of causality in the public world has as much of the contingent about it as our view of the private world. Thus a bloated, self-indulgent man is likely, sooner or later, to fall victim to a heart attack or stroke; a bloated self-indulgent nation is likely, sooner or later, to fall victim to inflation or conquest. We may even, for the sake of vividness, say 'it is bound to happen' – unless he takes a grip of himself, unless he has an abnormally strong constitution (my uncle Uriah never drew a sober breath and lived to ninety-five), unless he is, quite simply, lucky.

The political scientist takes exceptions to 'the rule' without too much fuss; when taking trouble to be precise, he will use such phrases as 'tends towards' or 'is likely to eventuate in' rather than 'is bound to' or 'leads to'. The determinist cannot be so nonchalant. He has to find a reason for every apparent exception to his rule. A has been followed by B, A_1 by B_1, A_2 by B_2, but why has B_n not followed A_n? Why does situation A_n in fact resolutely continue to obtain when all about it are B's, perhaps B's of various kinds but B's in some sense none the less? Why, for example, has the Emperor Haile Selassie continued in power for so long when all other African nations are self-styled democracies of one form or another? The easiest solution for those who believe in irresistible tides of history is to refer to the ancient traditional character of Ethiopian civilisation, with a grudging tribute to the way the emperor has maintained and adapted that tradition in order to give it a few more years of life. The determinist must resolutely resist the sneaking suspicion that in fact things may be the other way about – that the traditions of Ethiopia may be only a secondary aid to the retention of power by a very remarkable man.

If the determinist begins openly to study the effect of one man's personality on his times, he will find his determinism slipping away from him. If one man's strength can prevent the realisation of x-ism, if another man's weakness can bring about x-ism by a failure of maintenance, what becomes of 'the inevitable triumph of x-ism'?

We are left with something embarrassingly like the vulgar individualism of Disraeli: 'There is nothing like will; everybody can do exactly what they like in this world, provided they really like it. Sometimes they think they do, but in general it is a mistake.'[1] It is entertaining to guess how many French Marxists ever even attempted to deal seriously with the extremely awkward fact of General de Gaulle, for thirty years the palpable, living refutation of the Marxist theory of history.

The determinist is licensed to study the individual's pursuit and retention of power only in terms of the accomplishment of a revolution, peaceful or otherwise. The individual is a drop of water in the stream of history and only worthy of study because he is in that stream and not in a backwater. The thesis that this drop of water might change the course of the stream is not to be admitted.

Such an attitude produces colossal intellectual problems. At the collective level we see the conflict between the initiatory role of the cadre and the alleged spontaneity and inevitability of the revolution; at the individual level, we see the conflict between the leader as expresser of the enlightened general will and the leader as baleful beneficiary of 'the cult of personality'.

These conflicts produce distortions of history and of government at least as great as those bred of Machiavelli's version of the battle paradigm. The latter is simply the study of how the Prince may maintain himself in power and preserve or create sufficient strength and independence for his domain so that he may accomplish his desired objects. This study of power is a specialised branch of political science; it is relevant equally to the accomplishment of good and of bad objects. But, being in its own and subsequent centuries associated more with the bad, it quickly fell into disrepute. This disrepute was deepened by the rising popularity of the flattering notion of the general will. The very moral neutrality of the Machiavellian method does affront to our susceptibilities. We do not like to think that we are at the mercy of our rulers, even though we reserve the right to complain about them. We do not like to think that the accomplishment of our noblest impulses depends not on our own nobility but on the competence and honour of those we have elected to power or in whose usurpation we have acquiesced. In our hearts we know that we are, to a greater or lesser degree, underlings and we do not like it. Still less do we like the possibility that this servitude may be a necessary consequence of any conceivable form of social organisation, and the more necessary the more complex the organisation becomes. Hence our yearning for the old simplicity, provided of course that we still have access to modern medical facilities, contraceptives, transport and a varied diet. This is not to say that the citizens of Ruritania could not enjoy and would not benefit from a much greater say in their own affairs. In fact the conceivable limits of participation are very wide. We may imagine for example a rural soviet in which every villager is consulted on every matter. But even in a philadelphia we would be at the mercy of the competence and diligence of our fellows. Even if the worker, the peasant and the intellectual each takes his turn at delivering the milk, the man on duty still has it in his power to deprive the entire soviet of milk by driving the cart into the ditch. The look-out man can decide whether the battle is won or lost by whether he gives his warning of the enemy's approach early or late. Those who would reverse the logic of technology and attempt to stamp out the division of labour should realise the limits of their endeavour. It is impossible to stamp out power. It is impossible to stamp out a man's responsibility for his fellows. There is much to be said for spreading power as widely as possible, but pluralism does not diminish the quantity of power existing in a society. It merely distributes the responsibilities for exercising that power.

Power, when shorn of the mysteries in which both its admirers and detractors have wrapped it, is merely the ability to act. When people talk of power tending to corrupt, what are they referring to? Obviously the ability to act for good or for ill. Acton's dictum may be taken in two senses: first, that man is predominantly bad and that any increase in his power must lead to an increase in evil up to the point where he enjoys absolute power and therefore dispenses absolute evil. This melancholy view is not unsupported by historical evidence. But we assume that Acton and those who quote him are not merely elaborating some popular version of the doctrine of the Fall. We may assume this because Acton's dictum is popular and the doctrine of the Fall, involving as it does not only the 'high-ups' but every human being, is not. It is more likely that most people use the dictum in the second sense: namely, that the acquisition of a particular measure of power brings with it a particular liability to corruption and that as power increases beyond that measure corruption increases geometrically. If a man exercises less than that particular measure of power, let us say, as a humble clerk, householder and parent, his temptation to corruption may be regarded as minimal. At the other end of that scale we get Hitlers and Stalins.

This is the view which has obliterated the 'Machiavellian method'. The study of how power is obtained, let alone of how it should be obtained, is regarded as tainted. Even at the humblest level, a man who wishes to become a local councillor may be abused as 'power-hungry'. And when in office, if he acts unpopularly he will be called 'a little Hitler'. This of course keeps those in authority on their toes, but it has had a calamitous side-effect. The study of the acquisition and exercise of power is considered a black art, witness the popular use of 'Machiavellian'. 'Leader' is immediately translated into 'Führer' or 'Duce'; in a weaker sense, the concept of 'leadership' is taken to be synonymous with attempts to impose values whose tendency is dictatorial. We shall not here attempt to decide whether these criticisms are justified, whether Acton's dictum is true. We merely observe in passing that the power of the executive has undoubtedly increased in most western democracies over the past half-century; yet we doubt whether that increase has been unpopular with more than a small minority. Equally, the vast majority of decisions taken under that increased power have been, broadly speaking, popular at the time of taking, though their consequences have often proved unwelcome to both rulers and ruled. The wartime powers of Roosevelt and Churchill were certainly tremendous. Yet popular complaints about the exercise of these powers were few. Whether Roosevelt and Churchill were spiritually corrupted by those years is a different question; we are dealing with the outward effects of their powers.

Our main concern is that the possible infections of power should not deflect us from its study, any more than we should abandon the study of sewage disposal because of the concomitant stench. Power, like sewage, is here to stay. To avoid offending sensitive noses, we shall talk not of political 'leaders' but of 'actors'. This has a convenience of a twofold sense: the politician as a deed-doer and the politician as a role-player. The alternation between coincidence and contrast in these two aspects is fascinating and important. This alternation can only be studied by a polymorphic approach.

If we believe that all politicians are crusaders, obsessed by a single coherent group of ideals, we shall expect their deeds to correspond exactly to their role-playing. When we find no such exact correspondence, we shall conclude that all politicians are crooks. If, on the other hand, we believe that politicians are interested solely in the pursuit and retention of power, we shall expect no such exact correspondence. We shall dismiss their role-playing as mere playing to the gallery, and we shall analyse all their actions exclusively in terms of a calculus of power. Neither of these approaches gives anything more than an extremely limited view of the world. This is not to say that they are not valuable branches of the study of power, as long as it is realised that they are only branches. We must understand that the politician is motivated by a number of considerations other than those mentioned above. Let us take the common situation where a politician promises A in his election address, and in office performs B. There are several possibilities, for example:

—He never intended to perform A. He promised it only to win votes.

—He wanted to perform A, but circumstances have changed so much since the election that he is constrained to perform B.

—Since arriving in office, he has discovered new evidence which leads him to conclude that his original support for A was ill-advised.

—His colleagues are set on B and he goes along with them in return for their support on C and D which he regards as probably more important than A.

—A was quite possible, but he lacked the courage to carry through with it.

—A was not possible, but he thinks that B is the next best thing . . . .
And so on. Now the purist will still say that the politician should resign and that all his explanations amount to no more than pleading 'politics is a dirty game, full of shabby compromises'; however honourable the politician's intentions during the election campaign, by performing B he has rendered his prospectus false. The purist's cry at its noblest, when not tinged with rancour, rends the heart. There is no answer to it. Certainly it is no answer to say 'the world is not like that'. The purist is not arguing about what the world is like. He is arguing about how a good man ought to behave.

But equally we are not arguing with the purist. We are discussing how men, good and bad, actually do behave. And we are discussing the nature of good and bad government. And it is sad but true that the collective and the individual do not coincide. For while bad men usually produce bad government, good men – we mean sincere men,

men of good faith and good morals too for that matter – do not necessarily produce good government.

The questions we must ask are in no sense mysterious. They are such questions as: how do certain people obtain power of an established kind? How do others invent for themselves new kinds of power? How do both sets maintain or fall from power? What sort of people are they? Why do other men submit to them? How are the actors affected by the desires of the audience? How do they themselves change or create the desires of the audience? How far do the actors affect the scenery? How far does the scenery affect the actors? What drives the actors to create their roles? How, when and why do their roles differ from their deeds?

Common to all these questions is one assumption: the actors are men in the real world whose doings are of great interest and importance to themselves and to the audience. On them depends much of the success of life's evening out. We in the audience may be feeling out of sorts, the acoustics may be poor, the play may be a dull one. But the actors still have the power to increase or to diminish our happiness by their performance. The determinist who believes that politicians are but drops of water in the stream of history will not be sufficiently interested to ask questions about them. For him a molecule is a molecule. He shares with the cynic ('all politicians are corrupt') and the purist ('sincerity is all that matters') the belief that any relationship between the actors and the audience can only be superficial and static. The actors are simply hired players, of dubious morals and unfit to be buried in consecrated ground. They are animated versions of stylised masks, to which the audience responds with equally stylised boos or applause.

Yet such a view of the political drama has itself a stylised quality amounting to sterility. It is prevalent not only among people who have no interest in politics but also among the professional Tadpoles and Tapers who can see no further than 'registration' or 'a good cry'. This sullen determination to be bored results, like most forms of boredom, from inattention to reality. Release from this condition, for good or ill, follows from a more intense awareness.

And nowhere is this sense of release more powerful than when the subject is the political actor himself. This is the moment when he realises that he is not simply a man in the world but one who is engaged, or hopes to engage, in the 'endless adventure'; when he ceases to regard himself merely as one who happens to be politicking (when he might just as well be driving a lorry or fishing) and instead recognises the degree of his specialisation. For the purposes of modesty it is no doubt right for him to go on regarding himself as merely 'the chap on sentry-go this week'; but the excitement persists in the dawning consciousness that *he is a sentry* whether for a day or a year, with all the sentry's duties, boredoms, susceptibility to panic and fire at shadows, susceptibility to sleep, need to maintain discipline, even at the risk of seeming unfriendly to his comrades. We do not pretend that this consciousness strikes only the politician so dramatically. It is to be found in any activity which involves both professional skill and moral responsibility. The doctor, the lawyer and the parson must all, if they are to practise their trade well, develop a consciousness both of self and of the relation of the self to the world with which it must deal; a *professional consciousness*.

This, for the most part, professional men learn by practising their profession; and politicians are no exception. Academic political scientists are frequently amazed by revelations like Harold Wilson's statement that he had never read Marx. Yet in truth such reading is in large part irrelevant to the business of politics, even to the business of running a revolution – Castro, for example, was hardly a skilled dialectician when he threw out Batista. Conservative politicians in Britain frequently take as their guide not some work of Burke or Disraeli but *The Endless Adventure* by F. S. Oliver[2]. Baldwin in particular admired this long biography of Walpole, more particularly for the lessons it gives about the profession of politics. Churchill wrote of Baldwin in *The Gathering Storm:*

> He seemed to me to revive the impression history gives us of Sir Robert Walpole, without, of course, the eighteenth-century corruption – and he was master of British politics for nearly as long.[3]

Leo Amery claims even that 'the book had a disastrous effect upon a mind already temperamentally disposed towards a Walpole policy of inertia'.[4] This comment may be true of Baldwin, but in so far as it reflects upon Oliver it indicates only the cast of Amery's own mind– absolute, disdainful of compromise, almost the caricature of the intellectual in politics with the sole softening peculiarity of also being Tory. For it is just the distinction between flexibility and inertia which Oliver puts so well. He describes his subject thus:

> We cannot look back upon our history without having it borne in upon us, how often those who succeeded in gaining power and keeping it

were fitted by their peculiar temperaments and capacities for dealing with the special needs and conditions of their respective epochs.

Walpole is one of the most conspicuous examples of the man who came at the right time. And he is interesting for the further reason, that he is the archetype of the *normal* politician who forces his way into the highest positions. His virtues and his defects are alike characteristic of the craft he followed. He had a strong, clear, practical judgment. He was valiant and steadfast. His crowning merit was faithfulness to the king he served and to his country. Neither fears nor temptations could ever shake his fidelity. At the same time, it would be senseless to deny that he was a self-seeker, an opportunist, and a man without any tincture of book-learning or philosophy.[5]

Oliver accepts too easily the shams and impostures of political life: he believes that politicians are and have to be more cynical than in fact they are or need to be: he understands little about the relationship between rulers and ruled; his is the world of club politics, of 'having a word' with old so-and-so about such-and-such, an enclosed, self-regarding world where men's reputations are made or unmade in a single debate, where it is the opinions of one's peers and not that of the people which counts. No doubt much of Oliver's reputation among politicians is due to the fact that he is so fond of them. He regards them as a cheerful, uncomplaining, unflurried lot endowed with a down-to-earth wisdom. Anyone who has seen the House of Commons panic at some trivial setback which leaves the rest of the country unmoved will hardly give that assessment unqualified support. Indeed there are strong dramatic reasons why a debating chamber should overreact. What is the use of a muffled sounding-board?

All the same, *The Endless Adventure* has the very rare merit of defining politics as a profession and not as some spiritual vocation (in the monastic sense). Oliver illuminates the down-to-earth, *commercial* quality of the political process; this commerce between men demands pedestrian administrative qualities, no less than a readiness to settle for a half a loaf and a willingness to soldier on in face of the insults of opponents and the indifference of everyone else, to shrug off failure. All this is true and important. And the politician who does not pick up this lesson early in his career will not last very long. In other words, politicians must develop a professional consciousness to be both effective and successful.

THE DANGERS AND PLEASURES OF POWER

Any discovery, however rewarding, may be stultified or perverted. There are immediate dangers for the political actor in the development of a greater consciousness. He may become so absorbed in the analysis of his own self and its relation with other selves that he becomes incapable of fashioning the simplest actions to correspond to the desires and necessities that he has encountered. He cannot cope with the richness of the relation.

This immediate danger is an oscillation between the actor's consciousness of his own inadequacy for his role and his determination to overcome that consciousness by cutting a grand figure. It is beautifully caught by V. S. Naipaul in *The Mimic Men*. The narrator, a discredited and exiled West Indian politician, recalls his days of power:

Yet how could we see, when we ourselves were part of the pattern? The others we could observe. We could see them in their new suits even on the hottest days. We could see the foolish stern faces they prepared for the public to hide their pleasure at their new eminence. We could see them coming out of restaurants with their 'secretaries'. We could see them shirtsleeved – their coats prominent on hangers – as they were driven in government cars marked with the letter M, on which they had insisted, to proclaim their status as ministers. The car, the shirtsleeves, the coat on the hanger: the fashion spread rapidly down the motorised section of our civil service and might be considered the sartorial fashion of our revolution. At sports meetings they went to the very front row of the stands, and over the months we could see the flesh swelling on the back of their necks, from the good living and the lack of exercise. And always about them, policemen in growing numbers.

They were easily frightened men, these colleagues of ours. They feared the countryside, they feared the dark, they grew to fear the very people on whose suffrage they depended. People who have achieved the trappings of power for no reason they can see are afraid of losing those trappings. They are insecure because they see too many like themselves.[6]

But these are only the superficial burns of power. All political actors bear such scars, although there is an inverted variety of the affliction which may be termed the Escorial Variant. Here the sophisticated actor takes pleasure in his rejection of the trappings; he controls empires from a small, bare room. His bedroom contains only a hard pallet and a white washstand. Such spartan quarters are, however, usually located in the middle of a magnificent palace. Mr Macmillan refused all honours for himself but he delighted in patronising his aristocratic connections. The parallel is not with such rare examples of a genuine dislike of the trappings of power as that of the Emperor Charles V but rather with Marie Antoinette's pleasant hours playing milkmaid at Le Hameau. The Escorial Variant may therefore be dismissed as but another aspect of the limousine-and-secret-police syndrome.

But the political actor's consciousness of inadequacy produces a deeper and more serious disillusionment. It is the disillusionment born of the confrontation between rhetoric and reality. V. S. Naipaul describes its onset in a post-colonial society, but it is to be found wherever a previously excluded group, whether of the Left, the Right or the Centre, comes to power (and in a milder form whenever the means of attaining power have to be adjusted to the means of maintaining it):

> We began in bluff. We continued in bluff. But there was a difference. We began in innocence, believing in the virtue of the smell of sweat. We continued with knowledge, of poverty and power. The colonial politician is an easy object of satire. I wish to avoid satire; I will leave out the stories of illiteracy and social innocence. Not that I wish to present him as grander or less flawed than he is. It is that his situation satirises itself, turns satire inside out, takes satire to a point where it touches pathos if not tragedy. Out of his immense violation words come easily to him, too easily. He must go back on his words. In success he must lay aside violation. He must betray himself and in the end he has no cause save his own survival. The support he has attracted, not ideal to ideal, but bitterness to bitterness, he betrays and mangles: emancipation is not possible for all.[7]

These scars, both material and spiritual, are born of a consciousness, however barely realised, of inadequacy in the political actor. It is a consciousness of the disproportion between the actor, the mere forked radish, and the importance which he has for the millions in the audience. At first sight its effects may be confused with the reverse complaint: the consciousness of *adequacy*. Distressing as it may seem, there are in fact political actors who find no difficulty at all in sustaining their roles to the satisfaction of themselves and, for a time at least, of their audience. Such actors find nothing random in the fact that they alone should have been selected for the limelight out of the millions who could have attended the auditions. Granted such an outlook, there can be but one explanation for the actor's prominence, namely that he is indeed a remarkable and talented person. It is only reasonable therefore that he should devote a good deal of attention to himself. Thus sprouts the public narcissus.

While being conscious of the outside world, in fact revelling in it, his logically inevitable centrality leads him to see himself as its hub: the father of the little people, ever responsive to their wishes, moving them to tears, to deeds of heroism if need be, moving with catlike tread and gracefully encircling embrace among the awed clog-folk. This is the stereotype of the 'Machiavelli', the man who uses his insights purely for his own glorification. Surely the dangers here are far worse than mere narcissism; are not such skills of manipulation liable to produce a Hitler? This objection is the origin of the Machiavellian bogyman, and it is misconceived. Conscious manipulation is, it is true, common to a Hitler and a Disraeli; we may charitably accept that the manipulation of a Gladstone is unconscious. But these are little more than the tricks of the trade. The true political consciousness is essentially consciousness of self: who one is, what world one is living in, and what one is about. Disraeli rarely, if ever, forgot that he was a middle-class Jew who longed for fame and who was in love with an idea of England and of its institutions which did not match the reality of the Industrial Revolution but which was none the less noble and pleasant and might by analogy and projection help to solve some of the problems which existing techniques had failed to solve: poverty, the concentration of industrial power, the Tory Party's lack of direction. Hitler, on the other hand, could of course give a clear account of the resentments and longings of post-Versailles Germany, but we doubt whether he could give any account of his own character and motivations which had much relation to reality. Certainly *Mein Kampf* gives little away in that direction. Nevertheless, he was a brilliant master of the tricks of the trade. Albert Speer in his memoirs shows how Hitler moderated voice, language, pitch, gestures, clothes when addressing a sceptical university audience; the hysterical Chaplinesque uniformed puppet at the mass rally was as much 'putting on an act' as was the sincere young lover of German culture talking humbly to people of higher education than himself. But to be a good actor is not to know oneself; it is to know one's audience.

It is a common fallacy to suppose that self-knowledge is necessarily passionless, to suppose that the actor's consciousness of how he himself ticks must lead him to tinker with the mechanisms of others without having any fellow-feeling for them. On the contrary, a heightened awareness is more likely to stimulate than to deaden fellow-feeling. A doctor will call in a colleague to examine his own family for fear that his overwhelming affection for the patient may lead him into a false diagnosis, whether alarmist or over-optimistic; he himself might magnify a child's chill into pneumonia, or minimise his wife's cancer into heartburn. The treatment gains in sense and science by his keeping away from the bedside; but his own emotions may well become more not less intense because of his feelings of powerlessness or a sudden irrational distrust of his colleague's medical skill. On the other hand he may, if a person of more stolid temperament, sit down peacefully to watch television in the confidence that he has done all he can. In the same way there is no universal consequence of political self-consciousness or of the consciousness of the relation between the political actor and those upon whom he acts. In the last resort the degree of sympathy experienced depends on the temperament of the actor. But in most cases where the sympathy between actor and audience is imperfect it is because the consciousness is also imperfect. One actor may develop an obsession about his own destiny (the narcissus); another may bend too readily to the wishes of the audience even when he is better informed than they are and knows that their demands are short-sighted (the trimmer); another, through the discovery that certain hackneyed lines retain a popular appeal even when (or particularly when) repeated over and over, may come to think that his hearers are mere childish lumps of clay, apt only for his deft manipulations (the demagogue). These failings represent an imperfect consciousness of self, however sure their grasp of certain aspects of the actor–object relation. Is it too optimistic to believe that if the narcissus, the trimmer and the demagogue were *fully* conscious of the narrowness of their approaches to political action, they might be shamed into a broader vision?

Of necessity our criteria as to what constitutes 'a full consciousness' must be open to debate. No doubt had Woodrow Wilson been alive at the time of publication, he would have vigorously contested the Freud–Bullitt[8] reading of his inner life; and most of us would tend to agree with him. This is not to say that Wilson was not a great self-deceiver with very erratic perception both of his inner life and of the outside world. Yet it is on his own perceptions that we, the external observers, have to depend in analysing him. When the subject's perceptions are reasonably reliable, our task is easy. We just tidy up a few loose ends, put the record straight here and there. But the trouble with unreliable perceptions is that we can no more rely on them being false than we can on them being true. We cannot assume that when X says 'I am like this' he must really be not-like-this, because he is such a self-deceiver. This is the vulgar error of the Freud–Bullitt study. We may have to admit in the end that reliable readings of the personality of a public man are only possible when the public man has given us a body of reliable evidence, in other words when he has already told us what he is like.

If we were to take a political actor whom we see as predominantly of a daemonic and romantic inclination, Winston Churchill, and confront his shade with Anthony Storr's reading of his inner life,[9] we might arouse equally pungent rage. No great man, particularly one of the old school, is pleased to regard himself as a mere bundle of accidental qualities dumped on a physical frame by a whim of those who stood round his cradle. Only in modern times and especially in the United States has it become fashionable to regard the exegesis of one's own psychic life as a pilgrim's progress towards the new paradise – 'an integrated personality'. Churchill might consider such an undertaking, however tactfully done and modest in scope, as writing down not merely of himself but of the glory of the individual, in short as a cheeky intrusion. Yet Churchill, even when revelling in extraordinary power, did retain a considerable degree of clarity about his own personality. He may have had to prettify the picture of his neglectful mother in order to keep himself going (but would we rather that he had looked on her with cold contempt?). Yet he recognised that he was motivated solely by ambition, that outside the political struggle life held little real interest for him. As his hero Savrola put it:

A people's good! That, he could not disguise from himself, was the direction rather than the cause of his efforts. Ambition was the motive force, and he was powerless to resist it. . . . Vehement, high daring was his cast of mind. The life he lived was the only one he could ever live; he must go on to the end.[10]

The famous avocations – bricklaying, painting, prose-writing – were merely forms of therapy, pastimes, training sessions. The real business was elsewhere. Churchill spoke several times in terms which echo Napoleon's: '*Je n'aime pas beaucoup les femmes, ni le jeu, enfin rien; je suis tout-à-fait un être politique.*' He knew this, just as he knew that a certain level of activity was necessary to fight off his recurrent melancholia, 'the black dog'. Churchill, too, we must recall, was intermittently capable of self-mockery.

This is not to say that he was a model of professional self-consciousness. Far from it. His overbearing and impulsive manners, his refusal to listen to frequently excellent advice, his romantic fantasies – all these are well documented. But even in this political actor who liked to present himself as daemonic, and indeed was impressive in that role, self-consciousness was developed to a considerable degree, as it never could be in a Hitler figure. It is hard to imagine Hitler describing himself as 'devoured by egoism' as Churchill does.[11] This consciousness of self, not naturally a strong point (he never gained much grasp of what others thought of him and his actions), was sharpened and revived by the rough-and-tumble of parliamentary debate, by the merciless daily judgment of his colleagues and opponents. And it is this consciousness of self which modified Churchill's erratic intuition and which gives him an essentially civilised aspect despite his wilder characteristics.

Churchill is both the writer of *Savrola* and Savrola himself. He is, as all political actors must be, the analyst of humbug, the humbugger and the humbugged all in one. He knows that Savrola/Churchill is motivated by ambition. As an actor he is ready to use an actor's tricks to further that ambition; for example, though barely a believer, he will sprinkle his peroration with invocations of the Almighty. But it is hard to decide who is being humbugged in this passage from his war memoirs on becoming prime minister: 'I felt as if I were walking with destiny, and that all my past life had been but a preparation for this hour and for this trial.'[12] This recalls Gladstone's entry in his diary shortly after becoming prime minister in 1868: 'I ascend a steepening path with a burden ever gathering weight. The Almighty seems to sustain and spare me for some purpose of His own, deeply unworthy as I know myself to be. Glory be to His name.'[13]

Henry Fairlie[14] quotes this passage with a shudder and contrasts it with Macmillan's reaction to becoming prime minister in 1957: 'Where is the Chief Whip? We're off to the Turf to celebrate.' We could also add here Disraeli's delight at having climbed to 'the top of the greasy pole'. Certainly honest delight is a much more attractive greeting to power than lamentation over a God-given burden. We find in the breeziness of Macmillan and Disraeli an assurance that our lives will not be unduly interfered with for the accomplishment of some great end. We believe that this cheerful acceptance of the comic and sporting aspects of the struggle for power must bring with it a modest view of the duties of power. We have learnt to distrust the language of the holy war and of the man chosen by God. Such an instinct may seem sound when we examine the records of Supermac and Dizzy. But cheerfulness is not necessarily the sign of sound government. Nor is public good humour a token of a warm heart. We still remember the joviality and peasant wit of Stalin. Consider also these words of Bolingbroke, a lively and perceptive writer, but by no means a sensible or attractive political actor. In contrasting the relative satisfactions to be obtained by the philosopher and the politician he says:

He, who speculates in order to *act*, goes on and carries his scheme into execution. His labour continues, it varies, it increases; but so does his pleasure too. . . . While a great event is in suspense, the action warms, and the very suspense, made up of hope and fear, maintains no unpleasing agitation in the mind. If the event is decided successfully, such a man enjoys pleasure proportionable to the good he has done; a pleasure like to that which is attributed to the Supreme Being, on a survey of his works.[15]

This is a true picture of political action. Yet it is rather repulsive. Although we expect politicians to be ambitious and energetic – indeed we may even concede that without ambition and energy nothing much will get done – we do not like to see them exercising these qualities too openly and with too much visible enjoyment. We may be attracted by the idea of the lion as a great hunter while being much distressed at the sight of a lion tearing a young deer to pieces.

Almost all the qualities which may make for good government may on close inspection prove unattractive to the sensitive observer. If a politician is jovial, we smell a rat in 'his false smile'; if he is solemn and doleful, he depresses us, we suspect him of hypocrisy. If he is ambitious, he threatens dictatorship. If he is unassuming, he must be lazy. If he is detached, he is cold-blooded. If he is passionate, he is dangerous. Even that quality of amiable cynicism turns sour under our microscope. We begin to speculate: 'If this fellow thinks about things in the way that we do, why is he not on our side of the fence?

Why is he over there with the windbags and the petty tyrants? He must be playing a double game.' After all, we as taxpayers did pay for the erection of the greasy pole. Does it not therefore deserve a little respect?

This double mind which we have about the nature of the political actor bedevils the *polis*. We want him to be like one of us. Yet we want him to be different, not to say superior. He wants to show us that he is one of us; yet he wants to show us that he is superior (otherwise why would he be where he is?). This paradox, this tension, is an essential feature of a healthy relationship between the politician and his audience. For if we all agree that he is a superior being, he will be tempted to treat us as inferior beings. On the other hand, if we just regard him as an ordinary chap who has struck it lucky, he is likely to act down to correspond with everyone's expectations of him. If, for example, everyone including the prime minister expects the prime minister to take bribes, it is a safe bet that the prime minister will take bribes.

It is the very safeness of this bet which attracts the money of so many able observers of the public scene. Don Quixote's Rosinante is a long shot in whom no man of the world would invest a penny; dreams of ideal ladies and of great glory to be won are only dreams. Sancho Panza's mule, on the other hand, is a short-priced favourite. Expect the best of men, and you will be disappointed time and again. Expect the worst and you will be right often enough to rub along. It is the opposite of Pascal's bet, for it is based on the belief that the world is not such an intolerable place as to make any endeavour to change it better than none, whereas Pascal, being but ill-adapted to the delights of the senses, felt that we were so lapped in misery that the stake at risk was almost negligible. Yet how far does this 'realism' in fact correspond to reality?

As W. H. Auden points out:

> At first sight Sancho Panza seems a philistine realist. 'I go,' he says 'with a great desire to make money'; it may seem to the reader hardly 'realistic' of Sancho Panza to believe that he will gain a penny, far less an island governorship by following Don Quixote, but is not the philistine realist who believes in nothing but material satisfactions precisely the same type to whom it is easiest to sell a nonexistent gold mine?[16]

Thus Sancho Panza's 'realism' may serve as a healthy corrective to Don Quixote's idealism: but, taken in isolation, each attitude is as misleading as the other. Cynicism is not only no better a guide to men's motives than credulity; the one is almost meaningless without the other. Fénelon says:

> Indeed, men are unfortunate that they have to be ruled by a king who is like them a man, for it would take gods to set them right. But Kings are no less unfortunate, being mere men, weak and imperfect, to have the ruling of a great multitude of sinful and deceitful individuals.[17]

No doubt many will find this as astringent a corrective to the exuberant optimism of politicians as does Jouvenel.[18] Similarly, it is a pleasure to the sceptic to come upon the supernatural figure of the legislator in the middle of Rousseau's *Social Contract*. After much heaving and clanking, Rousseau suddenly announces that mere mortal man cannot teach us to throw off our chains:

> In order to discover what social regulations are best suited to nations, there is needed a superior intelligence which can survey all the passions of mankind, though itself exposed to none: an intelligence having no contact with our nature, yet knowing it to the full: an intelligence, the well-being of which is independent of our own, yet willing to be concerned with it: which, finally, viewing the long perspectives of time, and preparing for itself a day of glory as yet far distant, will labour in one century to reap its reward in another. In short, only Gods can give laws to men. . . . The real miracle, and the one sufficient proof of the legislator's mission, is his own greatness of soul.[19]

Never was there a more poignant cry for a Messiah. And we recall the cautious and conservative constitutions that Rousseau suggested for Poland and Corsica. For the flight from Utopia springs from the same insistence on perfection as the search for it; sentimentality is the cynic's bank-holiday in politics also. And yet how vapid is this mode of discourse; it is a network of tautologies. If we presuppose a legislator who is so wise that everybody will listen to him, then everybody will listen to him. If men were not imperfect, they would not need rulers; for every man would be master of himself. We have to discuss the problem of rulers just because men are imperfect. The pessimism of Rousseau and Fénelon amounts to saying that the problem of government would be soluble only if there were no problem. This pessimism, like the optimism of Marx or of Rousseau himself on a cheerful day, is essentially a demand for mathematical exactitude. 'To set them right' (Fénelon, *'Les meilleures règles'* (Rousseau) equals 1 on a scale of amelioration where 0 is total corruption and 1 is perfection. If the legislator be a mere man, how can he render the world perfect when he is himself imperfect? He must therefore be an outside force, a god. For even if we mortals attain by our own efforts something which seemed close to perfection, we could not be certain unless we had, as it were, some external seal of approval. Mr X may have made what seems to us a wonderful job of governing the country. But how do we know that Mr Y could not have done even better? And Mr Z? The only case in which we can be certain is if Mr X is the Messiah, for by definition nobody can improve on the Messiah, otherwise he would not be the Messiah.

But how do we decide if Mr X is the Messiah, or not? We can check his police record, question his wife about his personal habits, examine his knowledge of economics. But these procedures seem somehow inadequate. The truth is that, having proceeded thus far with rigorous deduction in this quest for certainty, we must now make a daring leap into the unknown. Either Mr X must say 'I am your Messiah'. Or the hand-out (Mr X's backers, family friends, co-believers, etc.) must say 'This is your Messiah'. Or the public must shout in unison 'He is our Messiah'. For any degree of permanent recorded success, some combination of these three assertions is to be desired. Certainly some supportive evidence that Mr X is indeed the Messiah before, during and after his proclamation as such will strengthen his claims: for example, healing the sick, military victory, making the trains run on time. Rousseau's *'grande âme'* might by itself not be accepted as sufficient proof of the legislator's mission. Yet the essential and crucial factor in the hallowing of Mr X as a Messiah is the proclamation that he is one; if this does not 'take', Mr X will be cast out as a crank.

This familiar phenomenon is a leap from the proposition that 'only a god could rule us' to the proposition that 'a god is in fact ruling us now'. The reason for this leap is that we suspect we might give way to despair if no god appeared; the whole drama would seem too shabby to be worth sitting through. A star actor more often than not *is* a better actor than the supporting cast; there is after all no overwhelming reason why the able should not be preferred. But the importance to many in the audience is not the fact that Mr X acts better but that he is a star, proclaimed and demanding as such affection and admiration. For these theatre-goers, the pleasure in watching Mr X extract the last syllable of value out of a tenth-rate play is as great as that in seeing him walk through a masterpiece;

and this because he is an accepted hero who makes not just the play but the whole theatre seem an exciting place to be, in fact the only place worth being.

It is easy to say that we must throw off such a puerile quest for certainties, that we should judge Mr X solely by what he does and that our love should be based only on his genuinely admirable qualities. And we know that Mr X should be muttering to himself night and day: 'I am one of them, I am not a Messiah.' Yet there are several reasons why this determined ordinariness is rarely achieved, why in some senses it may be impossible to achieve. Jouvenel claims that 'the worthiest and wisest men engaging in politics are least apt to experience the sporting enjoyment described by Bolingbroke'.[20] In so far as 'worthiest and wisest' are associated with the 'cautious, unromantic and down-to-earth', this proposition is self-fulfilling. Jouvenel is merely describing the kind of political actor whom he finds most sympathetic. But if we are talking in terms of measurable political achievements, we may find it more difficult to associate worthiness and wisdom exclusively with that particular type of temperament. We can find Attlees, Erhards, Walpoles and Butlers who have introduced new institutions or presided over old ones with great success and a minimum of personal display. Yet we cannot ignore the Churchills, Lloyd Georges and Roosevelts whose great contributions are inseparable from their 'sporting enjoyment'. And these contributions are not just the explosive result of the contact between dramatic personalities and dramatic moments of war or economic crisis. Churchill and Lloyd George played as crucial a part in the broadening of the welfare state before the first world war as did Attlee in the similar process after 1945. Equally we cannot ignore the failures of undramatic personalities (with solid records of achievement) to rise to dramatic moments largely through failure of the imagination – Asquith, Hoover, Neville Chamberlain.

TEMPERAMENT AND THE PUBLIC PERSONA

If it is admitted that a drab, undramatic personality is not necessarily a sign of worthiness or wisdom, we must take the varieties of public men as the stage presents them to us. We have the right to demand that they make the best of themselves; we cannot ask that they should be other than environment and temperament have made them. By the time the actor is on stage, it is too late for the audience to demand that his figure be thinner or his voice less resonant. We can only shout for his dismissal and replacement by somebody more suited to the part. Anthony Powell describes the overwhelming impact of Lord Alanbrooke's personality thus:

> His [Vavassor, the porter's] attention, my own too, was at that moment unequivocally demanded by the hurricane-like imminence of a thickset general, obviously of high rank, wearing enormous horn-rimmed spectacles. He had just burst from a flagged staff-car almost before it had drawn up by the kerb. Now he tore up the steps of the building at the charge, exploding through the inner door into the hall. An extraordinary current of physical energy, almost of electricity, suddenly pervaded the place. I could feel it stabbing through me. This was the CIGS. His quite remarkable and palpable extension of personality, in its effect on others, I had noticed not long before, out in the open. Coming down Sackville Street, I had all at once been made aware of something that required attention on the far pavement and saw him pounding along. I saluted at admittedly longish range. The salute was returned. Turning my head to watch his progress, I then had proof of being not alone in acting as a kind of receiving-station for such rays – which had, morally speaking, been observable, on his appointment to that top post, down as low as platoon commander. On this Sackville Street occasion, an officer a hundred yards or more ahead had his nose glued to the window of a bookshop. As the CIGS passed (whom he might well have missed in his concentration on the contents of the window), the officer suddenly swivelled a complete about-turn, saluting too. No doubt he had seen the reflection in the plate glass. All the same, in its own particular genre, the incident gave the outward appearance of exceptional magnetic impact. That some such impact existed, was confirmed by this closer conjunction in the great hall. Vavassor, momentarily overawed – there could be no doubt of it – came to attention and saluted with much more empressement than usual. Having no cap, I merely came to attention. The CIGS glanced for a split second, as if summarising all the facts of one's life.
> 'Good morning.'
> It was a terrific volume of sound, an absolute bellow, at the same time quite effortless. A moment later, he was on the landing halfway up the stairs.[21]

If the situation had called for a soothing committee chairman rather than a man who could radiate energy and purpose 'down as low as platoon commander', it would have been futile to ask Alanbrooke for a less disturbing performance. The only solution would have been to replace him with a quieter man.

Of course temperamental range is far wider and less fixed than, say, the range of a man's voice. Many men are capable of quite deliberately selecting a particular octave of public behaviour, not simply because it harmonises with their given temperament but because that octave seems to them to harmonise also with the demands of the times or the job in hand. Anthony Powell, later in the same work, describes Lord Montgomery in such terms:

I tried to reduce to viable terms impressions of this slight, very exterior contact. On the one hand, there had been hardly a trace of the almost overpowering physical impact of the CIGS, that curious electric awareness felt down to the tips of one's fingers of a given presence imparting a sense of stimulation, also the consoling thought that someone of the sort was at the top. On the other hand, the field marshal's outward personality offered what was perhaps even less usual, will-power, not so much natural, as developed to altogether exceptional lengths. No doubt there had been a generous basic endowment, but not of the essentially magnetic variety. In short, the will here might even be more effective from being less dramatic. It was an immense, wiry, calculated, insistent hardness, rather than a force like champagne bursting from the bottle. Observed in tranquillity, the former combination of qualities was not, within the terms of reference, particularly uplifting or agreeable, except again in the manner their synthesis seemed to offer dependability in utter self-reliance and resilience. One felt that a great deal of time and trouble, even intellectual effort of its own sort, had gone into producing this final result.[22]

Here it would be perfectly relevant to question the public persona, Anthony Powell's Montgomery having chosen that persona by an act of will. Indeed, many people, both military historians and laymen, have since questioned the value of that persona. The defence of this artificial cult and culture of personality is as follows: an army which is not winning battles must have its morale improved. Reinforcements of men, arms, food, concert parties will help. But the cheapest and also the indispensable element is confidence in the man at the top; to instil confidence, the man at the top must be visible. In earlier wars a Wellington could visit every hollow square in the heat of battle. In a vast, modern army the general is likely to be a more remote figure. He must rely therefore on artificially induced visibility. Ergo, he must wear a sweater and a cap with two badges on it.

In politics, a leading actor must be visible for these reasons:

—To inspire confidence and loyalty in his close supporters.

—To maintain contact with the uncommitted public and, if possible, to inspire them too with confidence and loyalty, though these will necessarily be pale shadows of the intense feelings of his own supporters.

—To prevent his eclipse by a rival who is more highly visible than himself.

In the present, visibility is necessary to carry his supporters and the rest of the population with him in those enterprises which he has already in hand. But visibility is also a necessary precaution for the future. The actor must maintain himself in power to carry on with those lines of action which he believes to be right.

What, then, is the secret of those political actors who have prospered despite apparently being invisible to all but their closest associates? A joke was current in Tory circles for many years to the effect that 'an empty cab stopped outside Buckingham Palace and Mr Attlee got out of it.' Yet Clement Attlee led the Labour Party for twenty years and the nation for six. Despite several plots by his leading colleagues to depose him, when he retired it was principally for reasons of age and failing health. How are we to explain this paradox? It is generally admitted that Attlee was a man of strong and resourceful character, but if he had been unpopular in the country and hence a liability to his party, he would have been quickly unseated, whatever his skills of political infighting. The truth is that Lord Attlee's plain, unadorned manner corresponded to public demand. He did not choose that plainness, though he was certainly conscious if not proud of it. In fact his plainness generated all the more popularity because it was so obviously straightforward. It had no taint of false frankness about it. Attlee was a reassurance to the public that the more exotic talents of Cripps and Bevan would not be allowed to get out of hand. He was also a symbol of a plain man's government that would have the *sense* as well as the compassion to reorganise society on 'progressive' lines. Attlee's refusal to be 'stylish' was in itself a style, and a cultivated one. To appear on the public stage is inevitably either to adopt a new style or to project a natural style. We in the audience are little concerned whether it be the one or the other so long as the result corresponds with our notion of how the part should be played. From the point of view of the actor, the 'sporting enjoyment' may take several forms, but it will rarely be absent:

Mr X may take pleasure in speaking his mind at the top of his voice.

Mr Y may take pleasure in modestly reflecting the views of his hearers.

Mr Z may take pleasure in showing sympathy with the views of his hearers while attempting to move their minds in the direction of his own. This may be done with passionate, highly coloured advocacy or by a tactful blurring of the object.

We may make moral judgment about the relative values of these styles; we may talk of vainglory, of egotism, of time-serving, of hypocrisy. The public stage dramatises and magnifies the temptations and challenges of life. But in the science of politics, we are concerned primarily with effects; not with 'was Mr X's speech noble or base?' but with 'did it achieve its purpose?' and 'was that purpose desirable?'

DEVIOUSNESS AND PRINCIPLE

When Eisenhower was president he was constantly ridiculed for the poor grasp of grammar he displayed at his press conferences and for his excessive addiction to golf. In his obituary notices he was dismissed as an affable but mediocre man. Yet Eisenhower led the greatest invasion army in history to a successful conclusion. He had a considerable hand in deciding the postwar political structures of western Europe. He was twice elected president of the most powerful country in history. During his presidency he ended another war and prevented further wars from breaking out all over the world. At home, prosperity increased with only a minor faltering. Some progress was made on the granting of full civil rights to racial minorities.

This is a record of success which only a handful of men in history could equal. Yet many observers are content to attribute it to a mixture of luck and charm – 'the gift of getting on with people'. Is it not odd that this mixture, though certainly potent, is otherwise usually associated with those who have just failed to reach the top of the greasy pole or who cling there only a moment or two before being knocked down by some more determined or talented rival? The truth is that Eisenhower was an extremely formidable and gifted political actor. As an allied commander, a 'political general', he is at last beginning to be appreciated.[23] Yet his political achievements remain closely guarded by a detached, chilly nature operating behind that infectious grin. Murray Kempton puts the matter superbly:

> It was the purpose of his existence never to be seen in what he did. When he fired Sherman Adams, his chief of staff, as a political liability in 1958, Adams thought it was Nixon's doing. While he was coldly measuring the gain or loss from dropping Nixon as his vice-presidential candidate, Nixon thought it was Tom Dewey's doing.
>
> When this gesture proved insufficient, Eisenhower accommodated what was inevitable, if transient, and even offered himself up as battle trophy for Goldwater's brief triumph at the San Francisco convention. It was a situation where, the surreptitiously neat having failed, the heroically messy could hardly succeed. The useless employment of further resources would have been an affront to that superb sense of economy which made Eisenhower a soldier successful just [by] being so immune to notions of glory and to pleasurable anticipations of bleeding ...
>
> No thought was to be uttered undisguised; the face had as many ranges, indeed as many roles as there are sins to commit, because it was an instrument for hinting without ever quite saying. Even the syntax was an instrument. When things were at their stickiest in the Formosa Strait, James Hagerty, his press secretary, told the president that the best course would be to refuse to answer any questions at all on the subject if it came up at his press conference.
>
> 'Don't worry, Jim,' [the president] told him as [they] went out the door. 'If that question comes up, I'll just confuse them.'[24]

And again, of Eisenhower's memoirs:

> There is the sound of trumpets, the fog of rhetoric, then just for a moment the focus of the cold intelligence.
>
> The president-elect goes to Korea.
>
> 'We used light airplanes to fly along the front and were impressed by the rapidity with which wounded were being brought back for treatment; evacuation was almost completely by helicopter since there were no landing fields for conventional planes in the mountains. Except for sporadic artillery fire and sniping there was little action at the moment, *but in view of the strength of the positions the enemy had developed, it was obvious that any frontal attack would present great difficulties.*'
>
> All else would be conversation; one look had decided Eisenhower to fold the war.[25]

Mr Kempton summed up these recondite qualities on the occasion of Eisenhower's death in the third month of President Nixon's administration:

The *effect* of General Eisenhower as a president is above all else the thing Mr Nixon wants; but the general's rules for performance were very closely held, although very closely watched by Mr Nixon – as evidenced by the acuity with which, alone among observers, he once described his great commander as 'more complex and devious in the best sense of the word than most persons imagine'.

It was General Eisenhower's trick never to neglect the pieties in moments of ceremony and never to observe them in moments of decision; he never did a foolish, let alone a wicked thing, for a high-minded reason.[26]

For many people today, it will seem inconceivable that devious could have a 'best sense'. Yet the epithet simply means 'off the beaten track'; in political terms it implies the avoidance of the set response to the set situation. We place a high value today upon 'originality' but we do not give equal value to the deviousness required to produce original work. Similarly, Murray Kempton's epigram on General Eisenhower and the pieties is a hard text for today. The modern reader is inclined to say that either General Eisenhower believed in the pieties, deeply and sincerely, in which case his neglect of them was deplorable. Or he did not believe in them, in which case his observance of them was hypocritical. This is a false antithesis. Eisenhower both believed in the traditional Republican things – individualism, thrift, *laissez-faire* – and was prepared to disregard them when circumstances seemed to him to demand it. Where he went wrong after behaving in accordance with Republican principles, the reason was more likely to be a failure to secure for himself the right mixture of advice rather than an excessive adherence to principle (for example, his conduct of the American economy during his second term). No doubt those whose own lives are ruled by emotion will feel distaste for others who can master and understand their emotions and beliefs. In fact the usual procedure is either, if hostile, to deny that the masterer has any feelings ('Mr X is a cold fish, he only believes in Mr X'); or, if friendly, to claim that the masterer is all feeling ('Mr X will make a great president, he believes in his country'). So low does sound reasoning stand in comparison with sound feelings. Who loves Odysseus for his cunning, though to be cunning is only to be kenning, to know how to, and 'I ken' is the same as 'I can'? Such epithets quickly become degraded; and then we have to find a new word to describe these unromantic but essential aspects of competence. Will a 'can-do man' soon come to mean the same as a con-man? 'Do', we may notice, already has this pejorative sense when the object is a human being. Until we understand how 'devious' may have a best sense, we shall never understand political actors nor how they translate their personal abilities and inclinations into political action. The conflict between presentation and personation, between detachment and involvement has been central to the study of the theatre since the days of Schiller, if not of Aristotle. It has not yet flowered as it should in the study of politics. For this neglected science has not a Stanislavsky to its name, still less a Brecht to spar with him.

Perhaps we may finally clarify this idea of the political actor by making the metaphor more precise. An actor-manager of the old school, for example Sir Beerbohm Tree, is faced with a variety of considerations in putting on a play.

—He must endeavour to ensure that the play makes money or at least does not bankrupt him. If he loses all his money or the confidence of his backers, he will be able to put on no more plays, however splendid.

—He must try to keep together a good company. This will require delicate techniques of 'man management' – the sort of thing that is taught in cruder form in the labour relations departments of business schools.

—He will wish to put on plays that he 'believes in' – that is, which he believes to have merit of some kind. Apart from his exciting repertoire of favourites, he will be on the lookout for new material.

—He must maintain his own acting skills if he is to keep the confidence of the public and of his own company, if he personally is to remain a big 'draw'.

Now each of these aspects of his task is in itself a science – finance, man-management, literary-theatrical criticism, acting. And an actor-manager who is deficient in any one of them will not last long. Indeed, the difficulty of mastering all four sciences has led to the virtual disappearance of the actor-manager. When we speak of the art or science of the actor-manager we include all these sciences individually plus an overarching, coordinating technique. The four aspects we have mentioned are of course overlapping: if, for example, our hero does not act well, his play may make less money. But even if we were able to classify his tasks so precisely that there was no overlapping, there would still be some coordinating aspects omitted: for example, the effect on company morale of himself always taking the leading role, although the box office may demand a certain degree of one-man-bandsmanship – or the conflict between the need to make money and his desire to put on the plays he likes (or why would he be in the business at all?). In other words, though we may divide up his tasks for the purpose of description, we must not forget that the job is an organic assignment.

Similarly with the political actor. We cannot separate his acting ability from his organisational ability, still less from his 'pre-political' endowment of prejudice. For he does not arrive on the stage purged of all prejudice by some intense dramatic training; he does not make his début as a blank sheet of paper on which experience scrawls stage directions such as 'pursuit of liberty', 'obsession with equality' or even 'exit left'. On the contrary, his prejudices are already fully formed; it is his acting technique, his communication with the audience, his talent at managing men and running institutions, his analysis of motive and situation, which require development. It is obvious that experience modifies the pre-political endowment. Yet pre-politics is not only temporally but logically prior to politics. That is to say, even if a man's views on liberty are modified by political experience, they cannot find political expression, they cannot bring pressure to bear on reality until they are at least vaguely formed. A man's view about the merit of a possible act – for example, devaluation of the currency – may change overnight; but his object of stability or a favourable balance of payments remains unchanged. And even such an object is well towards the means-side of a means-ends spectrum. A man's attitude towards such basic ideas as 'liberty' or 'law and order' is likely to change very slowly over a long period of years, if at all. We know of sudden shocks – Wordsworth's disenchantment with the French Revolution, the making of 'Thirties Communists and their subsequent disenchantment with 'the god that failed'. But the reason in most such cases is a violent turn of events or an inescapable revision of the observer's picture of events in the light of fresh evidence rather than a deep change in the basic disposition of the observers. Whittaker Chambers joined the Republican Party after renouncing Communism and, when asked why, replied: 'I am an Orgbureau man'. Of course a switch of this kind does have profound *practical* consequences when the man in question is of political importance, although as observers of his conduct we are fascinated by the way his new beliefs mirror-image his old ones. But equally practically, such total switch-overs are very rare. It is more useful and more accurate to treat the pre-politics as a separate unchanging datum, and to record modifications only in the margin. It would be foolish, for example, to treat the American constitution as a fluid, ever-changing corpus and to publish each year its exact composition. The obvious method is to print it in its original form and stick on the occasional amendments. The political constitution of most individuals has an equally solid base. Even the trimmer, for example, is motivated continuously by a solid belief in accommodation. The only real change in *his* political constitution would be if he suddenly stood rock-hard for some principle. If we trace, for example, the careers of Churchill and Baldwin over thirty years, we shall find that Baldwin is always concerned to conciliate and accommodate, having before him a fixed goal of national harmony, while Churchill, with no fixed goal, is always concerned to find a rock on which to found a defence of principle. Both, of course, constantly change position on policy, Baldwin, bedouin-like, folding his tents silently and leaving not a trace, Churchill leaving great castles in ruins behind him. But neither ever changed his basic attitudes. Policy comes before persuasion, principle before policy, and prejudice before principle. Prejudice we call 'pre-politics', not because it has no relevance to politics – indeed it is more often than not the motor of politics – but because the political process has power to *change* it only over a very long period, perhaps longer even than a man's life. To assess a man's actions as if they were the result solely of 'desiccated' analysis and not also of passion and prejudice is a great error. But it is as great an error to assume that prejudice is the same kind of influence upon action as is analysis. In most men prejudice is far stronger. And it derives much of its strength from its accumulated solidity, from having rooted itself deeply over the years. Surprise is frequently expressed at the shameless inconsistency of politicians. But where great passions are not engaged, politicians quite often simply forget what they have said before and are unperturbed by accusations of inconsistency. And there is no necessary correlation between the depth of passion and the degree of practical importance involved. Tariffs which could decide a nation's economic future may seem to some a purely technical question while a small increase in health charges may be seen as the beginning of fascism.

The change in Enoch Powell's attitude towards Commonwealth immigration has stirred widespread speculation. In his political youth an ardent imperialist, he accepted something approaching a

Roman idea of British citizenship which would have resulted in a boundless influx of former colonial peoples into this country. In the late 1960s he aroused passionate reaction, both friendly and hostile, by his advocacy of the strictest possible control of immigration plus some measure of voluntary but government-encouraged repatriation. Paul Foot, in his lively tract,[27] attributes this change simply to political opportunism and shows that Mr Powell's interest in the supposed dangers of and opposition to Commonwealth immigration was only made public after the 1966 general election and Edward Heath's accession to the leadership. This argument is in one sense cogent but it also raises the question: why, if Mr Powell is so opportunistic, did he not seize the opportunity much earlier? After all, the topic of immigration had occupied a place near the centre of the political stage for some six or seven years. If Mr Powell's aim was merely to stake a claim to the leadership of his party by exploiting this topic, he would surely have been well advised to start earlier.

Without dismissing Mr Foot's explanation entirely, we may find it hard to accept it exclusively. David Watt comments:

His [Enoch Powell's] motives are not as simple as Mr Foot thinks. Like Gladstone and many other men of powerful emotions held down by powerful intellect, he has a volcanic cast of mind. It is never clear whether it is the emotion which cause the upheavals or whether it is changes in the intellectual structure; all one knows is that there is an explosion and the landscape immediately changes so completely that it is impossible to remember what it was like before.[28]

This seems a more perceptive reading of characters such as Powell and Gladstone. And yet we may wonder whether it is quite bold enough. The landscape does surely retain something of its outline after the explosion, however shattered the trees or scorched the soil. At all periods of his life Mr Powell has been driven by an overwhelming patriotism, and this not in a pleasantly contemplative affection for English pastures but violently and dynamically felt. He has, it seems, always longed to *make* something of his feelings for his country, almost in the sense in which one belligerent man in the bar asks another 'Do you want to make something of it?' His vigorous opposition to any derogation from the authority of the Queen's titles and to any slapdash reform of the House of Lords is more than a mere affection for things as they are, it is a precise, three-dimensional vision of the nation as a living organism, not a mere inert conjunction of circumstance. One whose job is to analyse, tend and purify that organism – namely a politician – is duty bound to delimit its size and ascertain its composition. He must in fact define citizenship, not again as an inert conjunction of legal clauses, but as a living molecular structure. His first attempt at definition – an attempt to give organic meaning to the Empire – fails. The Commonwealth into which the Empire is transformed is a sham, 'a gigantic farce' according to *The Times* article by 'A Conservative', generally assumed to be Enoch Powell himself.[29] Patriotism must be based on reality, not on dreams. Now that the reality of British power, particularly in India, has faded, to give any organic meaning to the concept of British citizenship we must turn to the only other readily available mode of realisation, the traditional reliance on racial and linguistic homogeneity. Mr Foot makes much of Mr Powell's 'abdication' from his great declaration that 'I have set and always will set my face like flint against making any difference between one citizen of this country and another on grounds of his origin.' But matters are not so simple. Let us get down to cases A and B in Wolverhampton. A is black, B is white. $Powell_1$ treats them alike, because they are for him both British citizens. But for $Powell_2$ A may no longer be a citizen; therefore it may be legitimate, even principled, to give B preference over him.

This may seem an odious switch in practice. If it conforms with Mr Powell's patriotism in its varying expressions, it does not conform with other well-known political prejudices in favour of, for example, the brotherhood of man or the need for stability and continuity of government particularly in its treatment of the individual (we are talking here of an area somewhere between equity and the rule of law). It may be that Mr Powell either holds these latter prejudices little or not at all (this is in fact not so; he is certainly very strongly attached to the rule of law), it is certain that he believes in them much less strongly than he 'believes in his country', as defined through citizenship. The effect of the change in that definition has indeed proved volcanic both in its effect upon our society and upon Mr Powell's standing therein. But we need not suspect Mr Powell himself of any deep change of temperament or prejudice. The lava certainly blurs the lines of the landscape but the bedrock never shifts.

IV

The High Comedy

WHY POLITICIANS ARE UNPOPULAR

Men of letters, as Burke says, being fond of distinguishing themselves are rarely averse to innovation. Persons of intelligence and sensitivity whose interest is drawn to politics expect a stimulus at least as sharp as that to be experienced through the performing arts and as much colour and warmth as there is to be found in the conversation of friends. They are frequently disappointed, not of course by the dazzling possibilities of Marx and Rousseau, but in the countervailing political theory and practice of Tocqueville, Peel, Baldwin, Metternich, Oakeshott. This, they will murmur, is humdrum stuff.

And certainly some of these latter political scientists are not unaware of the murmuring. Tocqueville, for example, writes:

> What I call the literary spirit in politics consists in looking for what is ingenious and new rather than for what is true, being fonder of what makes an interesting picture than what serves a purpose, being very appreciative of good acting and fine speaking without reference to the play's results, and, finally, judging by impressions rather than reasons.[1]

Professor Oakeshott talks of men in political activity sailing a boundless and bottomless sea; and adds 'a depressing doctrine, it will be said'.[2] Raymond Aron remarks that his has been described as 'a melancholy approach'.[3] In fact, Aron shows a cautious confidence in the possibilities of the future. He remarks acidly that 'in so far as Sartre-like political literature is considered normal, the attempt to think with lucidity and detachment which has always been the ambition of philosophers, must appear mysterious'.[4] True, but is this all?

The more closely the political scientist concerns himself with the humdrum practicalities of politics, the more he will share the odium endured by the practising politician. What is the nature of this odium? Why are politicians so unpopular? Raleigh summarises the usual accusation:

Why Politicians are Unpopular

Tell men of high condition
That manage the Estate,
Their purpose is ambition,
Their practice only hate:
And if they once reply,
Then give them all the lie.

Such a view is not confined to what one might call literary adventurers. Adam Smith writes of 'that insidious and crafty animal, vulgarly called a statesman or politician, whose councils are directed by the momentary fluctuations of affairs'.[5] And, as F. S. Oliver points out, Adam Smith 'enjoyed the confidence of Mr Pitt and the friendship of Mr Burke';[6] he was not one to shrink from the insensitive crudities of political conversation.

This feeling of revulsion goes beyond a healthy distrust of any politician's motives; it even goes beyond that distaste so many of us feel for the spectacle of someone 'on the make', a spectacle which is of course heightened by the spotlights of the political theatre. There is something more even than this. I mean a distaste for the *manner* of practising politicians both in public and private conversation. This distaste is to be observed even among those (political commentators, for example) whose life is lived in the political world and with politicians. Members of Parliament, senators, congressmen, deputies, are not an attractive breed. We shun the company even of those whose opinions we share. Why should this be so?

First of all, members of Parliament (which I shall use as a short-hand term for all elected representatives who are acting mainly in a political rather than an administrative function) take man and the world as they are. The doctrine of the Fall is their guiding rule. Men can be appealed to by promises of direct benefit to themselves – money, property, privileges, liberties. Self-interest, either individual or communal, is accepted as a major spring of human action. Now such an attitude does not imply that men may be moved *solely* by self-interest. Some politicians think so, the Boss Tweeds for example; but many, if not most, do not, and those are the ones whose unpopularity we are attempting to analyse. Nobody wonders why Boss Tweed was and is so strongly criticised; nor, we may note, does anybody seem very surprised that he should have been successful. The majority of politicians, like the rest of us, believe and act on the belief that people are moved partly by altruism and partly by self-interest. (We are not tackling here the complexity of defining altruism; the criterion prevalent in daily life is whether an event is of immediate direct benefit to its agent or to somebody else.)

The politician promises lower taxes; he also talks of doing our duty as a nation towards the poor. The individual offers his children sweets on condition that they are good; he may also speak of his own duty to his kith and kin. There seems to be little difference in the mixture.

The main difference is in fact one of scale. The politician is engaged on a vast and complex operation of balancing and reconciling interests. To make the operation manageable he must group the interests of individuals into blocks. But thereby the nature of his concern with those individuals at that moment is nakedly exposed; for they are collectively labelled 'the temperance vote' or 'the farming interest' or 'the housewife's vote'; they are shoved together into a depersonalised bundle, each part of which instead of being remarkable as a human being is remarkable only as sharing one particular quality (temperance, farming, housewifedom) with all the other parts of the bundle.

The professional manner is the defect of the professional consciousness described in the last chapter; to use a somewhat old-fashioned expression, it is a professional *deformity* and its repulsiveness derives from the professional necessity to treat people as objects. The bricklayer has no such problem; bricks and mortar are bricks and mortar. But the physician, the lawyer, and the politician all have to respond to the people around them both as fellow-beings and as cases for treatment. We may try to mitigate this impersonality by talking of the friendly bedside manner of a good doctor, the humanity of a good lawyer; but their professional qualifications are based on non-personal skills. Doctors are not awarded degrees for showing sympathy with patients; the essential test of a lawyer is whether he knows his law, whether he can correctly assign our case to the right forensic pigeon-hole. The doctor and lawyer are preserved from odium by the fact that we normally call upon them only in an emergency, when impersonal and accurate advice is the first essential, though even in such circumstances many clients and patients find the similarity between impersonality and inhumanity highly distressing.

Politicians, on the other hand, are, as it were, performing an operation or conducting a lawsuit which never ends. They are in full and constant view of their clients. And, worse still, they have to dissemble their function. For they are not supposed to possess *skills* in the sense in which the doctor and the lawyer possess skills; they are supposed to be blessed merely with a good heart and a sympathetic ear as if these were enough to run a country. We may perhaps wish to know about their administrative competence, but certainly not about their skill in balancing and reconciling interests – for these are low political tricks.

This conventional minuet can work on a small scale; a politician can talk to one of his constituents and both can go home in the happy conviction that they enjoy a warm and intimate relationship in which there is no hint of manipulation.

But in large distanced societies this happy conviction becomes a thin fiction. For the scale (of population, of geographical size, of institutional complexity) dictates a coarser classification, a cruder cross-referencing. Time is a crucial factor. How can a politician canvass a hundred thousand electors except by megaphones and television commercials? To stage a moment of intimate contact between politician and voter requires more and more artifice; the efforts to rig up spontaneous meetings during American presidential campaigns rebound upon the artificers. The politician appears more not less cardboardy as a result. And the efforts to appeal to various interest groups become more and more mechanical.

The levers of political persuasion are jerked to and fro with only the roughest attempt at secrecy; even those levers which are not connected with straightforward self-interest, for example equality before the law and aid to the poor, come to be barely distinguishable from the most naked appeals to greed and envy – merely because they are all in the same signal box. As soon as the ordinary passenger peeps into the signal box, all the mystique of the railways disappears from him. Trains cease to miss each other by divine intervention, the level crossing gates are no longer open and shut by magic; all depends on the skill and alertness of an elderly man sweating in a small room. The passenger may well lose not only his worship of the iron horse (and a modern man cannot feel more than a twinge of regret for the passing of such obscurantist veneration) but also his affection for it and his confidence in its workings.

Mary and Martha

It is futile to deny the existence of a genuine problem when the politician ceases to be a holy man and becomes a mere mechanic.

And the natural temptation for the politician faced by the indifference, contempt and lack of confidence of his public is to try to turn himself back into a holy man again. Such genuine holiness as there is in politicians is therefore a second-order, self-conscious sort of thing. It consists in the *avoidance* of saintliness, in the accepting of the imperfect and the dedication to its repair. There is in this a real humility, however overlaid with vulgar vanity (as opposed to conceit). The motivation is merely a longing to be loved – 'the love of fame' as it is usually described, for example by Disraeli – and only in rare cases a love of power for its own sake. This simple but rarely recognised fact is evident from the study of the continual failure of democratic governments to use even those powers that they can exert without encountering strong opposition. Ian Gilmour's *The Body Politic*[7] gives examples from recent British history. But the same is observable in all stable democracies where the ruling power does not have to throw its weight about to secure itself against violent overthrow. Politicians have on the whole fewer and less strong opinions than those who despise politicians and also less strong drives to enforce those opinions which they do hold; but politicians have a far stronger yearning to be liked and admired than most of us. They hope to achieve this popular respect by performing services for people. I mean to put this in a flat way; we do not need to invoke grandiose conceptions of 'dedication' and 'service'. We are talking here simply of errand-boys or charladies – 'the lady who *does* for me' as the idiom has it.

Is there something genuinely fine in this limitation of scope? 'Who sweeps a room as for thy laws makes that and the action fine.' Or is the limitation so inherent that there can be no question of allotting praise and blame? Is it merely that officious little men who relish the feel of busy-ness and the equivocal illumination of celebrity are bound to go into politics? Perhaps both. If this is how politics are, then this is the sort of person who will become a politician. But on the other hand, if political arrangements make our lives better in some degree, then the agents of that improvement deserve a few well-qualified words of thanks. Of course if political arrangements appear to make our lives worse, then we may curse the politicians.

For it is not our task here to work out a scale of spiritual refinement, to assess the relative merits of the Marys and the Marthas. The Bible's answer is clear enough and so is the instructive response of our hearts to the man who dares absolutely to demand perfection. The political scientist is concerned with the relative *functions* in politics of the Marys and Marthas. And the truth is that most of the business of politics lies in Martha's field, to wit:

—The reconciliation of interests.

—The maintenance and repair of institutions.

—The routine of administration.

—The attendance to grievance.

—The maintenance of dialogue with the electorate.

The latter task, as we have shown in earlier chapters, is the most important. It is also the most tedious and time-consuming, consisting as it does of an immense volume of trivial courtesies, mutual expressions of respect, soothing of grievances, whether genuine or chimerical, clarification of muddles and misunderstandings. Only a tiny fraction of the dialogue bears any practical fruit; yet not one syllable can be omitted. It is rare indeed to find a Mary who can go ungrudgingly through this grind. She will usually rely on her Marian qualities in 'constituency work', that is to say on her capacity to inspire affection by the mere radiance of personal magnetism rather than by hard work. It is doubtful how long a constituency may be held by this means alone without the supporting legwork. The Kennedy machine, for example, has been praised for its durability; leaving aside the two remarkable tragedies which must inevitably help to perpetuate in legend the public affection for the family, we should remember that not merely has an extremely tough, large-scale, old-style political organisation supported the 'charisma' all along, but the foundations of the organisation were firmly in place before the charisma first cast its aura.

All this is not to say that Mary has no part to play. Her duties are crucial, namely:

—The articulation of moral outrage.

—The focusing of hope in crisis.

—The insistence on principle.

These duties obviously have a long-term function. They keep some kind of moral harmony in the community. They imbue local history with a noble drama of which people can be proud. They give heightened expression to the principles of civilisation which form the common currency of ordinary men and indeed of the Marthas who attend to their political arrangements. But the Marys have a crucial short-term function as well. To put it bluntly, they save the state;

either by fighting or by moving the people towards a reform so morally essential that its omission will mean permanent division in the community. In both cases the political Mary is intensely *active*. The wartime activities of Chatham, de Gaulle, Lincoln, Churchill, are obviously Marian; noble, dramatic, inspirational. That quality corresponds to the peacetime suasions of Lloyd George, Bevan, Martin Luther King and of course countless revolutionary leaders. These latter depend on seeing peacetime as a permanent war, with continuing violence being done to the oppressed. Such an attitude contrasts sharply with the attitudes of Baldwin, Burke or even Lincoln (in his attitudes towards everything except secession) towards divisions in society, namely that a combination of certain reforms and a general attitude of conciliation could heal such divisions; in fact that the normal business of brokerage could deal with the situation. The latter represents essentially the outlook of Martha; that the existing realities both of men's lives and of men's minds are sufficient for our moral purposes. A few rearrangements, a little more effort, a friendly word in the right ears at the right time, and society can repel any invading poison. The Mary, on the other hand, sees the organism as so essentially corrupt that a new moral antibiotic must be concocted; for the virus has become immune to palliatives and placebos.

It would seem therefore that we should hope for some mixture of Mary and Martha in our rulers. But experience shows that we are unlikely to find the qualities of each united in one person. The drive needed to produce results – what we used to call dedication – is so strong that it cannot coexist with a different kind of drive. We cannot demand that one man be simultaneously Montgomery, Alanbrooke and Eisenhower. The best that we can look for is a succession of Marys and Marthas, each arriving at the point of power at the moment when most needed. Such a coincidence of time, person and place is, not surprisingly, all too rare. Marthas usually know their place; not always, for the defects of their qualities – indolence and complacency in the face of remediable injustice – put up stout defences against radical action; those who attempt such radical action are denounced as untrustworthy rogues and hotheads. We should not forget in the afterglow of history that the denunciations of Disraeli and Churchill on these grounds were far from baseless. Nor should we forget that they did finally achieve power. The strength of the Marian appeal, its passionate association with the contemporary moral dilemma, gives it a leverage which the low-key appeal of the Marthas cannot rival, least of all in times of crisis. The Marthas therefore usually only delay necessary radical action; and they can defend even this delay with the valid argument that, more often than not, it is unnecessary or misconceived radical action which they are holding back.

The reverse situation is far graver. The Marys not only hold more important levers of persuasion; they very rarely appreciate the virtues of the plodding broker. For them the present is always a moment of high drama, a time for noble deeds, a crisis of moral challenge; they do not see why they should ever 'leave off'. Most modern dictatorships have been founded on such a view of the political process; and none of them has ever willingly left off. From Peron to Mao we find not merely that the dictator clings fiercely to personal power, he relies on a succession of personal initiatives to keep the revolutionary drama alive. Even those dictatorships (Franco, Salazar, Tito) which would appear to the outsider to have settled down after initial shocks into a cautious combination of amelioration plus repression are to the real insider, namely the dictator himself, merely going through a consciously quiet passage in a great symphony which even so is punctuated by new melodies, quietly introduced yet destined to play a great part in the finale; reorganisation of the structure of government or of the ruling party, for example. To the toiling peasant such changes may have no practical effect at all, but the dictator is genuinely convinced of their 'objective' significance. The 'great soul' overcomes the plodder by force, either of arms or oratory; but how is the plodder to convince the 'great soul' that the latter's moment is past and that it is time for modest stillness and humility to resume their throne?

THE BANALITY OF POLITICS

In Molière's *Le Misanthrope,* the choleric Alceste, impatient for certainty and sincerity, does not understand the value of his friend Philinte, an intelligent, placid, kindly man of the world; Philinte appreciates Alceste's absolute moral qualities and is also fond of him. Here only does he touch Alceste, who responds to Philinte's uncalculated affection for him. Yet this friendship does not deter Alceste from complaining ceaselessly to Philinte about the hypocrisy of the people he meets:

I'd have them be sincere, and never part
With any word that isn't from the heart.[8]

Philinte responds:

But in polite society, custom decrees
That we show certain outward courtesies. . . .
Alceste:
Ah, no! we should condemn with all our force
Such false and artificial intercourse.
Let men behave like men; let them display
Their inmost hearts in everything they say[9]. . . .

It is not as if Philinte was innocent of the world. His view of the world corresponds closely to Alceste's. Only he draws a stoic rather than a radical conclusion from that view:

Alceste:
Do you propose to offer lame excuses
For men's behaviour and the times' abuses?
Philinte:
No, all you say I'll readily concede:
This is a low, conniving age indeed;
Nothing but trickery prospers nowadays,
And people ought to mend their shabby ways.
Yes, man's a beastly creature; but must we then
Abandon the society of men?
Here in the world, each human frailty
Provides occasion for philosophy,
And that is virtue's noblest exercise;
If honesty shone forth from all men's eyes,
If every heart were frank and kind and just,
What could our virtues do but gather dust
(Since their employment is to help us bear
The villainies of men without despair)?
A heart well-armed with virtue can endure. . . .[10]

It should be noticed that, although this attitude in itself could be described (and has been by such authorities as Faguet and Rudler) as misanthropic, it has a softer side which amounts to an affection for his fellow beings with all their faults.

Philinte:
Come let's forget the follies of the times
And pardon mankind for its petty crimes;

Let's have an end of rantings and railings,
And show some leniency toward human failings.
This world requires a pliant rectitude;
Too stern a virtue makes one stiff and rude;
Good sense views all extremes with detestation,
And bids us to be noble in moderation.
The rigid virtues of the ancient days
Are not for us; they jar with all our ways
And ask of us too lofty a perfection.
Wise men accept their times without objection,
And there's no greater folly, if you ask me,
Than trying to reform society.
Like you, I see each day a hundred and one
Unhandsome deeds that might be better done,
But still, for all the faults that meet my view,
I'm never known to storm and rave like you.
I take men as they are, or let them be,
And teach my soul to bear their frailty;
And whether in court or town, whatever the scene,
My phlegm's as philosophic as your spleen.[11]

Not only in these lines but in his conduct Philinte shows a patient humanity and tolerance.

As a result of a reluctance to compromise, Alceste becomes caught up in a lawsuit and a row with a prickly poet; for the same reason his affair with the dashing young widow, Célimène, is doomed from the outset. Throughout all these troubles, Philinte sticks to his side, offering him good advice, getting him out of a tricky situation with the Tribunal des Maréchaux,[12] even refusing to press his suit with Eliante, whom he loves, until he is certain that Alceste, whom *she* loves, does not want her.

Molière thus makes it perfectly clear that Philinte is not a treacherous and wordly time-server. His devotion to Alceste is remarkable. Yet we would not cross the street to meet Philinte; he is, as Molière intended, a banal figure, polished until everything of interest has been rubbed away.

Alceste, on the other hand, is a perpetually fascinating character, endlessly the topic of conversation (his own and other people's), blind to the desires and characters of other people (why otherwise would he have taken up with Célimène?), obsessed with self. He believes that his lawsuit will be remembered by posterity; he would even rather lose it, because that would give him the right to curse the wickedness of men. A great comic figure.

And yet through the ages a large number of people have been unable to accept *Le Misanthrope* as Molière wrote it. They could not accept that a banal realist should be in a sense the hero and a noble idealist the clown. Many if not most of the Romantics rebelled against the text in this way; Alceste has from time to time been played as an almost completely serious hero. Musset called him a herald of the better truth. Michelet saw him as the hangman of hypocrites and hence a forerunner of the French Revolution. The greatest of all these rebels against Molière was Jean-Jacques Rousseau.*

The burden of Rousseau's attack on the play is that Molière has falsified and vulgarised reality to get cheap laughs. '*Il fallait faire rire le parterre.*' Rousseau complains that Alceste is not a true misanthrope, who would indeed be a monster, but a man of bitter sincerity who hates in men only the evil which they do. It is unfair to mock such a man by grafting on to him irrelevant characteristics – personal vanity, anger over trifles, possessiveness in love. Now it is of course evident that such characteristics are far from irrelevant; they are typical of the man who insists on absolutes. And whatever Rousseau may say, they are comic weaknesses. The most glaring

---

* As Professor Maurice Cranston points out (*Politics and Ethics*, LSE Inaugural Lecture, Oct. 26th 1971, published London 1972), Rousseau loathed the theatre. In his Letter to d'Alembert, Rousseau depicts it "as an evil institution with no saving grace or merit, and the métier of the actor as a totally corrupt one. A word that recurs often in this letter is the word 'representation'. Rousseau attacked the theatre because fictions and falsehoods are represented on the stage as realities . . . About half way through, Rousseau asks: 'What is the talent of an actor?' He answers: 'The art of counterfeit: the art of assuming a personality other than his own, of appearing different from what he is, simulating passion while his feelings are cold, of saying something he does not believe just as naturally as if he really believed it . . .'

"Conscious, perhaps, that these words might put the reader in mind at once of politicians, Rousseau hastens to add that there should be no confusing the actor and the orator. 'The difference between the two is very great,' he writes. 'When the orator presents himself to the public it is to make a speech, and not to put on an act; he represents no one but himself; he fulfils only his own role; he speaks only in his own name; he does not say, nor should he say, anything other than what he thinks; the man and the persona are identical; he is where he should be, and he discharges the same duty which any other citizen in his place would discharge.'" We have already seen (particularly in I.iii.) how this distinction of Rousseau's between politician and actor, between the sincere and the counterfeit is not nearly so clear-cut in real life. Indeed, as Professor Cranston reminds us, Rousseau urges his own législateur to dissimulate and to suggest to the crowd that the proposals he himself has devised have been laid down by the deity.

proof that this is so lies in the character of Rousseau himself, Alceste to the life in all his strengths and failings. It is Molière's glory that, a century before the advent of the 'natural man', he should have analysed him so completely and sharply in Alceste. Rousseau quite fails to understand the subtlety of the characterisation, which consists precisely in the fact that Alceste is not a comic symbol of misanthropy in the same way that Tartuffe is a comic symbol of hypocrisy but a mixture of the sublime and the ridiculous. If it was a question of making the audience laugh, Molière knew far coarser, more sure-fire tricks of the dramatist's trade than he ever employs in *Le Misanthrope*.

But we are perhaps even more concerned here with Rousseau's portrait of Philinte:

> One of those men of the world whose maxims bear such a close resemblance to those of scoundrels; one of those mild and moderate people who always find that things are going well because it is not in their interest that anything should go better; who get on well with everybody because they don't care about anybody; who, with their feet under a good table, assert that it is untrue that the masses are hungry: who, with their purse well lined, take it amiss when people speak up on behalf of the poor; who, from the security of their own home, would watch the rest of the human race being beaten up, burgled and butchered without a murmur, seeing that God has endowed them with a sweetness of character which is perfectly designed for tolerating the misfortunes of others.[13]

In spite of all Molière's precautions, Rousseau has refused to see the Philinte of the text. For, time and again as we have seen, Molière emphasises that Philinte's stoicism is not just talk; its practical effect is loyalty, kindness and self-renunciation. The extent of Rousseau's blindness is shown by his description as '*maximes des fripons*' of remarks by Philinte which are clearly affectionately ironic (what Emile Faguet aptly describes as '*taquin*' or '*teasing*').[14]

Let us be clear about the lesson of the piece. In the Mary–Martha sense, Alceste *is* the hero and Philinte the straight man, the down-to-earth stooge. But Molière's point (one repeated again and again throughout his work, a strong moral centre which makes him the last if not the only real master of the high comedy) is that spiritual attitudes are incomplete without practical application; that we must look always to the *effects* of action and beliefs. The case here is plain; Alceste, a noble and attractive soul, leaves nothing but mess and misery in his wake; Philinte, a banal and *tarnished* soul, tidies up the loose ends with a disenchanted clarity. Molière leaves us with a dilemma which we may roughly express thus: is tarnishing the price of being human? Can we love our fellow men without getting our hands dirty? It is Alceste's self-absorption which destroys his tolerance, which makes him a genuine misanthrope, which of course the simple audience never doubted. It is in that sense that Burke rightly says that the theatre is a good school of moral sentiments.[15] A wicked act which a Goebbels or a Robespierre or a Stalin (or a Rousseau?) may be able to dress up as necessary in his propaganda will, when presented on stage, be flatly seen as wicked. Whatever the intention of the producer, the audience cannot help, to a greater or lesser extent, sharing in Molière's vision of the comic misanthrope.

The rebels against the text cannot accept this. For there follows from the play one crucial *practical* consequence; that we shall always love Alceste the more, but that we had far better be governed, both in our private lives and in our political arrangements, by Philinte. The unmitigated pursuit of sincerity has a disastrous effect upon our lives; it is far better to recognise the fallen nature of man and to organise some rough-and-ready temporary, alterable cage-structure to keep us from each other's throats while allowing us as much liberty as possible. But the rebels rattle the bars of such cages with a rising rage. They invent choleric dreams. Rousseau, for example, tells us how the characteristics ought to be distributed in the misanthrope:

> I mean that the misanthrope should have waged non-stop war on public vice and remained calm about the personal misfortunes which he himself suffered. In contrast, the philosophical Philinte should have regarded all social injustice with a stoical phlegm and have flown into a rage at the slightest ill which befell him directly.[16]

Well yes, characters like Rousseau's Alceste and Rousseau's Philinte do exist; but they are rarer, less psychologically true than Molière's versions. Rousseau's protagonists are, in my view, particularly uncommon in public life; a certain unity of temperament produces either Molière-Alcestes or Molière-Philintes. And it is incontestable that Molière-Philintes (Sir Robert Walpole, for example) produce far more congenial circumstances than Molière-Alcestes (Torquemada or Lenin). It is for this very reason that Rousseau felt driven to sketch out precisely how the play *should* have been written. A further fascination is that a later hand did in fact write a new play with the same characters. Fabre d'Eglantine, travelling actor, playwright, rascal who tagged on to the French Revolution and went to the guillotine with the Dantonists, wrote '*Le Philinte de Molière ou La Suite du Misanthrope*', successfully performed at the *Comédie Française* in 1790. In fact Fabre's piece was not primarily inspired by Rousseau's suggestion but by another play of the time which reflected an absurd Panglossian optimism. The interest in Fabre's piece is that he has had to carry Rousseau's suggestion a great deal further. For the drawback of Rousseau-Alceste was that, although deprived of personal pettiness, he would still be of little practical assistance to his friends or to the public. Certainly, '*le parterre alors n'aurait pu rire qu'aux dépens de l'homme du monde*', as Rousseau wanted; but they would be hardly likely to entrust their affairs to Alceste, as Rousseau, perhaps only half-consciously, also wanted. Fabre brings this out into the open. Philinte becomes a selfish, whining, middle-aged man. He is saved from arrest and bankruptcy by the disinterested services of Alceste. Philinte is here certainly a transformed character, but there is an even greater surprise when we come to look at Fabre's Alceste. Here we have, as Fabre-Philinte tells us, a real 'Don Quixote' who entirely neglects his own affairs in order to help others. The great difference between Fabre-Alceste and Quixote is that the former's help is of great practical benefit. In fact the new Alceste is hardly a misanthrope at all. He does, it is true, reject the grateful friendship of Philinte at the end. Henceforth 'I relegate you to the ranks of those cold beings who have lost all rights to the noble name of men, who are dead, stone dead for years before they actually die, and whom one is in honour bound to pity'.[17]

Fabre-Alceste is the wave of the future. He cannot afford to mix with the dried-up old 'scoundrels'. He is purged of all vanity, of all interest save the cause of humanity. So no doubt Fabre saw himself, just as Rousseau saw himself as Rousseau-Alceste and as Molière did *not* see himself either as his Alceste or even his Philinte. Yet in truth Fabre's one good quality was his theatrical talent. For the rest, his character shows a cold and scheming selfishness redeemed only by comic mishaps; Molière's Alceste without the purity of soul. Then suddenly, at the end of his life, Fabre's dreams come true; he tastes a little power and acclamation, he is surrounded by self-romanticising adventurers like himself (one of them, Collot d'Herbois, was even a strolling actor whom he had met in his travelling days), he *belongs*.

In that crowd of actors and journalists hanging round the Cordeliers we must see, as they saw themselves, the wave of the future. And we must remember how young they were. In 1789 Robespierre was thirty-one, Danton thirty, Saint-Just only twenty-two, Camille Desmoulins twenty-nine. Fabre himself was thirty-nine, almost mutton dressed as lamb. All of them were guillotined in 1794. 'The politics of rationalism are the politics of the politically experienced.'[18]

Well, and why not? Why should not honest, passionately sincere hearts and minds bring a fresh honesty and sincerity to government? The masses are hypnotised by the dreary puppetry of the conventional theatre (in modern terms by bingo and telly); is it not a glorious thing to confront them with living reality, to 'take the people out of the theatre and into the streets', as Georg Büchner's Camille Desmoulins says in Büchner's remarkable play, *Danton's Death,* written at the age of twenty-one, two years before his own death? The answer is that it may be glorious but it is not good government. For government is by nature a banal skill but a skill. That skill is learnt little by little over a lifetime; its fruits are slowly and painfully gathered and must be carefully stored. Walpole – coarse, limited, cautious, patient – gave his country twenty years of comparative peace and prosperity; Fabre d'Eglantine thought up the charming names for the Republican calendar. It may seem unfair to compare a lightweight with a heavyweight, a mountebank with a man of outstanding ability, but we must take Fabre and his kind as they claim to be, makers of a people's destiny. Achievement must be the criterion. And what achievement can the Dantonists claim? They were merely amateurs in a game in which the real professionals like Talleyrand had withdrawn to the sidelines. Any professional jockey will testify that his most terrifying experience has been when he has strayed into a bunch of amateur riders. To talk about their enthusiasm and freshness at such a moment would be ludicrous; they are simply highly dangerous to themselves, to each other and to the onlooker.

Unremitting attention to a limited professional skill breeds a limited mind; but it breeds also a steady and undistracted mind, with an eye for the hidden snag, the crucial detail. As Burke says 'I have never yet seen any plan which has not been mended by the observations of those who were much inferior in understanding to the person who took the lead in the business'.[19]

To some the work may seem dull stuff. The sharpest mind is

dulled by the constant flow of similar but not identical dealings, the lack of plan or pattern, the only progress a slow accretion of professional wisdom. Such a business will not attract for long those with large imaginations and ample passions. Again Burke records:

Almost all the high-bred Republicans of my time have, after a short space, become the most decided, thorough-paced courtiers; they soon left the business of a tedious, moderate but practical resistance to those of us whom in the pride and intoxication of their theories, they have slighted as not much better than Tories.[20]

The principles suggest themselves, prompted by our hearts – that is to say the beliefs and desires acquired by inheritance, interest, passion or intellect. The practice – the implementing and reconciling of those principles – requires attention and study and perseverance. The politician's cry is the reverse of the smart tradesman's: we could give you the impossible right away, the possible will take a little longer.

Can political science, then, offer no relief from the banality of the day's business endlessly repeated? Certainly, there is no respite from continuity; all attempts to freeze reality are false and doomed – the Reich that will last for a thousand years, the withering away of the state in the fullness of Socialism. Yet we should carefully distinguish the banality of the political process from the material that is, so to speak, being processed. To describe the rules of a game is a dry and tedious business; it is only when we see or take part in an actual game that it all comes alive. And here we have an intensified fascination in that not only would the moves, tactics, strategies be absorbing enough if played with mere cards or counters, as indeed they are in certain board games which mimic barely the complexity of human affairs, such as L'Attaque, Diplomacy, and Monopoly (I say 'barely' because such games leave out, for example, all the tender side of our natures), but in real life we ourselves are the playing cards. We do not therefore need to add any metaphysical decoration to the political process in order to enhance our lives. An act of charity or community is satisfying enough in itself and well enough backed with the authority of both the religious and the humanitarian ethic to need no embellishing as, say, 'a step towards Socialism'.

And indeed when we use the notion of banality, in connection with politics, we do not intend thereby to diminish politics. We wish merely to point out in forceful fashion the everyday – *alltäglich* –

quotidien nature of political activity. Only if we regard life itself as dull could we regard politics as dull and seek to liven it up with some political religion (which has been the constant intention of radicals since Rousseau). We may note here the wonder of the good scientist not just at his own discovery of some part of the mechanism but at the beauty of the whole. It is only those of cold hearts and muddy understanding who do not receive such intimations and are forced to fabricate their own clouds of glory.

A man has half an hour to spare before leaving to catch a train. What is he to do? Have a row with his wife, play with his children, read a good book, read a bad book, pour himself a drink, prune the roses, ring up an old lover, write to his aged mother, kill himself, play patience, go to sleep? For the extreme man, the Alceste, such a burden of decision has to be faced every minute of every day; most of us can survive only under the partial sedation of routine. But nevertheless a glorious multiplicity of choice flickers even through our drugged minds – anger, affection, wisdom, gluttony, devoutness, diligence, charity, lust, loyalty, self-destruction, sloth, despair. A world of such strong and conflicting emotions needs an army of brokers, just as a multiplicity of taxes breeds swarms of accountants. Every day we are broking with ourselves and our families, our own groups broking with others, nations with other nations.

It is in fact the very fascination of the daily activity that makes the political actor so heedless of political theory. The parallel is with the science of science, until recently a startlingly neglected subject. Who wants to study the historical emergence of the experimental method, or indeed to analyse and criticise the way in which the method is being applied to one or other of the natural sciences? The appeal of practical work in the laboratory is too strong. The method is a rough and ready thing. But it works. Only the scholar will puzzle over its philosophical justification. This explains the comparative dearth of books about politics as it is actually practised and the plethora of books about politics as it is not, and in many cases never could be practised. For it is the failure of nerve before the problems of life that drives people to seek mystical solutions whose emptiness is shown by their total failure to relate to political reality. It takes a certain steadiness, almost a lack of imagination, to make a start upon a vast, rambling problem which viewed as a whole looks unconquerable. But the carthorse plods on. It is surprising how large a load he pulls and with how little noise and fuss.

ACT II

You send an image hurrying out of doors
When you depose a king and seize his throne:
You exile symbols when you take by force.

And even if you say the power's your own,
That you are your own hero, your own king
You will not wear the meaning of the crown.

The power a ruler has is how men bring
Their thoughts to bear upon him, how their minds
Construct the grandeur from the simple thing.

And kings prevented from their proper ends
Make a deep lack in men's imagining;
Heroes are nothing without worshipping,

Will not diminish into lovers, friends.

                              Elizabeth Jennings: 'Kings'

With the progress of time, there arose as leaders of unmusical illegality poets who, though by nature poetical, were ignorant of what was just and lawful in music; and they, being frenzied and unduly possessed by a spirit of pleasure, mixed dirges with hymns and paeans with dithyrambs, and imitated flute-tunes with harp-tunes, and blended every kind of music with every other; and thus, through their folly, they unwittingly bore false witness against music, as a thing without any standard of correctness, of which the best criterion is the pleasure of the auditor, be he a good man or a bad. By compositions of such a character, set to similar words, they bred in the populace a spirit of lawlessness in regard to music, and the effrontery of supposing themselves capable of passing judgment on it. Hence the theatregoers became noisy instead of silent, as though they knew the difference between good and bad music, and in place of an aristocracy in music there sprang up a kind of base theatrocracy.

Plato: The Laws, Book III, 700–1.
Translated by R. G. Bury.

I

Novelty and Sentiment

THE THEATRE OF NOVELTY

We have come far enough to try to encapsulate the contrast between the three old paradigms and the alternative notion of politics which has been outlined in the last three chapters. That contrast may be crudely put thus: implicit in all the old paradigms is the assumption that 'people don't know what is good for them'. And this is the assumption which the concept of politics-as-theatre decries. The knight in shining armour, the bright-eyed pilgrim, the social engineer in his white lab coat, each has a cause; and those poor mortals who cannot see the justice and wisdom of that cause must be forced, converted, engineered so that they do see it. Further, when the knight puts on the white surcoat with the red cross over his armour – when in short he becomes a crusader – he represents an even more powerful intention to *act upon* the desires, beliefs and affections of 'ordinary people'. The modern knight templar holds or held a party card or a little red book; but his lack of restraint, his *wilfulness* is the same as that of his medieval predecessors.

This basic belief that people do not know what is good for them, and must be taught the right way, is most brutally and nakedly presented by Lenin. In *What Is to be Done?* he condemns 'slavish cringing before spontaneity'.[1] The masses will not awake of their own accord; they must be roused by the experts. 'Modern Socialist consciousness can arise only on the basis of profound, scientific knowledge. . . . Socialist consciousness is something introduced into the proletarian class struggle from without and not something that arose within it spontaneously.'[2] Lenin claims that spontaneity leads to the domination of 'bourgeois ideology'; that is why the Socialist movement must be 'infected with intolerance against all those who retard its growth by subservience to spontaneity.'[3] The professional revolutionaries must push on the workers 'from outside'; and they must do so 'a hundred times more forcibly than before'.[4] Revolutionaries 'have not the time to think about the toy forms of democracy . . . but they have a lively sense of their *responsibility*, because they know from experience that an organisation of real revolutionaries will stop at nothing to rid itself of an undesirable member.'[5] These grim words add the final touch to Lenin's rejection of working-class spontaneity: 'The only serious organisational principle the active workers of our movement can accept is strict secrecy, strict selection of members and the training of professional revolutionaries.'[6]

But this belief in the need to impose a new consciousness upon the masses is not confined to Lenin; it is not the excess of the man forced into revolutionary activity by exile or the secret police. It is the central tenet of the Communist faith, as crucial to that faith's literary academics as to its political hatchet-men.

Georg Lukács, in his famous essays of the early 1920s,[7] claims that his analysis 'establishes right from the start the distance that separates class consciousness from the empirically given, and from the psychologically describable and explicable ideas which men form about their situation in life.'[8] This class consciousness is an ideal to which even the most revolutionary workers can only approach. And it can be known and defined only by the Communist Party, which 'is assigned the sublime role of the bearer of the class consciousness of the proletariat and the conscience of its historical vocation. . . . Only through discipline can the party be capable of putting the collective will into practice'[9]. . . . 'The discipline of the Communist Party, the unconditional absorption of the total personality in the praxis of the movement, [is] . . . the only possible way of bringing about an authentic freedom.'[10] And, most chilling of all, the party 'is sometimes forced to adopt a stance opposed to that of the masses; it must show them the way by rejecting their immediate wishes. It is forced to rely upon the fact that only *post festum*, only after many bitter experiences, will the masses understand the correctness of the party's view.'[11]

Only thirty years later, only after the death of Stalin, did this attitude begin visibly to alter. Lukács joined the Hungarian revolt. At the very end of his life, seven weeks before he died in 1971 at the age of eighty-six, he at last accepted that:

. . . there must be a permanent dialogue between the party and the workers, so that [the party] may know what questions are troubling the workers, what matters are of deep concern to them at any given time. . . . This is why a permanent contact is necessary, and this contact is what I call democracy, the democratisation of our society. Without such a democratisation, I do not believe that we can carry out economic reforms.

Bureaucrats always believed that they knew what was right for the masses, 'which is certainly not true. . . . If one speaks to the workers, one always sees that they want something quite different from what the bureaucracy wants to give them.'[12]

This kind of virtual recantation is more the exception than the rule. In this century, few leading Marxist thinkers at any stage in their lives have shown sympathy towards or even interest in what people actually want. Marcuse, for example, says bluntly that the masses cannot distinguish 'between true and false wants and interests, nor between true and false enjoyment'.[13]

It is sometimes argued, largely because Marxists themselves so argue, that the dividing line between Communists and Social Democrats should be drawn here. Social Democrats, we are told, do believe in 'spontaneity'; they respect and respond to the expressed wishes of the people they represent. True, Social Democrats operate in a rigorously legal manner; they respect the results of elections that go against them; they are content to let a fair number of sleeping dogs lie; they do not overthrow every measure of the previous governments. The practical effect of such regimes upon the lives of ordinary people could hardly be more different from the effect of Communist regimes. And yet we may question whether it is not the Social Democrat's attitude of tolerance and civility – a disposition born of individual temperament and communal tradition – which accounts for this difference, rather than his theoretical view of the world; his respect for the feelings and customs of other people is expressed in practice, not theory.

Antonio Gramsci, the Italian Communist, defended himself against accusations of 'spontaneism' with the claim that in his Turin movement

 . . . the element of 'spontaneity' was not neglected and even less despised: it was *educated*, it was directed, it was purified of everything extraneous that could pollute it, to make it homogeneous, but in a living manner, historically efficient, with a modern theory. . . . This unity of 'spontaneity' and of 'conscious direction', that is, of 'discipline', is precisely the real action of the subordinated classes, to the extent that it is mass politics and not simply an adventure of groups that claim a relationship to the masses.[14]

Gramsci denies that there is a dividing line to be drawn between 'spontaneism' and 'discipline'; in real political action the two elements must be fused. Is such a view so very different, in theory at least, from that of many Fabian Socialists and Social Democrats? For example, take this argument of Professor Joan Robinson, a sympathetic interpreter of Marx:

> ... it is generally admitted that the individual is inclined to spend less on education than is desirable on general grounds. Certainly, few children would freely spend on education as much as their parents think right, and if the parents may coerce the children, it is difficult to argue that the state ought not to coerce the parents. The same argument is admitted to apply to the question of medical services. And health is affected not only by sanitation and bottles of medicine, but by diet, housing and clothing. The authorities under Socialism, guided by scientists, can make wiser decision for the individual in all these matters than he can make for himself.
>
> The sphere of action of the competitive pricing system, once all these exceptions are admitted, has been greatly narrowed. And it must be still further whittled away. For it is obvious that in reality advertisement, fashion and the custom of society dictate the actual expenditure of individuals far more than the text-book principle of 'equalising marginal utilities', and if individuals, left to themselves, allot their expenditure between goods under influences which have no ultimate rational justification, it seems hard to maintain that the Socialist authorities ought to be guided by the decisions of individuals, reflected in the pricing system, rather than by any other plan which may recommend itself to them.[15]

The nub of this argument is, perhaps unintentionally, clear. The masses are like children, ill-informed and easily led astray. Compare here these famous words of Douglas Jay, a leading parliamentarian and minister in the postwar British Labour Party:

> Housewives as a whole cannot be trusted to buy all the right things, where nutrition and health are concerned. This is really no more than an extension of the principle according to which the housewife herself would not trust a child of four to select the week's purchases. For in the case of nutrition and health, just as in the case of education, the gentleman in Whitehall really does know better what is good for people than the people know themselves.[16]

Compare further the whole thesis of Professor J. K. Galbraith, the hero of the liberal hour, in *The Affluent Society*:

It will be obvious, however, that this view [the classical theory of the market economy] depends on the notion of independently determined consumer wants. In such a world one could with some reason defend the doctrine that the consumer, as a voter, makes an independent choice between public and private goods. But given the dependence effect – given that consumer wants are created by the process by which they are satisfied – the consumer makes no such choice. He is subject to the forces of advertising and emulation by which production creates its own demand.[17]

Throughout the spectrum of progressive politics we shall find the same underlying belief strongly held – the belief that the masses are not qualified to exercise choice. They cannot tell right from wrong, true from false, the excellent from the shoddy. Their incapacity extends from education to washing machines, from social security to transport, from the arts to the family. This belief is based on a crude version of behaviourism, though it is not usually stated in this way. Man is the sum of his conditioning. It is therefore possible for political theory and practice to condition him correctly. Moreover, there are evil and/or misguided men at large who will coalesce into evil and/or misguided political systems which will continue incorrect conditioning; it is therefore a moral duty for the enlightened man to join the struggle to enforce correct conditioning. Left to themselves, the masses will go astray. In particular, the 'cult of spontaneity' always leads to the dominance of bourgeois ideology. The natural forces of politics, the free interplay of our desires, can end only by denaturing us.

We must therefore be forcibly taken to the theatre like school children, not for our own immediate satisfaction but for the good of our souls. There we shall see a drama of a new and unfamiliar kind, what I have ventured to call the theatre of novelty. Its theme is simple: all traces of the old conditioning must be swept away by means of the destruction and discrediting of the beliefs and institutions which perpetuate it, and in its place a new conditioning must be imposed and hence the new man created. The feature of this new drama is that it permits the audience no right of criticism. This is logically inevitable; B. F. Skinner would not dream of allowing his rats to question the arrangement of the levers. To admit that the victims of the old conditioning have a right to criticise the new conditioning would be to admit that there may be some merits in the old conditioning. There can be no question of a debate with those who dare to criticise; they must simply be taken away and re-educated before they mislead others.

Equally throughout the progressive spectrum we shall find the opposite view pleading its case – the view that the masses are the best judges of what is good for them, in fact the only proper judges. This view is present in 'Left' Communism, in Anarchism and in Revisionism as typified by Khrushchev's notion of 'goulash' Communism. We find this view actually predominating in the mildest forms of Leftism; for example Jo Grimond, former leader of the British Liberal Party, describes what he takes to be left-wing attitudes: 'The Left is populist and not bureaucratic. It is committed to the primacy of politics over economics. It is fraternal and not paternal. It believes in the distribution and not the centralisation of power.'[18]

Yet in practice it is always the flavour of bureaucratic paternalism that characterises regimes of the Left. Even the American liberal J. K. Galbraith centres his economic strategy on wage and price controls. The same is certainly true of authoritarian, paternalist regimes of the Right. But in the latter case paternalism is the explicit, central tenet of the regime. Where the aim of the regime is to provide 'authentic freedom' for the masses, paternalism can at best be defended as a temporary means, a technique. Why does it tend to become the permanent motive force of the polity?

SOCIAL ENGINEERING

This tendency to bureaucracy is most easily understood if we examine its workings in the mildest climate – Social Democracy. Because the Social Democrat has abjured revolution by violence, in order to gain and hold power he must make considerable concessions to the actual demands of the public. In fact it is unfair to call them concessions. The urge to implement such demands, passionately expressed over a long period, is often what drives him to take up politics. Who could remain unmoved by the spectacle of a great trade union movement demanding universal opportunities for work or proper care of the sick and aged? The image of the British trade union movement as a carthorse, slow, strong and loyal, is a just and telling one; George Orwell in *Animal Farm* and Low in his cartoons used this image to great effect.

This genuine impulse has sparked off an aggrieved defence against

146

accusations that Social Democracy has authoritarian tendencies. It is claimed that the functions of authority in a Social Democracy are principally technical and explanatory, although it must have certain back-up powers against the irredeemably unenlightened. In the case of education, for example, it may be argued that in the interests of the children the authorities must at least compel school attendance; but, for the rest, the authorities are merely engaged in evolving a good educational system in cooperation with parents. It will be further argued that, say, the vast increase in the number of university places in Britain and the United States has been a natural response to public demand for higher education rather than the expression of a governmental prejudice in favour of giving a university education to the maximum number of people possible; or at the very least that it is both.

This is true. But it is an ingenuous and partial account of the process. The government admittedly acts as our agent, but we are permitted to give the agent only the most general instructions. The carrying out of the project is handed over to the *social engineer*. His power over the kind of service provided is almost total. And he is entrusted with the vast bulk of the funds available for the service, leaving alternative possibilities open only to the rich. In the case of education, for example, the engineer decrees the kind of school that the vast majority of us will attend; in the case of medicine, he approves only allopathic methods; in housing, he builds matchboxes or vast windswept housing estates for us. Consumer protest may eventually trickle through to alter or add to the engineer's plans; he may be forced to include religious or progressive varieties of schooling; he may be forced to build the kind of houses that people actually wish to live in. Yet even in those countries where public housing authorities do try to discover consumer preference, they never respond to that preference with the speed or whole-heartedness of the good private developer. For consumer preference is not the driving force of the public housing project; indeed, it will probably be a lesser influence upon the planners and architects than fashions within their own profession, because they depend upon the approbation of their colleagues for promotion rather than upon the approbation of the families who are to live in the homes they have built. Similarly, changes in the type of primary school or psychiatric hospital being built usually derive from the latest views of educationists and psychiatrists rather than from the feelings of consumers, whether as parents or patients. Lord Boyle, a former Tory education minister with a strong interest in social engineering, says that at the Ministry of Education 'overwhelmingly the biggest number [of new policies] originated from what one broadly calls the "education world", if you like, from the logic of the education service as it was developing.'[19] He shares with Anthony Crosland, a former Labour education minister, the apparent view that the demands of their own political parties were a tedious imposition compared with the recommendations of sociologists and educationists, that the views of the public, as mediated through the political process, were of less *interest* than the views of the social engineer, and were important only as a potential source of trouble. In fact, the views expressed at length by Boyle and Crosland in conversation with Professor Maurice Kogan should not have been collected under the title of *The Politics of Education*; the book should have been called rather *The Administration of Education*, or, better still, *The Engineering of Education*.

How far does the social engineer exceed his brief? Are we permitted to give him as full a brief as we would like? Should we be permitted to do so? The role of this enigmatic figure who has such a great influence upon our lives is perhaps most clearly explained and defended by Sir Karl Popper in *The Open Society*, without doubt one of the most seminal works of our time.

With much of this lucid and forceful book it is hard to disagree. Popper claims to find a historicist strain running through and bedevilling the western tradition of political thought. The aim of his enquiry is 'to show that we may become the makers of our fate when we have ceased to pose as its prophets.' It is therefore directed principally at the major prophets of the western tradition: Plato, Hegel and Marx. We shall not here attempt to elaborate Popper's masterly isolation and annihilation of some of the elements in the historicist strain: the belief that the future is somehow contained in the past and that the future is thereby predictable or even inevitable, the belief in an ideal essence of which the world we perceive through the senses is but a corrupt, flickering shadow, the belief in the divinity of the state, the belief in the chosen people or the chosen class whose mission is assigned to them by God or history. These beliefs Popper rejects. The future is what we choose to make it. The search for essences is futile and frequently harmful; things are what we choose to call them. Indeterminism and nominalism. We can heartily agree with Popper on both these points. And most of us would also agree that the state

148

is not of divine origin, its worship not the chief end of man. Equally there is no reason to believe that any one class or race should have been allotted by the Almighty missions totally denied to their fellow men. We would agree further in according both to Plato and Marx a large measure of respect for what Popper describes as their 'independent sociology' – that is their analysis of the effect of institutions as opposed to that of individuals upon the course of human history. If we are less bound by modish jargon, we might be content to remark that, among their largely meaningless or actively harmful teaching, both Marx and Plato give us powerful insights on how the world works. It may seem that, in accepting Popper thus far, we accept him virtually *in toto*. For did not *The Open Society* emerge as a counterblast to the historicism, state worship, dictatorship and plain wickedness of Hitler and Stalin? This is perfectly true. But by accepting Popper's destructive points, we do not necessarily accept his alternative construct. The alternative, the open society, is much more sketchily treated; nevertheless the few strokes with which it is outlined are so clear and sure and the subject of so much copying by later, inferior hands that Popper alone is sufficient source. Every non-Marxist Radical today (and covertly some Marxists too, namely those who have tried to chuck out the historicism, and take on only the egalitarian, humanitarian message supported by a heavily emended version of Marxian sociology) accepts in one way or another the concept of the open society.

The general drift of Popper's work is a contrast between historicism and the attitude of social engineering, the latter being typical of the open society. These are described as being 'diametrically opposite',[21] and yet both are to be found in Plato's work. Popper defines the social engineer thus:

The social engineer does not ask any questions about historical tendencies or the destiny of man. He believes that man is the master of his own destiny, and that in accordance with our aims, we can influence or change the history of man just as we have changed the face of the earth. He does not believe that these ends are imposed upon us by our historical background or by the trends of history, but rather that they are chosen, or even created, by ourselves, just as we create new thoughts or new works of art or new houses or new machinery. As opposed to the historicist who believes that intelligent political action is possible only if the future course of history is first determined, the social engineer believes that a scientific basis of politics would be a very different thing; it would consist of the factual information necessary for the construction or alteration of social institutions, in accordance with our wishes and aims. Such a science would have to tell us what steps we must take if we wish, for instance, to avoid depressions; or if we wish to make the distribution of wealth more even, or less even. In other words, the social engineer conceives as the scientific basis of politics something like a *social technology* (Plato, as we shall see, compares it with the scientific background of medicine), as opposed to the historicist who understands it as a science of immutable historical tendencies.[22]

Popper gives an example:

> ... we may consider a police force. Some historicists may describe it as an instrument for the protection of freedom and security, others as an instrument of class rule and oppression. The social engineer or technologist, however, would perhaps suggest measures that would make it a suitable instrument for the protection of freedom and security, and he might also devise measures by which it could be turned into a powerful weapon of class rule.[23]

Quite so, but is not Popper describing here the difference between two jobs, not two attitudes? The *historian* gives his view of how the police came to be as they are. The Home Secretary reforms the police. In that case, there would be no difficulty in finding both attitudes in Plato's work. We would not even need to say that he deals with one question from the historicist point of view, another from that of the social engineer. For within his discussion of a single problem, he could be historicist when referring to the past and a social engineer when looking to the future. Nobody could deny that the actions of Marxists when in power represent a colossal programme of social engineering. Their historicism of course dictates this intensity; 'everything must be just so, because history says so' – they cannot allow any haphazard accretion. In what sense, then, can historicism and social engineering be said to be 'diametrically opposite' any more than a retailer and his wholesaler are diametrically opposite? They simply operate at different stages in the process. Popper says, 'the engineer or the technologist approaches institutions rationally as means that serve certain ends and as a technologist he judges them wholly according to their appropriateness, efficiency, simplicity, etc.'[24] Yes, but so does the historicist. He even shares certain purposes with Popper, equality for example. The difference between them lies in the gods to whom they bow down – the historical process on the one hand and what we may roughly describe as humanitarian morality on the other. This difference is enormous and has enormous consequences in actions recommended or undertaken. But the differences between Popper's actions and the historicist's actions are not due to any differences over the *theory* of social engineering. The historicist's interest in the past relates only to his theory of ends; he does not respect the past in his actions. The past merely 'proves' that he is right. The social engineer has equally little respect for the past. But he is also uninterested in it because it has nothing to tell him. His is an open society in the sense that he is ready to undertake any action which will help to promote his ends. Well, then, the Popperian may reply, is there not here a contrast between this attitude and that of the historicist, for the latter's determinism means that the future is as preordained as was the past? Is not this a 'closed society'? In one sense it is. For the historicist, ours is not a world of infinite possibility. Certain things are bound to happen in the inevitable progression towards the millennium; our task is only to hasten that progression. In that sense, the historicist world is a closed one. But that is not precisely the sense in which Popper uses the notion of a *closed* society.

For Popper the closed society is 'magical or tribal or collectivist . . . the so-called organic or biological theory of the state can be applied to it to a considerable extent'.[25] Its social customs are rigid: 'It is determined by taboos, by magical tribal institutions which can never become objects of critical consideration.'[26] Change in such a society is comparatively infrequent and 'not based upon a rational attempt to improve social conditions'. All in all, Popper says, 'the transition from the closed to the open society can be described as one of the deepest evolutions through which mankind *has* passed'.[27] In other words, the closed society is dead or dying. We live now in a world of social changes unrestrained by taboos.

It would seem then that the sharpest contrast must be between social change and social stasis (the extreme of which Popper calls 'the arrested society'). That is surely the simplest definition of the difference between 'open' and 'closed' societies. Simplest because it takes account of the actual effects on our lives. In considering a new National Health Service, for example, we shall be more interested in how and whether it works than in whether it springs from a determinist Marxism or from a free-wheeling humanitarianism. If we are to be nominalists, as Popper urges, function is all-important. Popper may claim that he is less dogmatic, more open-minded than the historicist, but they are both proponents of social change; their interest lies in furthering social change, not in resisting it. There is of course an immense difference between 'Utopian' engineering of the Marxist type and the 'piecemeal' engineering which Popper favours. Popper's preference is certainly more sympathetic. Yet Popper and Marx are both on the same side of the fence. They both believe that the world of stasis is gone for ever and that continuous social change is here to stay. Both are dedicated to the theatre of novelty, rather than the theatre of sentiment. Both recognise drawbacks in this situation; Popper talks of 'anonymity and isolation' and consequently 'unhappiness'[28] because of the decay of 'real social groups' – approximately the same thing as Marx means by 'alienation'. Marx believes all this can be overcome by Communism; Popper considers such a view to be an unrealistic demand for the return to an organic or tribal society. In his view the gains of our present society outweigh the losses. By more piecemeal improvements we can further lessen the losses. He passionately attacks the idealisation of 'an indeed more "organic" and "integrated" past'.[29]

In the Middle Ages, he says for example, 'to the miseries of constant war, political and social disintegration, there was added the dreadful affliction of inescapable, mysterious and deadly disease. Mankind stood helpless as though trapped in a world of terror and peril against which there was no defence.'[30] Similarly, Professor J. H. Plumb writes of 'the decay of the family structure and the growing independence of adolescent life' as a result of the loosening of 'the vice-like grip of the past'.[31] He continues:

Wherever we look, in all areas of social and personal life, the hold of the past is weakening. Rituals, myths, the need for personal roots in time are so much less strong than they were a mere hundred or even fifty years ago. In education and economic activity the past has ceased to be a guide to the present, even if bits of it still litter and hamper the development of both. In family and sexual relations the past offers little understanding and no comfort. Of course there are areas of resistance, but they are islands of conviction in a surging sea of doubt. In these aspects, at least, if the past is not dead, the rattle of death can be heard.[32]

Technology has demolished taboo:

The taboos of the dead no longer cast their shadows across the bed. To me this loosening of time's stranglehold is far from wholly bad. The past in its personal as well as its social dimension has been full of nightmares.[33]

All this has happened because of the very recent emergence of history as a scientific enquiry on analytic lines.

The past being dead (and broadly speaking a good thing too), the rational man must set to if he is to create a healthy future. He will use the tools of social engineering and he will be guided by humanitarian moral principles (Popper and all 'Social Democrats', 'Progressives', 'Radicals', etc.) or by a scientific theory of historical development (Marx). This analysis and these solutions have gained such sway among students of politics that it may be at least salutary to enquire whether the analysis is accurate and whether the solutions are either admirable or inevitable.

Marxists at least deal with the question of what is to be done when the wishes of the masses do not agree with the wishes of the social engineers of the party. Their answer is clear. The party's duty is not merely to disregard the short-sighted wishes of the masses but to engineer their very consciousness until it does agree with that of the party. Popper ducks the problem. He talks vaguely of 'the construction or alteration of social institutions, in accordance with our wishes.' But he does not examine fully who 'we' are. He does not really consider the relationship between the engineer and his clients, which is the crux of politics. He does talk of trial and error, of the engineer going back to the drawing-board when a particular scheme fails. Failure would naturally include rejection by those people whom the scheme is supposed to benefit. But why should we assume that the social engineer is likely to be right at all? Upon what theory does he make his trials and his errors? Upon rational humanitarian morality, we presume. But what if rational humanitarian morality does not precisely chime with public opinion or with the way we have traditionally preferred to make our social arrangements? Is the social engineer to return chastened to the drawing-board and reframe his plans in accordance with public feeling? Or is he to impose the original plans, invoking morality as his justification? Popper speaks always of piecemeal *reform*, of altering institutions or of constructing new ones. But what if we do not want reform, alteration or innovation in a particular field, what if in that field at least we prefer a closed to an open society? Popper's answer, though never made explicitly, is clear. If the existing situation conflicts with humanitarian morality, then the social engineer must press for reform. There may seem to be nothing wrong with this; a man must say what he thinks and fight for what he believes to be right. But we must consider exactly who *this*

153

man is; the social engineer, in Popper's open society, enjoys a good deal of power – not untrammelled power, Popper is sympathetic to pluralism – but a good deal of power none the less. And his primary aim is to reform society in accordance with rational humanitarian principles. He is intentive and not attentive. He may be baulked by the limits on his powers or by the recalcitrance of the public; but he will never cease trying to impose his blueprint. He takes his orders from moral principles and not from the people. And to that extent he, too, like the Marxist but in a far milder and more sympathetic way, comes to believe that very frequently 'people don't know what's good for them'. As a consequence, he too wishes primarily to act upon society rather than to act for society.

THE THEATRE OF SENTIMENT

To this general view the theatrical paradigm opposes two distinct but connected propositions, one normative and the other descriptive. Put baldly, they are these.
– On the whole, people do know what is good for them.
– Whether they do or not, they will sooner or later get their own way, unless prevented by force.
Politics-as-theatre adds a third connected proposition, this one concerning the duties of the actor.
– The political actor, being a sentient moral being like any other man, has a *duty* to strive for what he personally believes to be good; but his *profession* is to satisfy his public.
In examining and qualifying these propositions, we shall draw copiously upon the works of Edmund Burke. We shall do so for two reasons; first, because nobody before or since has put the matter better, second because he did so in opposition to the first great fusing of the three old paradigms in the shape of the French Revolution. The menace of Jacobinism imbued Burke's arguments with a freshness and immediacy which give added force to what in some degree are commonplaces, taken for granted in practical life but too often neglected or rejected in political theory.

Now the opinion of Burke held by those whom we may generally term the social engineers does not appear to be excessively high. Popper, it is true, refers to Burke's 'appreciation of the significance of tradition for the functioning of all social institutions',[34] but he does not bother to speculate too closely on how, if at all, the notion of 'tradition' fits or could fit into the open society. Popper also lumps Burke in with the 'state-worshippers'.[35] And he contrasts Burke's view that 'the laws of commerce are the laws of nature, and therefore the laws of God' with Marx's view that the only inexorable laws of society are its laws of development.[36] In Popper's eyes, of course, both propositions are more or less nonsensical; we are the masters of our fate, so that our political arrangements and institutions cannot be dictated by inexorable laws. Plumb complains of Burke's method:

Why should a rationalist, intellectual approach to the problems of human organisation seem either stupid or wicked or both, when such problems as man has solved – control of power, the diminution of diseases, etc. – have been achieved by their application? Why should a reliance on intellect be regarded as foolishly optimistic or wildly idealistic, and an addiction to tradition, ancestral wisdom and the mysteries of Providence be the hallmark of sound judgment? Burke clothed in the eloquent language of religion and ethics the nakedness of private greed and public oppression.[37]

Professor Stuart Hampshire, in an otherwise lucid and not unsympathetic summary of Burke's views on the state of civil society as the true state of nature, suddenly bursts out:

Burke's rhetoric was mere assertion. It was not proof or even argument. He was not clear and he was not consistent. He saw less far into the future than the philosophical radicals and the men of the Enlightenment, less far certainly than Condorcet. He had a confused and superstitious idea of providence within history. He was often merely reactionary and frightened.[38]

Such criticism may be excited by Burke's attachment to the *status quo* and his distaste for innovation. Yet other writers of a conservative temper do not tend to stir such anger; the political ideas of Coleridge and Hume, for example, correspond to aspects of Burke's thought, but neither would be likely to be dismissed by Bentham with the vehemence he applied to Burke as 'a madman, an incendiary, a caster of verbal filth'. Indeed, eminent Victorians like Morley and Leslie Stephen were ready to recognise him as a kind of utilitarian of some distinction whose 'mysticism' could be set aside as what Morley called 'a really singular trait', an amiable eccentricity. Unfortunately for such convenient judgments, modern scholars have established two facts. First, Burke believed in the natural law.[39] This belief in the natural law in the Thomist sense means that 'behind his conception of the order of society lay always the grand idea of the order of the universe',[40] a divine moral order. It can no longer be supposed that Burke was, as Harold Laski put it, 'a utilitarian who was convinced that what was old was valuable by the mere fact of its arrival at maturity'.[41] Secondly, the modern sociologist finds that, whatever his intentions as a social engineer, he can draw an adequate picture of man in society only by allotting a central place to belief systems and institutional loyalties. And it is in the analysis of such systems and loyalties that Burke excels. As Alfred Cobban points out,[42] when we consider the pallid and shallow empiricism of the eighteenth century as instanced in Condillac or La Mettrie, we see the originality and intellectual energy which permeates Burke's description of human psychology. The discovery, then, in Burke both of an exponent of the natural law and also of a formidable political sociologist presents a considerable challenge to those who do not only wish to remake the world but realise that they cannot do so without also remaking 'human nature'. For Burke's major effort of synthesis is to link the beliefs that men do hold with the beliefs that they should hold by saying that our conception of the beliefs they should hold must be drawn from experience; and therefore there must be a presumption that the experience of the ages, as distilled in our laws, customs and institutions, must contain at least strong intimations of the natural law. He makes use of the Lockean weapons of sensism and empiricism which the radicals had thought their own exclusive property; but he turns them to the opposite purpose.

More awkward still, the influence of Burke has spread far beyond those Conservatives who have tried to claim him exclusively for themselves. Charles Parkin says:

Burke's relevance is less to either one of the political parties of modern England than to the English political community as a whole . . . as a formulation of the moral beliefs on which English society had been formed, his work was central to the political activity of his own time, and remained thereafter an accurate expression of the enduring principles of English political and social life.[43]

It would be more exact to talk not of England but of the English-speaking world, for Burkean thought permeates American political life, not to speak of its effect upon former British colonies. Democrats, Social Democrats and Liberals are marked by that influence as well as, if to a lesser degree than, Republicans, Conservatives and

Christian Democrats. If Burke were only the spokesman of the die-hards, radical critics could comfortably write him off as a picturesque backwater in the stream of history. But as the exponent of a living tradition of thought, he remains for alert radicals the enemy within the gates. It is because Burke's theatre of sentiment is grounded on sociological observation that he so threatens the claims of the theatre of novelty to be 'scientific'.

The contention that Burke rejected reason is false. His respect for reason is profound, reiterated and genuine. What he rejects is rationalism in the sense of sole reliance upon cogitation *a priori*. The weakness in Professor Plumb's argument is the implied claim that *exclusive* reliance on reason and *exclusive* reliance on tradition are the only possibilities and that Burke chooses the latter. But Burke makes it clear that it is rationalism and not reason which he rejects:

> I do not vilify theory and speculation. . . . No, whenever I speak against theory, I mean always a weak, erroneous, fallacious, unfounded or imperfect theory; and one of the ways of discovering that it is a false theory is by comparing it with practice.[44]

Burke ends the *Reflections* by describing himself as a man who 'when the equipoise of the vessel in which he sails may be endangered by overloading it upon one side, is desirous of carrying the small weight of his *reasons* to that which may preserve its equipose'.[45] This thought is obviously a reflection of Halifax's notion of trimming.

A lesser objection is that Burke is not a systematic thinker. Even Russell Kirk, his admirer and exegete, says:

> Framing a system to refute the assumptions of egalitarianism was a task uncongenial to Burke's nature. Even when he set himself doggedly to it, as in the *Reflections*, he could express principles in the abstract only for a few consecutive paragraphs.[46]

Burke himself says of the *Reflections*, undoubtedly the most comprehensive of his writings, containing as it does almost all the elements of his political theory:

> Indulging myself, in the freedom of epistolary intercourse, I beg leave to throw out my thought and express my feelings, just as they arise in my mind, with very little attention to formal method.[47]

Certainly the steps in his argument come to our gaze in a disordered sequence. But each fragment of the argument is complete and sizeable.

We are not dealing here with a heap of rubble, which may come from a variety of different buildings and which has been smashed in such small pieces that only a lunatic would attempt to put them together again. We are dealing rather with one of those children's jig-saw puzzles which contain no more than, say, a dozen pieces which fit perfectly and need only a child's skill to complete. With Burke we may simply rejig the order, casting aside some of the purely ephemeral matter, not because it is not apt or relevant to the problem in hand but because it tends to obscure the main line of argument. Thus easily stripped and rejigged,[48] Burke's political theory is rational, clear and almost always basically consistent, though with sharp variations of emphasis. And throughout it is dedicated to scientific method:

> The science of constructing a commonwealth or renovating it, or reforming it, is, like every other experimental science, not to be taught *a priori*. . . . We must look to the evidence. . . . I cannot stand forward and give praise or blame to anything which relates to human actions and human concerns, on a simple view of the object, as it stands stripped of every relation, in all the nakedness and solitude of metaphysical abstraction. Circumstances (which with some gentlemen pass for nothing) give in reality to every political principle its distinguishing colour and discriminating effect. The circumstances are what render every civil and political scheme beneficial or noxious to mankind.[49]

What, then, does the recourse to experience, the evidence, the circumstances, the practice (all are legitimate names for different aspects of the political scientist's checking) reveal to us? A picture of the world very different from that described under the label of the open society:

> You see, Sir, that in this enlightened age I am bold enough to confess that we are generally men of untaught feelings; that instead of casting away all our old prejudices, we cherish them to a very considerable degree, and, to take more shame to ourselves, we cherish them because they are prejudices; and the longer they have lasted, and the more generally they have prevailed, the more we cherish them. We are afraid to put men to live and trade each on his own private stock of reason; because we suspect that the stock in each man is small, and that the individuals would do better to avail themselves of the general bank and capital of nations and of ages. Many of our men of speculation, instead of exploding general prejudices, employ their sagacity to discover the latent wisdom which prevails in them. If they find what they seek, and they

seldom fail, they think it more wise to continue the prejudice, with the reason involved, than to cast away the coat of prejudice, and to leave nothing but the naked reason; because prejudice, with its reason, has a motive to give action to that reason, and an affection which will give it permanence.[50]

Burke then starts by asking not what is good for us and how is that good to be brought about, but rather by enquiring into what we actually feel to be good for us and into how we have come by these feelings. It may be argued, as Marxists do, that this method dictates its own conclusions; that is to say, if we examine by means of 'bourgeois logic' people's actual feelings, we shall be bound to attach to them an importance, to endow them with a validity which for the Marxist is illusory. It is at this point that a fearful suspicion may cloud certain minds. Is it possible, after all the efforts of the social engineer to arrogate to himself sociological methods as his private tool-kit, that sociology may turn out to be far more useful to the conservative?

For Burke undoubtedly describes the beliefs and practices which govern our daily business. He does not deal with the technological innovations which the proponents of the open society regard as having wrought so colossal a change in our lives. But, leaving aside the question of whether we light our houses by means of oil lamps or by nuclear-powered electricity, and ignoring for example the influence of the motor car on the way we live, it is undeniable that most of our *social* arrangements are governed by 'prejudice' as Burke describes it – from the constitution of the House of Lords down to the rules of procedure at a revolutionary meeting. So too are our opinions about our social arrangements. Professor Plumb may believe that, for example, traditional views of the family and sexual relations 'are islands of conviction in a surging sea of doubt'.[51] But sociological research indicates even today that our convictions in these matters are much harder to shift than is sometimes imagined. The cattle outnumber the grasshoppers both in number and substance. The 'unprejudiced' are a minority, active and restless, but yet a minority. Those who assume otherwise 'take the deviation from the principle for the principle'.[52]

Men do not trade each on his own private stock of reason, not because this stock in each man is useless or irrelevant but because it is small. We avail ourselves of the general bank and capital of nations and of ages largely for reasons of convenience. It would not be superhumanly difficult for any intelligent man to work out rules of procedure for an orderly public debate which would allow as many people as possible to have their say; he might well work out something very like the system so many of us use – the impartial chairman, the proposer and opposer, resolutions and amendments, question time, the rules of order. But we are satisfied with the system as it is: not merely to invent but to build up general public acceptance of and confidence in a new system would be a life's work.

There is another observable advantage in prejudice:

Prejudice is of ready application in the emergency; it previously engages the mind in a steady course of wisdom and virtue and does not leave the man hesitating in the moment of decision, sceptical, puzzled and unresolved. Prejudice renders a man's virtue his habit; and not a series of unconnected acts. Through just prejudice, his duty becomes a part of his nature.[53]

Prejudice then is the commonest fuel of public passion. How is it acquired?

To be attached to the subdivision, to love the little platoon we belong to in society, is the first principle, the germ as it were, of public affections. It is the first link in the series by which we proceed towards a love to our country and to mankind. . . .

No man ever was attached by a sense of pride, partiality, or real affection, to a description of square measurement. He never will glory in belonging to the Chequer no. 71, or to any other badge-ticket. We begin our public affections in our families. No cold relation is a zealous citizen. We pass on to our neighbours and our habitual provincial connections. These are inns and resting places. Such divisions of our country as have been forced by habit and not by a sudden jerk of authority, are so many little images of the great country in which the heart found something which it could fill. The love to the whole is not extinguished by this subordinate partiality. Perhaps it is a sort of elemental training to those higher and more large regards, by which alone men come to be affected, as with their own concern, in the prosperity of a kingdom. . . .[54]

We must stress again that all this is observation, not prescription. It may be possible to replace family affection by affection for the kibbutz or the commune if the substitution is made more or less in the cradle. But in that case we are merely enlisting our children in a different little platoon; we are not abolishing the press gang. We may add in passing that such a substitution seems to have a perilous effect on the larger loyalties. Not merely does it not submerge those larger loyalties in a direct, undifferentiated love for all mankind, it adds a more rancorous edge to such affections as patriotism and trade unionism. This seems in part to be the result of the efforts needed to make the substitution. Burke believes that 'it has been the misfortune (not as those gentlemen think it, the glory) of this age, that everything is to be discussed, as if the constitution of our country were to be always a subject rather of alteration than enjoyment'.[55]

The more strenuously politicians attempt to alter the nature of our affections, the more fiercely we cling on to the objects of those affections, the more bitterly we mourn those that have been taken from us. Instead of its cells being naturally renewed, the smooth skin of society is artificially inflamed. Insecurity breeds fear and suspicion. 'Your constitution has too much of jealousy to have much of sense in it. You consider the breach of trust in the representative so principally that you do not at all regard the question of his fitness to execute it.'[56]

Individual affections coagulate into group affections which in turn harden into institutions; the actual formation of institutions may be an unforced process of accretion (such as political parties, trade unions) or it may be achieved by a succession of single legislative strokes (local government, the welfare state). But even in the latter case the new institution is usually built upon the ruins of some previous and far from dissimilar institution. At the least, it is a political response to the sudden clotting of public affections. For example, it had been more or less vaguely felt for centuries that slavery was wrong and that the poor were handicapped in the courts. But only in the last few years before action was finally taken did the abolition of slavery and legal aid come to seem not only desirable but possible and urgent. The hopes of scattered individuals and groups clotted into a public outcry so loud that authority had to respond to it.

It will be observed that we have already very much broadened the ground of public affection. This is inevitable. If we love the little platoon, we are bound to love also its property, its rights, its rituals. We do, it is true, sometimes hear of a child who despises his parents' way of life, the home in which he was brought up, all the property and attachments of the parental world and who yet claims to love his parents; but again it is a matter of observation that such a love is feeble and easily smothered by distance or the years. Those who make a permanent home in our affections almost always bring their baggage with them.

A politician, to do great things, looks for a *power*, what workmen call a *purchase*.'[57] The best of social engineers cannot build a house on sand. Whatever the motives for his 'experiments and readjustments', he needs a purchase to dovetail them into the body politic. If he works with the grain, if he adjusts his own purposes to fit in with popular institutions and to meet the public desire for the maintenance and improvement of those institutions, the implementing of his purposes will be easy. If he works against the grain, if his plans do violence to everything that the people hold dear, there are two possible outcomes, not mutually exclusive: first, riots, war or revolution (George III's taxes on the American colonies); second, total failure of plan, although it has been implemented by force (collectivisation of Russian agriculture). Persuasion is the critical factor in political action, not something to be tacked on after the analysis is complete. 'We compensate, we reconcile, we balance.'[58]

Burke makes us feel the overwhelming *power* of the people, the weight of popular institutions, the accumulation of attachments to the world around us. That same weight drives radicals to talk of detonating a vast bomb under the edifice, of 'smashing the system', for they despair of finding any *purchase* on the precipitous, towering walls; they flee therefore from the *difficulty*.[59] Yet what possible appeal can their bomb-talk make to the people at large? Certainly they can raise a few followers by promising the demolition of a specific, unpopular institution. But the radicals themselves no longer share the naïve faith of Guy Fawkes. They are beginning to suspect what Burke knew: 'A certain *quantum* of power must always exist in the community, in some hands, and under some appellation.'[60] They shy away from this sad reality and try to conjure up a world in which it is not so, a community where power has withered away. Paradoxically, to make even the first halting steps towards such a community requires an exercise of power on a colossal scale, either by the dictatorship of the proletariat or by the leaders of the new coalition of the alienated (students, racial minority groups and other outcasts). The exercise of that power will be unwelcome to the majority of people; for it is again a matter of observation that people set a high value on peace, prosperity and security, all of which are threatened by the prospect of revolution. For Burke a liberty which does not lead prosperity and plenty in her train is very equivocal.[61] On the belief that omelettes cannot be made without breaking a large number of eggs Burke says, 'I am not sagacious enough to discover how this despotic sport made of the feelings, consciences, prejudices, and properties of men, can be discriminated from the rankest tyranny.'[62]

The conventional wisdom as advanced by Professor Plumb and many others is that we live in an age which thirsts for change. Certainly the grasshoppers make all the noise, as they did in Burke's day. But observe how reluctant any body of people is to accept any change which affects its own activities; in Britain, the trade unions and local authorities are obvious examples. Observe more generally with what ease conservative forces can regain control if they are allowed to do so through the ballot-box; this is as true in the United States in 1968 as it was in France in 1848. Only when the conservative forces are repulsively harsh or frighteningly weak does violent change stand a good chance.

Out of Burke's observations grows a further observation which is equivalent to the second proposition offered by the theatrical paradigm: namely, whether or not people do know what is good for them, they will sooner or later get their own way unless prevented by force. This great comatose bulk, the 'system', moves extremely slowly but also irresistibly. It takes a colossal explosion to smash it. This fact is well recognised both by Conservatives and Leninists. Social Democrats and Liberals are not so sharply aware of the strength of prejudice. As in the classic cartoon, they think themselves cast away on a desert island which is theirs to do with as they like when in fact they are standing on the back of an indolent whale liable to spout them hundreds of feet into the air.

At the same time Burke slips gently but not furtively from describing what people feel to be good for them to asserting what is in fact good for them. And he claims that, broadly speaking, the two are much the same.

Why? First, because most of the things people want are natural desires to which no one could take exception – peace, prosperity, security. Well, almost no one. R. H. S. Crossman has objected to the 'Roman orgy' enjoyed by workers in postwar industrial states. Many a revolutionary would denounce security as 'bourgeois complacency'. A colonel-figure, distressed by the supposed effeteness of modern young people, may think that another war would stiffen their moral fibres. And so on.

But most of us would feel such views to be quirky, perverse. We would point to the hard nature of most people's lives even in Britain or the United States today; we would point to the tragedy of early death, the moral as well as physical casualties of war and insecurity. But of course if pressed we are bound to admit that such arguments are ultimately based on our own particular (though widely shared) notion of what is natural – in short, on psychological criteria. On this situation – a commonplace in discussion between positivists and moralists – Burke has two general comments. The first is that our commonly held conceptions of what is natural are long-matured distillations of the natural law, mental pictures of the divine reality, by no means perfectly drawn but always deserving of respect. At the very least, then, our notions of what is natural demand the closest examination before being rejected in the name of some allegedly superior morality. There is, in Burke's word, a 'presumption' in their favour.

The second hinges on Burke's notion of political freedom. He points out that the Rousseauists claim above all that their morality will *liberate* us; and he argues that in fact they are trying to have it both ways by changing the meaning of the word 'freedom'.

LIBERTY IS LIBERTY

Burke says: 'If any ask me what a free government is, I answer that, for any practical purpose, it is what the people think so; and that they, and not I, are the natural, lawful and competent judges of this matter.'[63] It may be that if people demand certain freedoms or fail to demand others, they will be making foolish demands. But to be foolish is not to be unfree. Indeed the freedom to be foolish is itself a freedom. Certainly my friend's freedom to urge wisdom upon me is also a freedom; but so is my freedom to reject that wisdom. The Left's preoccupation is not with freedom but with wisdom (or more precisely with the type of society which it wishes to bring about and which it naturally deems wise). Freedom is a matter of open dialogue, not of hidden possibilities; its universe of discourse deals with demands actually made and either met or unmet.

But are there not just demands which could be and ought to be made but have not been made because the society has consciously or unconsciously repressed them? Very possibly. But that does not destroy the society's claim to be free. For we cannot apply the calculus of freedom to such possibilities until they have ceased to be hidden. We cannot say that a society is free or unfree on a particular question until that question has been put to the society's legal and social codes by those who feel themselves to be shackled in that particular respect.

The concept of women's liberation presupposes a women's liberation group. In many cases, unfreedom is clear from the outset. In ancient Greece, nobody attempted to deny the existence of slavery. Plato took one view about its desirability, Pericles a somewhat different line. The public question was: Is slavery necessary to produce a stable and prosperous society? Which goal should have priority? It would have been ludicrous to ask: are slaves unfree? In a milder form, modern wage slavery is certainly a constraint. While we are not legally compelled to arrive punctual and sober for work five days a week, the economic cost of not doing so may be considerable. But there is no 'repressed consciousness' here. We are fully aware of the constraint; we accept it as a necessary condition of a modern industrial state which provides us with a certain standard of living. We are also aware of alternative systems provided, for example, by the syndicalists. Our quarrel with these alternatives does not concern freedom; we do not say that syndicalism would be freer or less free, nor are we much moved even to define industrial freedom; our quarrel is a practical one. We may doubt whether the alternatives could be introduced without acceptable loss of stability and prosperity; or we may doubt whether the alternatives would not introduce new and equally unattractive constraints.

The practical test of a free society is clear. When demands are made, does the system respond quickly to those demands, either by granting them or by giving satisfactory reasons why they should not be granted? We may well say that a fourteen-hour day is slavery and therefore pass a law to limit maximum working hours to eight; but if our society is threatened by invasion and massacre, we may unhesitatingly suspend that law in order to maximise our defence effort. It would be perverse to claim that slavery had thereby been reintroduced.

It would be equally perverse to say that a free society should be tested by its readiness to listen to demands that have not been made or that the people have actually refused to make when urged to do so by itinerant ideologues. After all, until somebody within the society makes the demand, how can we know what it is? And if there is no demand, supply (by which we mean the fitting of the new demand into the existing legal and social framework and the adjusting of our existing priorities accordingly) would be a work of supererogation.

Frequently not only is unfreedom clearly established without any need for debate, but also the limits of freedom, as already laid down, make it plain on which side of the line a new case will fall. For example, although there may be no specific law against turning cartwheels down the middle of the street, it would obviously be forbidden under laws against breaching the peace and obstructing the traffic.

But why should we think always in terms of 'new' demands? Should we not rather be surveying the existing landscape of freedom in a society rather than minutely examining the borders through which new freedoms are trying to squeeze? Such an objection once again betrays an unduly static, essentialist view of politics. For the dialogue is open and continuous. Every day we find out by experience, both repeated and varied a million times, what society permits and does not permit. Where we sense injustice, to ourselves or to others, we complain; we are, so to speak, engaged in constant, often instantaneous litigation not only with authority in the sense of governments and councils but also with commerce, industry, transport, parents, children, spouses, employers, servants, associates, friends, enemies. We are non-stop consumer-testers of freedom. Each demand is not a new demand; but each test of that demand is a fresh test. Each day I find out whether or not the freedoms that I enjoyed the day before are still on offer. And I am the only person who can draw up my own personal report. It may be that the demands I rate highest are trivial or misguided; my scale of preference may be provincial and short-sighted. But only I can say whether I am free or not.

As Sir Isaiah Berlin points out:

... nothing is gained by a confusion of terms. To avoid glaring inequality or widespread misery I am ready to sacrifice some or all of my freedom: I may do so willingly and freely: but it is freedom that I am giving up for the sake of justice or equality or the love of my fellow men. I should be guilt-stricken, and rightly so, if I were not, in some circumstance, ready to make this sacrifice. But a sacrifice is not an increase in what is being sacrificed, namely freedom, however great the moral need or the compensation for it. Everything is what it is: liberty is liberty, not equality or fairness or justice or human happiness or a quiet conscience.[64]

For Burke it follows from this that in a free society:

The people are the masters. They have only to express their wants at large and in gross. We are the expert artists; we members of Parliament are the skilful workmen to shape their desires into perfect form and to fit the utensil to the use. They are the sufferers, they tell the symptoms of the complaint; but we know the exact seat of the disease, and how to apply the remedy according to the rules or art. How shocking would it be to see us pervert our skill into a sinister and servile dexterity for the purpose of evading our duty, and defrauding our employers, who are our natural lords, of the object of their just expectations.[65]

That is the underlying nature of the relationship (it is the reverse of the fatuous distortion introduced by Lord Shawcross – 'we are the masters now'). The politician may act purely in response to public pressure, he may act on his own initiative, hoping that the public will later come to see the advantages of his plan, or he may meet the sense of the people 'on the way', as Burke puts it earlier in the speech quoted above. But in all cases the people are the masters.

And it is crucial to note the terms that Burke uses to describe the profession of politics – 'expert artists' and 'skilful workmen'. Politicians are skilled (at least we must hope so) but they are *employees acting under our direct control*. They are acting for us. The 'social engineer' by contrast acts independently of our wishes when not actually in contradiction to them; his orders are dictated by the standards of his profession (rational humanitarian morality). He is aiming not for a free society but for a humane and rational one.

The social engineer and his supporters may therefore persist: 'Very well then, liberty is liberty. But is it the highest good? Is it right to prefer a free society as an overarching goal to a rational and humane society? Do people know what is good for them?'

For Burke there can be no genuine antithesis here. We do not have a choice between a free society and a rational and humane society. We have a choice between a free society and a controlled society. And he believes that 'it is better to cherish virtue and humanity, by leaving much to free will, even with some loss to the object, than to attempt to make men mere machines and instruments of a political benevolence.'[66] Our ability to 'enjoy' our institutions depends upon our freedom both to criticise or reform them and to keep them as they are – in a word, upon our freedom.

MYTH AND FUNCTION

This idea of enjoyment brings us to what seems to me a very bad mistake in many students of Burke. Popper, for example, says that

Burke wishes 'to make the state an object of worship'.[67] And he quotes in evidence for this Burke's statement that 'it is to be looked on with other reverence because it is not a partnership in things subservient only to the gross animal existence of a temporary and perishable nature.'[68] Popper interprets 'it' as meaning the state in the sense of 'the government'. But Burke makes it perfectly clear that he means the state in the sense of 'society'. In fact, he says, two sentences before the words just quoted, 'society is indeed a contract'. It is *society* that is this spiritual partnership. And so indeed it must be; why otherwise should we entertain towards each other feelings of trust, duty, affection and brotherhood? If it were not so, our society would be 'nothing better than a partnership agreement in a trade of pepper and coffee, callico or tobacco, or some other such low concern'.[69]

In fact, Burke is the opposite of a state-worshipper in the sense that Popper means. 'Government is not made in virtue of natural rights, which may and do exist in total independence of it.'[70] If it were so made we would indeed have to pay reverence to it, just as we do pay reverence to the Church which is the earthly representative of divine right. But no, 'government is a contrivance of human wisdom to provide for human *wants*'.[71] It is a mere machine for performing such tasks as preserving our liberties, restraining our passions, defending us against the enemy, succouring the poor and so on. 'The moment you abate anything from the full rights of men, each to govern himself, and suffer any artificial positive limitation upon those rights, from that moment the whole organisation of government becomes a consideration of convenience. This it is which makes the constitution of a state and the due distribution of its powers a matter of the most delicate and complicated skill.'[72]

These are things to be settled by convention for our convenience. They are to be conceived, in Popper's phrase, as 'means that serve certain ends'. Yet this only at the outset. As time passes, these means begin to generate affection; when Radicals complain of their rigidity, they are talking not of the machinery of convention but of the set attitudes which people have accumulated over the years towards it; the longer they have lasted and the more generally they have prevailed the more we cherish not only our prejudices, but their expression in our institutions. Why should this be so? Burke says because it is 'natural'. We may presume in the same sense that it is natural for a child to love his mother. Unless children are taught not to love their mothers, they will do so. If a child is taught that his mother is a murderess, he is, however, likely to evince a certain coolness towards her. History may indeed consist 'for the greater part' in a record of evil.[73] Yet those who look only at the black side run a great risk; 'because their minds are not only unfurnished with patterns of the fair and good, but by habit they come to take no delight in the contemplation of those things. By hating vices too much, they come to love men too little.'[74] To concentrate on the black side is an approach to reality which is both incomplete and unproductive.

It is far more effective to make use of the natural affection felt both by the political actor and the political audience for existing institutions than to start entirely afresh; for the existing institutions not only give the actor a guide to what should be done, they put him in sympathy with the audience and assure him of public support. The social engineer of Popper's metaphor has no such guide or rope to save him from falling. He stands in a strange land. He knows the theory of stresses, he knows how much weight the bridge *ought* to be able to bear, but he does not know the past history of the bridge – its age, its composition, whether it has already been weakened by too much strain. And he does not know the native language so that he cannot ask the local inhabitants. Interpreters are unreliable. He is always liable to be tricked or lied to, or to give offence by unwittingly infringing local taboos. He has to do it all out of his head.

Burke's politician, on the other hand, is a local man. He has grown up with the people and he naturally shares their affections. He is set apart only by the nature of his task. This alone forces him to work harder, to find out all the facts, to listen more. Yet underneath all his accumulated wisdom and behind all the tricks of the trade must lie a man who shares the preconceptions of his time and place. The man who does not share these preconceptions may make a memorable dictator, but he will not make a politician.

In the same way that progressive critics have confused the reverence due to the spiritual partnership of society with the affection paid to long-standing and reasonably efficient institutions, so they have been confused by Burke's notion of Providence. We shall not treat this question at length. Burke's main point is that God hates nothing that He has made. And His purpose is working itself out in the history of mankind, though we may not be able to fathom it. It would in fact be bizarre to conceive of a Supreme Being who had no purpose.

But this in no way shackles our free will. Nor does it imply that 'all is for the best in the best of all possible worlds'. Our duty is simply to obey the dictates of our religion. Whatever one may think of such a doctrine, it is neither perverse nor recondite, being merely the mainstream belief of the Christian Church.[75] As the future course and total purpose of history ('Providence') are hidden from us, we are left to do the best we can in our feebleness and ignorance. Man operates with complete freedom within his own context, the natural world. The implication of that freedom is to throw more rather than less responsibility upon our shoulders. Here the critics of Burke's 'superstitious confusion' go furthest astray. The grace of God, being an unmerited privilege, brings with it a correspondingly great duty to use our best rational and moral endeavours. This sturdy attitude is the very reverse of the heathen gibbering an impotent fear before the wrath of God as expressed in a thunderstorm.

The important point here is that Burke believed both that the Christian religion is true and that it is a valuable source, if not the primary source, of social harmony: 'We know, and what is better, we feel inwardly, that religion is the basis of civil society, and the source of all good and of all comfort.'[76] Religion is 'the grand prejudice, and that which holds all the other prejudices together.'[77] This is a sociological remark whose justness does not depend upon the truth or falsehood of religion itself. Those who believe ardently in Christianity, as Burke himself undoubtedly did, may wish to see its influence expand for that reason; but those who believe ardently in social harmony, as Burke did too, may also wish to see any or all religions grow in influence without necessarily accepting any or all religious doctrines. Burke was as ready to defend the faith of Irish Catholics or Indian Hindus as the faith of Protestant Englishmen. Indeed, the link between the truth and the social value of a religion is that one man's passionate belief in the truth of his own religion ought to lead him to appreciate the depth and hence the social value of other people's beliefs in the truth of *their* religion – ought in fact to lead him towards tolerance. The strength of Burke's attack on Warren Hastings (it has appalling weaknesses) rests upon this appreciation of religion as in a secular sense the keystone of public affections, from which must follow tolerance of religions other than one's own. Religious tolerance is a modern virtue of which modern political theory has found it singularly difficult to take account. Of course liberal progressives concede the right of any man to believe what he will and to worship as he will; totalitarian regimes do not concede even that right. But liberal theory breaks down when faced with the questions of proselytisation and of religious education of children.* The matter is set aside by means of a shamefaced and often temporary acquiescence in traditional practice. But religious observance and the consequent solace can flourish only in a full-blooded *enjoyment* of tradition and custom. We are dealing here not with the truth value of a religion, nor with the relative merits of organised religion and private communion with the numinous, but with its measurable effect upon the internal harmony of communities and of individuals. Organised religion, Burke believes, does us good; and where it is not at present doing us good, it is better to repair the defects than to destroy the whole fabric. For, 'in vain shall a man look to the possibility of making such things when he wants them. The winds blow as they list. These institutions are the products of enthusiasm; they are the instruments of wisdom. Wisdom cannot create materials; they are the gifts of nature or of chance; her pride is in the use.'[78] George III in America, Hastings in Bengal, the National Assembly in France – all were attempting to smash priceless objects which could never be reproduced.

Biographers of Hastings have managed convincingly to defend his financial probity and administrative impartiality against Burke's intemperate attacks. But to this greater and deeper charge they have only been able to argue that traditional Indian culture had already been smashed beyond repair and that Hastings, who regretted this as much as anyone, could only start *de novo*. This defence is amply refuted by the evident survival of a great quantity of Indian culture right up to the present day through two hundred years of British rule and the Nehruism (so reminiscent of Hastings himself) which succeeded British rule.

Certainly Burke gives close attention to the structure of the myths that animate the mind of the individual and the movements of society. But he cannot be described as a 'structuralist' in the modern sense; for his interest in the myths is severely practical. For Burke the relevance of the myth lies at the point where it directs or encounters social events. He is not concerned basically with the original 'deep' structure of the myths, but with the way their flowers scent the air and pollinate each other. His interest lies determinedly above ground.

* This breakdown is tellingly displayed in the arguments surrounding the US Supreme Court's decisions on the propriety of religious services in state schools.

Still less is Burke concerned with whether the myths are in some sense true. Those moral truths which he appeals to as being 'natural' fall outside the scope of his sociology. They are pre-political, to be invoked in political discourse and action without argument. For example, slavery is abhorrent to moral sense; it should be abolished. In such a case we need no reference to the origin of the custom of slavery or to the myths which have sustained it. Slavery is simply wrong.

But where no such general moral principle is involved, the myth (in the sense of traditional prejudice and justification of prejudice) is all-important. And Burke is totally clear in his argument on this point. There is none of the confusion of categories which bedevils the dialogue between Marxists and structuralists; to wit, which is the 'reality' – the myth as perceived by the natives, the myth as analysed by the scientist, the external world which has conditioned and shaped the myth, or the mind of the myth-spinner? It is such confusions which have led scientists to invent lubricating devices such as the theory that the roots of myths must be unconscious. This is akin to the Freudian belief that the important drives must be hidden. Such a belief is necessary to support the corollary that by bringing the submerged part of our minds to light we can solve our emotional problems, that knowledge will make us happy. There is also a less endearing aspect to this attitude, namely that sociologists like to get the bulge on the rest of us, to learn the secret of how we all tick; their satisfaction is much diminished if some of us do in fact already have a reasonably accurate understanding of how we tick. There is a good deal of doubt about how far, if at all, mythic structures need to be unconscious in order to survive effectively. There is also a great reluctance among social scientists either to examine or to admit this doubt, for by so doing they would be admitting the limits of their own magic power.

Burke himself is lucid and empirical. Myths may be conscious or unconscious; they may arise out of inner feelings (for example, family affection leading to patriotic myth) or out of an external situation (for example, the need for stability leading to hereditary monarchy). In both cases they result from a natural logic; it is not too much to say that it would be odd if something of the sort did not happen. If we are forced to think about the myth, it becomes conscious; if we are not, it does not.

Throughout the troubles over the difficulties of succession to the

English throne in the sixteenth, seventeenth and early eighteenth centuries, acts and declarations of Parliaments constantly and openly stressed the need for 'certainty of succession'. At the same time, they fall to what Burke calls 'a pious, legislative ejaculation' and declare (we are talking here of the accession of William and Mary but the tone is common to other such occasions in our history) that they consider it 'as a marvellous providence; and merciful goodness of God to this nation, to preserve their said majesties *royal* persons, most happily to reign over us on the *throne of their ancestors*.'* No question of choosing a cycling sovereign. And yet the object of the whole exercise – certainty of succession and hence political stability – is stated as bluntly as directions in a bicycle repair kit. We accept the divine nature of the myth while fully aware of its practical use. This would seem to be a frequent occurrence in myth and ritual; the knowledge of hygienic or medical reasons for a certain taboo (for example, on the eating of pork) has never prevented the devout observance of that taboo. For Burke the point of the Declaration of Rights is not that it introduces a 'deviation' from the principle of hereditary monarchy, but that it reaffirms the importance of the principle. This is presumably the kind of attitude which Professor Plumb and others criticise as 'unhistorical'; that is to say that it concentrates not on the appearance of a new element in society but on the continuation of the old. Of course the rise of a strong centralised monarchy under the Tudors, and the dynamite added to this explosive charge by the Catholicism and Divine Right of the Stuarts, precipitated more than what Burke dismisses as a mere deviation. He is indeed on weak ground if we take his judgment as relating to the relative historical importance of, first, the continuation of the reverent forms of the monarchy, and secondly, its unprecedented confinement within a constitution.

But Burke is making not a diachronic historical judgment but a synchronic sociological one. He claims that people like Lord Somers at the time of the Declaration of Rights *thought* the continuation of the reverent forms of the monarchy (what Bagehot would call its 'dignified' aspect) very important; and this belief made these forms in fact very important. The only diachronic element in Burke's argument here is his claim that the English had this belief even at a time of revolution, that the English kept it still in his own day at another time of revolution, and that the passage of years had strengthened that

* Burke's italics.

belief. The English are conscious of the mythic nature of the belief; but that does not weaken its strength as a stabilising factor in the community.

The boilermakers' union in Britain starts every meeting with the display of a board, or box, called the Dispensation, and with the same speech: 'Upstanding Worthy Brothers, we are now assembled together to transact the business of this society: I hope, therefore, that you will deal fair and impartially in any case that may be brought before you, in honour to yourselves and to the credit of the Society to which you belong.' Candidates for membership have to stand outside the room and knock three times after a ceremony in which brotherly love is stressed, together with 'a sacred devotion for the elevation of the Order you are about to enter'. Now the union's members are clearly aware of the archaic nature of the language and ritual; the union president, Mr Danny McGarvey, refers jovially to the initiation ceremony as 'Knock three times and ask for Doris'.[79] But these formalities have the purpose both of stressing the long history of the union (in particular its origins as an illegal secret society) and of providing a framework for civilised, rational discussion. What may appear to the outsider as antiquated mumbo-jumbo is in fact highly practical, endowing the institution with authentic authority and giving the members a focus for their loyalties. And it is the members who consciously make the decision to keep the myth in operation. Whatever its errors of policy, the union has in fact a long-standing reputation for sticking together and being singularly free of corruption.

Burke of course does not pretend to be an sociologist; he is defending a society which he loves at a time when it is threatened. He describes the myths of the people with mingled irony, affection and wishful thinking:

Thanks to our sullen resistance to innovation, thanks to the cold sluggishness of our national character, we still bear the stamp of our forefathers. . . . We have real hearts of flesh and blood beating in our bosoms. We fear God; we look up with awe to kings; with affection to Parliaments; with duty to magistrates; with reverence to priests; and with respect to nobility.[80]

A wildly exaggerated picture of reality; but no more exaggerated than the reverse picture which sees merely a discontented proletariat groping towards revolutionary consciousness. And it explains, as the reverse picture does not, a great part of subsequent English history. Why should the English cherish such beliefs? Because it is 'natural' to do so; that is to say there is no reason not to do so. It is 'subtilising us into savages' to have atheists as preachers, madmen as law-givers. And the merit of such natural acceptance of authority and affection (what we lump together under the name of tradition) is a plain practical one.

At this point we reach the boundary of the political scientist's field of analysis. He has shown the principles and processes that typically produce a stable and harmonious society which allows for peaceful change when needed without allowing anarchy. He cannot say (though of course Burke can and does) whether the impulses which have supported those principles and directed those processes are based on valid moral or religious beliefs. That is not his task but the task of the moral philosopher or theologian. He may, however, remark, as Burke does, that a political science which is unsupported by moral or religious beliefs is at best a crude behaviourism. Without religion as the basis of civil society men become little better than the flies of a summer. A clever man may teach fleas to jump through hoops but there is not much glory in it for the fleas.

Burke takes as axiomatic two propositions which are now quoted as 'discoveries' of modern sociology/ethnology: to wit, that man is a cultural animal and that man is a myth-making animal. Man does not exist 'stripped of every relation, in all the nakedness and solitude of metaphysical abstraction' any more than does the object of his gaze. Whenever we are invited to consider the latest breakthrough in the social and human sciences and to gasp with wonder at the new all-revealing jargon – transactional therapy, *le cru et le cuit*, Gestalt psychology, game theory – we are likely to find the core of the new doctrine perfectly and sharply defined in a single phrase of Burke's. To claim this is not always to claim any great originality for Burke; some of what he says is soundly platitudinous, which is to say that it is based on common observation of common phenomena.

These days we are well aware of the identity of the spec builder who built all those heresies which are now being dismantled at enormous expense; it was the essentialist, the man who believed in the concept-as-thing rather than the concept-as-function. The Platonic Idea rooted itself so deeply into our intellectual life over the centuries that whenever we pulled up one growth, another used to sprout. At last we are beginning to understand that on the whole we are likely to make more progress by examining how things work rather than by defining the ultimate elements of which they are composed. Today we believe (or at least Chomsky, Laing, Lévy-Strauss, etc. all do), that syntax rather than etymology is usually the fruitful field of study. Burke never doubted this rule of thumb.

MYTHIC OBJECTS

This belief that function, process and praxis are more significant for the study of human society than substance and essence is peculiarly modern. And it has led to a peculiarly modern impatience in defining what Burke would have called 'prejudices', the strongly held basic beliefs which are the constituent elements of political dialogue. The modern student is more concerned with the prevalence of 'belief systems', their patterns of distribution, their relation to other belief systems, and the use to which they are put, rather than with their inner nature, composition and moral value. He may indeed refuse to answer the question of moral value on the ground either that the question lies outside his province or that the question is in fact meaningless; 'ought' cannot be derived from 'is' except on the criterion of consistency within a given language (if x is a soldier, then x ought to be brave). In the case of the Greek military regime quoted above,[81] we may analyse M. Papadopoulos' attempts to establish legitimacy by placing his regime in a tradition of Hellenistic/Christian inspiration; we can assess these attempts on the criterion of whether his actions are consistent with that tradition. We can do the same with the efforts of President Nasser of Egypt and more recently Colonel Gadaffi of Libya to place their respective regimes within a tradition of Islamic Socialism whose natural culmination is a federal Arab republic. Similarly with the attempts of Dom Mintoff, prime minister of Malta, to establish his own regime as the culmination of a long tradition of a Maltese struggle for independence. The island's annual national festival marks two sieges, by the Turks in 1565 and by the Axis powers in 1940–3. Mintoff's message to the islanders on the occasion of the 1971 festival asserted that under the rule of the Grand Masters, the Maltese were oppressed by a social system which deprived them of the right to own property. But they shared Christianity with their overlords and this made them feel they had something to cherish which made up for oppression. So when the Turks forced their way into the harbours the Maltese 'put up a resistance which ranked with the greatest known in those times. Malta survived the siege and Europe had good cause to be grateful to her.' During the second world war, Mr Mintoff continued, Malta was likewise under an alien power. The island was 'a colony and suffered the indignity and poverty of a colony . . . our people for the second time beat off the Nazi and Fascist siege . . . and once again Europe had much to thank us for.' But the third great event in Malta's history 'is the brightest one in the history of our country. Our people awoke and became alive to the fact that they had as much right to be free and independent in their own country as other nations of the world. For the first time in their lives our people are saying to outsiders: "My country is my own and I shall use it as I think fit for the benefit of my children".'[82]

It is easy enough to evaluate the historical accuracy of these claims and the historical validity of linking them to form a pattern. But if we do this, and nothing more, we shall restrict ourselves to drawing a certain type of conclusion. For example, if we question whether Mintoff's renegotiation of Malta's defence and aid agreements with Britain represents such a significant loosing of the ancient shackles (similar arguments took place years before the granting of independence), we might conclude that Maltese independence is a chimaera, that in reality the island is now passing through a stage of neo-colonialism, and that Mintoff's three events are evidence not of the ancient spirit of independence of the Maltese people but of the necessary subjection of the island to the strategic and economic interests of the great powers of the day (because of Malta's geographical position). Yet to draw such conclusions is to miss the point; Mintoff's aim is not to illuminate the history of Malta but to create in his audience a new consciousness which sees in him, not a prime minister more or less competent than his rivals, but the embodiment of Maltese national unity and aspirations and which sets the highest value on those aspirations. The historical events referred to are mythic objects, symbols shaped by the mind for its own purposes, not dates in a chronicle published for the furtherance of knowledge.

This making of symbols is seen at its most dramatic and lyrical in the Irish struggle for independence. On Easter Monday 1916 Patrick Pearse stepped out in front of the Dublin Post Office and read out the famous proclamation:

POBLACHT NA h–EIREANN
THE PROVISIONAL GOVERNMENT
OF THE
IRISH REPUBLIC
TO THE PEOPLE OF IRELAND

IRISHMEN AND IRISHWOMEN: In the name of God and of the dead generations from which she receives her old tradition of nationhood, Ireland, through us, summons her children to her flag and strikes for her freedom. . . .

There are several elements in this proclamation – the emphasis on a republic, the alleged support of foreign allies, the guarantee of 'religious and civil liberty, equal rights and equal opportunities to all its citizens' – but as Professor F. S. L. Lyons points out, 'it is essentially historical in conception. The intention is to link the present with "the dead generations" and to establish 1916 as the latest link in a chain stretching back over three centuries. *This* insurrection was not to be regarded as a sudden, opportunist explosion, but rather as the logical development of a long-established nationalist tradition.'[83]

The soil was prepared, well dug for generations, fertilised with blood of martyrs. The actors became legendary heroes, marmorealised by Yeats that same year:

> I write it out in a verse –
> MacDonagh and MacBride
> And Connolly and Pearse
> Now and in time to be,
> Wherever green is worn,
> Are changed, changed utterly:
> A terrible beauty is born.[84]

The sixteen executed men had joined the pantheon of martyrs. They had found 'new comrades' in Elysium, Lord Edward Fitzgerald and Wolfe Tone. Yeats himself might be apprehensive, melancholy, stoical about the consequences of it all:

> Too long a sacrifice
> Can make a stone of the heart.
> O when may it suffice?
> That is Heaven's part, our part
> To murmur name upon name,
> As a mother names her child
> When sleep at last has come
> On limbs that had run wild.[85]

178

But the impact of the event was too great for such discriminating, equivocal reaction to be generally shared. Even the place became hallowed. When the British government interned Catholics in Northern Ireland in August 1971, it was outside the General Post Office in Dublin that Sinn Fein held a protest meeting. Nor is the Easter Rising itself the sole example of a fleeting feeling or circumstance in Irish politics being caught and frozen into marble. A year after the rising, in defiance of the authorities the Irish Republican Brotherhood organised a great demonstration at the funeral of one of their leaders who had died in prison after forcible feeding; the IRB did this under the transparent disguise of the Wolfe Tone Memorial Committee; the martyrdom of the hero of 1798 was being re-enacted in a metaphor. Tone in fact cut his throat in jail while under sentence of death. His speech from the dock did not reach the emotional intensity of Robert Emmet's but was none the less moving in its courage and dignity.[86] But this is not all. As Professor Lyons points out, the odd title of the committee 'recalls, in the obliqueness of its terms of reference, the old Emmet Monument Association of Fenian days. Emmet, in his speech from the dock, had said: "When my country takes her place among the nations of the earth, *then*, and *not till then*, let my epitaph be written." Since Tone's objective had been the same, the "Memorial Committee" had presumably a similar monument – a free country – in mind for him.'[87] Never was a myth, a metaphor, made more literally concrete.

But may not the Irish struggle be atypical in its constant stress upon history and tradition? Does not, for example, the fact that the proclamation starts in Gaelic indicate that it may be only this peculiarly traditional brand of nationalism which demands the crystallisation of myth around historical figures and incidents? And may not a pure Radical movement dispense with such comforting ornament? Radical movements do of course emphasise, often ferociously, the need for the obliteration of old symbols, the longing to see 'the last king strangled with the guts of the last priest' (a desire expressed as early as 1733). Burke himself quotes Rabaud de St Etienne, a leading member of the National Assembly, as saying:

Tous les établissemens en France couronnent le malheur du peuple: pour le rendre heureux il faut le rénouveler; changer ses idées; changer ses loix; changer ses moeurs; . . . changer les hommes; changer les choses; changer les mots . . . tout détruire; oui, tout détruire; puisque tout est à recréer.[88]

And Tristan Tzara, one of the founders of Surrealism, wrote in 1918:

> Honour, Country, Morality, Family, Art, Religion, Liberty, Fraternity had once answered to human needs. But nothing [remains] of them but skeletons . . . There is a great negative work of destruction to be accomplished. We must sweep and clean.[89]

If even the skeletons must go, the new man in the new society surely has no need of myth or symbol to sustain his faith.

Yet time and again we are struck by the harking back of revolutionaries to past models of revolution and their heroes, and by the way those memories are incapsulated in myth and symbol. Even in the midst of vital struggles which might be thought to consume all mental and spiritual energies, the making of myths and symbols continues, sometimes with even greater intensity than before, precisely because the struggle is so demanding that only myth and symbol can refresh the warrior. Instant nostalgia is in fact the particular morbidity of revolutionary circles; in no other milieu do we find such an eager longing to marmorealise the recent past, for the simple reason that the revolutionaries have destroyed or denied all preceding pasts.

Bastille Day was never more magnificently celebrated than in 1790. The festivities lasted more than a week. The ruins of the Bastille were 'floodlit' with lanterns and embellished with a huge 'tree of liberty' surmounted by a gigantic phrygian cap. Carlyle's ironic description of the scene is matchless.[90] June 20 1792 – the third anniversary of the Oath of the Tennis Court – was celebrated with barely less splendour. Another fête was to honour the Constitution of 1793 – and the date chosen was of course 10 August, the first anniversary of the Storming of the Tuileries. The burial or reburial of Voltaire, Rousseau, Mirabeau, Marat – on each occasion there were processions, orations, feasts, and on each occasion a myth was consciously formed or smashed, just as the decision to add Stalin to or subtract him from Lenin's mausoleum was not done merely for the convenience of the embalmers.

Many such traditions continue to this day, for example the custom of naming revolutions and revolutionary movements after their month or date of origin. After the French *septembriseurs* and the men of Thermidor come the Russian Decembrists of 1825, echoed consciously by the Decembrists of the Moscow Rising of 1905 and finally by the Octobrists of 1917. Fidel Castro's movement of 26 July offers a classic example; 26 July was the date of Castro's attack on the

Moncada Barracks in 1953. The attack was not exactly a military triumph, though it achieved real political significance by the savage treatment of those Castroites who were taken prisoner. Its significance was as an initial growth point for revolution. In 1953 Castro was not a convinced Marxist, though clearly a revolutionary of the Left. At one time his group referred to themselves as The Youth of the Centenary.[91] The Centenary was that of the birth of José Martí, the greatest of Cuban independence leaders, poet, romantic, imprisoned as a schoolboy merely for writing a letter which accused a fellow student of treachery for walking in a Spanish parade,[92] killed in battle on a white horse. Professor Thomas points out that the last line in one of his most famous poems –

I shall die with my face to the sun –

was adapted forty years later to stand as the opening line of the hymn of the Spanish Falange. Myth knows no doctrinal niceties. When the white Rhodesians declared their independence from Britain in November 1965 they borrowed shamelessly from the preamble to the American Declaration of Independence of nearly two hundred years earlier, omitting only the embarrassing contention that men are created equal.

Castro and his friends then saw themselves in the tradition of the legendary Martí, as witness the proclamation which was to be read after the capture of the radio station in 1953:

The revolution . . . recognises and bases itself on the ideals of Martí . . . The revolution declares its absolute and reverent respect for the constitution which was given to the people in 1940 . . . In the name of the martyrs, in the name of the sacred rights of the fatherland. . . .[93]

How characteristic of the mythic, rhetorical nature of revolutions is the universal rule that the first objective must be the capture of the radio station. The practical purposes of calming the public and terrifying the loyal troops into submission shade into the more nebulous but no less essential purpose of promulgating the new myth, the need for the new regime to define itself.

After the attack on the Moncada Barracks the Hymn of Liberty, a marching song of imprecise but irreproachable sentiments, was re-named The Hymn of 26 July; the movement itself was re-named later, shortly after Castro came out of jail. While in prison he had pamphleteered with energy and brilliance. One of his main aims was the creation of a mythic golden past to throw the tyranny of Batista into sharper relief:

> Once upon a time there was a republic. It had its constitution, its laws, its civil rights, a president, a Congress and law courts. Everyone could assemble, associate, speak and write with complete freedom. . . . There existed a public opinion both respected and heeded: all problems of common interest were freely discussed . . . the whole nation throbbed with enthusiasm. . . . [94]

Not only did Castro attempt to create a usable past for Cuba, he also drew from history a host of arguments in order to legitimise armed rebellion:

> The authority of Montesquieu, John of Salisbury, St Thomas, Luther, Melanchthon, Calvin, Milton, Locke, Rousseau and Tom Paine were invoked for rebellion; the American, English and French revolutions were mentioned, as well as the Cuban leaders of 1868–98 (Agramonte, Céspedes, Maceo, Gómez and Martí). Always there was a hint of the role played by fighting: Maceo was quoted as saying liberty is 'not begged for but won with the blow of a machete'. [95]

Before Castro discovered the even greater force of Marx's method of historical pattern-making, he had evolved a familiar brand of revolutionary tradition. All history presses for the overthrow of tyrants, all philosophy and morality demand it; the revolution will not only overthrow the tyrant, it will also restore the golden age, the form of government which gives true and lasting expression to the genius of a people.

Examples of similar techniques in the manufacture of myth are legion. The Spartacists echoed in their very title the tradition of drawing legitimacy from historical authority. Rosa Luxemburg's famous speech, 'On the Spartacus Programme,'[96] is based on the theme that 'great historical movements have been the determining causes of today's deliberations' (the founding of the German Communist Party). The evolving views of Marx, Engels and others are traced in parallel with the dramatic events they reflected or helped to create: the Communist Manifesto and the February Revolution of 1848, the Paris Commune of 1871 and the reissue of the Manifesto in 1872, the Erfurt Programme of 1891 and the collapse of German social democracy in 1914 – these are points on the graph of history whose position establishes beyond doubt the significance of the final point, the present moment; they are stations of the cross which prove that this is the true resurrection.

Daniel Cohn-Bendit and his supporters, while proclaiming their intention of creating an entirely new style of revolutionary movement, followed traditional practice so far as to call their party *le mouvement du 22 mars*. American practice is somewhat different. In the United States political life is saturated with the questions of legality arising from the separation of the three branches of government and the determination of their powers in legal terms. As a result, the most striking conflicts between the revolutionaries and the established authorities are to be seen in the courts and usually depend upon the interpretation of some phrase in the American Constitution, most often in the Bill of Rights; in the eyes of the revolutionaries these confrontations highlight the failure of modern American reality to match the historical promises. They are thus both spurs to revolution and a means of reviving the spirit of the golden age, or rather the golden blueprints, of 1776, 1787 and 1791. In such court cases a custom has arisen by which the groups of defendants are referred to by their number and the location of the court: the Chicago Seven, the Catonsville Four, the New Haven Nine, the Boston Twelve. Attempts have been made to export this custom. Black militants in London's Notting Hill, charged with riot and assault during a protest march in support of the West Indian owner of the Mangrove Restaurant who was having difficulties with the police, called themselves the Mangrove Nine.[97]

It is this universal instinct for celebration, 'our part to murmur name upon name', that Orwell satirises in *Animal Farm*. After the animals rebel and expel farmer Jones, their rousing song, 'Beasts of England', 'spread with astonishing speed. . . . Any animal caught singing it was given a flogging on the spot. And yet the song was irrepressible. The blackbirds whistled it in the hedges, the pigeons cooed it in the elms, it got into the din of the smithies and the tune of the church bells. And when the human beings listened to it, they secretly trembled, hearing in it a prophecy of their future doom.'[98] And each fresh skirmish with the counter-revolutionary humans is immediately and consciously transformed into legend:

There was much discussion as to what the battle should be called. In the end, it was named the Battle of the Cowshed, since that was where the ambush had been sprung. Mr Jones's gun had been found lying in the mud, and it was known that there was a supply of cartridges in the farmhouse. It was decided to set the gun up at the foot of the flagstaff, like a piece of artillery, and to fire it twice a year – once on October the twelfth, the anniversary of the Battle of the Cowshed and once on Midsummer Day, the anniversary of the Rebellion.[99]

But are not such terms – numbers, dates and the like – merely convenient shorthand? In long, intense political discussion we cannot be expected to refer each time to 'Dr Benjamin Spock, the Reverend William Sloane Coffin, *et al*'. No indeed; and were such practices found to be isolated locutions in a mass of plain, direct speech, they could be dismissed as mere conveniences. But the repetition of these locutions over long periods of time, the motives, both conscious and unconscious, for choosing these locutions and not others, the links between the naming of names and the explicit development of a historical tradition – the evidence of all this is too weighty and too worldwide to allow us to talk of convenience or even coincidence. Clearly the revolutionary leader is doing much more than using language as a practical tool and adding a few new locutions to deal with fresh circumstances; he is attempting to breathe a new and different life into language. We should not forget that Rabaud de St. Etienne talked not only of destroying everything but also of *changing* customs, things, words. A new mythic universe has to be created.

So far we have been discussing the myth-making of those who are bent on radical change. But it is important to remember what they are up against as compared with the defenders of the *status quo*. Unless the Radicals have the good fortune to come at the end of a long tradition of political initiatives undertaken in the same spirit as their own, their language will be thin, coarse, unsatisfying. The Irish rebels, for example, were lucky to possess both a long history of political revolt and a rich tradition of *cultural* independence; the French revolutionaries less so, for though their actions were a concentrated response to an increasingly widespread language, the language of Rousseau, by itself that language was not rich enough to sustain a *post*-revolutionary culture. Superb though it might be as an instrument for arousing indignation and the passion for liberty, by discrediting the traditional culture as repressive, artificial and hypocritical it left a bleak void which the stage managers of the Revolution did their best to fill with their new calendars and their Festivals of Reason.

It may be objected that, while these symbols may be rather more than shorthand terms, they are still only decorations which for the sake of elegance and ease of recognition follow a common style. The trademark of a firm may be imprinted upon all its products without stirring any deep emotion in the customer; at most the sight of the mark will create a lukewarm preference for that firm's goods, certainly not an intense loyalty. Precisely so; the measure of the mythic importance of a symbol is the power of the emotion which it arouses. We are lukewarm about the firm's trademark because we are lukewarm about the differences between consumer goods, but few of us are lukewarm about revolutions. On the other hand, it is conceivable that a man who had spent his life working for that firm might experience deep emotion on suddenly seeing the old trademark again; the symbol might concentrate, focus all the experience of his working lifetime. In the same way, the attack on the Moncada Barracks or on the Dublin Post Office or on the Tuileries epitomises a whole struggle, a whole history of felt economic and political oppression. That oppression could be given full expression in a vast library of military, parliamentary, economic and social records; but for practical political purposes, for rallying support to a common banner, it can be expressed only by a symbol. The myth must stand for the reality, because the reality is too complex, too hedged with qualifications and contradictions to be capable of bearing the weight of popular aspirations and affections; the myth is sturdy, its story-line simple, its moral unqualified.

The myth has to contain and define the political emotion which it symbolises. Similarly, the rhetoric in which the myth is clothed has to tone in with the political reality, for if there is a clash in any great degree, the myth ceases to be fully effective; instead of *reinforcing* the political emotion, it weakens that emotion by introducing the very note of complexity and doubt which the myth was formulated to avoid. Castro succeeded in establishing his myth in Cuba where Guevara failed in Bolivia, not because the physical, political or economic conditions in the two countries were so markedly different, but because the Bolivian Indians took a different attitude from the Cuban peasants towards those conditions. The mythic blueprint that Guevara had brought with him from the Sierra Maestra did not express the Indians' hopes and fears; to them it was unmistakably a foreign import. Guevara, it seems, did attempt to modify the blueprint as he went along; yet the resulting complexity not only failed to make much impact upon the Indians but tended to weaken the faith of Guevara's own closest supporters.

It is because the myth must correspond to the feelings of the audience that close study of the *nature* of the myth is often more rewarding than the conventional attempts of the anthropologist and sociologist to study the *use* to which the myth is put. For the nature of the myth serves to define *the idea that the audience has of itself.* Peoples reveal in their national myths what kind of people they think they are. In the banal grace of Baldwin's evocation of the English countryside, we feel the secure sense of identity, the basic contentment of a nation which had not been seriously invaded for nearly nine hundred years and which had retained a strong national identity throughout that period. Baldwin writes, for example:

When I think of England when I am abroad, England comes to me through my various senses – through the ear, through the eye, and through certain imperishable scents. . . . The sounds of England, the tinkle of the hammer on the anvil in the country smithy, the corncrake on a dewy morning, the sound of the scythe against the whetstone, and the sight of a plough team coming over the brow of a hill, the sight that has been seen in England since England was a land, and may be seen in England long after the Empire has perished and every works in England has ceased to function, for centuries the one eternal sight of England. The wild anemones in the woods in April, the last load at night of hay being drawn down a lane as the twilight comes on, when you can scarcely distinguish the figures of the horses as they take it home to the farm. . . . These things strike down into the very depths of our nature. . . .[100]

Baldwin conjures up a landscape to be *enjoyed*; it is a gentle, watercolour landscape, the counterpart of the placidity and kindness of the English people; it is also a *permanent* landscape, the product of centuries of peace and security. Nor is this theme a mere rustic archaism. In his long series of speeches on the need for reconciliation in industry – starting well before the General Strike and continuing until his retirement as prime minister eleven years later – which form his most distinctive contribution to English political life, he creates a myth of an equally harmonious industrial past grounded on the experience of his own family ironworks:

It was a place where I knew, and had known from childhood, every man on the ground; a place where I was able to talk with the men not only about the troubles in the works, but troubles at home and their wives. It was a place where strikes and lock-outs were unknown. It was a place where the fathers and grandfathers of the men then working there had worked, and where their sons went automatically into the business.

It was also a place where nobody ever 'got the sack', and where we had a natural sympathy for those who were less concerned in efficiency than is this generation, and where a large number of old gentlemen used to spend their days sitting on the handles of wheelbarrows, smoking their pipes.[101]

Baldwin admits that this harmonious community was highly atypical even in its heyday and not to be found in big industrial towns; moreover, such communities have now been swallowed up in 'one of those great combinations towards which the industries of today are tending'.[102] He dwells on this pleasant picture, therefore, as a deliberate act of myth-making, a sketch of things as they should be, not as a piece of historiography. Baldwin's long and firm hold on power in competition with men who were then and are now regarded as more 'able' illustrates how apposite were the myths he created, how closely they reflected the deepest feelings of his audience. Only if we look at Baldwin in the light of these myths can we begin to understand 'appeasement', the determined rejection of the risk-strategies of Churchill, Lloyd George and Mosley, the peculiar force with which Baldwin used the traditional incumbent's slogan of 'Safety First', and the special revulsion Baldwin and many others felt against the political, financial and amorous manoeuvres of 'the Goat'. Lloyd George was the demon of energy, the infinitely fertile source of ideas, representing boundless possibilities of change; he had come to disturb the landscape, while Baldwin came to cherish it. In that subtle interaction between the political actor and his times (discussed in I. iii) the spirit of the age calls forth the man, but the man then reinforces that spirit, even while he is defining it.

By contrast, the rhetoric of General de Gaulle was born of the insecurity of France, a land blessed by nature for all purposes except military defence and political stability, a land invaded four times in the last hundred and fifty years. Before the war, in *The Army of the Future*,[103] de Gaulle was already defining the elements of his mythical France, a landscape loved and possessed, yes, but for how long? In his call to arms – more precisely, his call to adopt modern military methods – there is a noble evocation of the great moments of French history, an evocation which is yet drenched in an acid, melancholy realism. His prose is indeed an alarum, as poignant and stirring as the sound of Vigny's horn in the depth of the wood, echoing Roland's at Roncesvalles – a national epic in which the nation never stirs until the perpetually recurring eleventh hour:

The rumbling echo of the thunder with which Napoleon overthrew his adversaries is still to be heard. However, of the great conflicts in which our destiny was at stake, how many started calamitously! How many absurd defeats has that evil genius cost us which, at Crécy and Poitiers, made us, faced by the English archers and cavalry, confide our cause to the naïve weapons of chivalry. . . . It is, of course, very fine and very pleasant to discover, in our extremity, Le Grand Ferre, Joan of Arc or Duguesclin, to contrive so well after Saint-Quentin as to drive Philip II from Paris, to be victorious at Denain when everything seemed lost, to frighten the already triumphant Prussians at Valmy, to strike again after Sedan with the mere stump of a sword, to win as if by a miracle the battle of the Marne. Nevertheless, these escapes from the brink of the abyss do not, on the whole, offset the large number of initial errors which make history echo with the agonising cries of our chiefs: the grim orders of the day of Joffre and Gallieni; Gambetta's adjuration: 'Lift up your hearts!'; Danton's outcry: 'The country is in danger'; the sad utterance of Louis XIV: 'There is no happiness in our age!'; Francis I's sorrow: 'All is lost save honour!'; the Maid's tears over 'our piteous condition'; the despair of Philip VI in flight: 'Open the door! It is the wretched king of France!'[104]

Yet for all his fierce urgency, his military pessimism, de Gaulle is secure in his enjoyment of a French national identity. His stance is ironic, even patronising, but none the less affectionate, comparable to though less sentimental than Burke's description of 'the cold sluggishness of our national character'. Comparing the French with the sinister gothic contrasts of the German character, de Gaulle writes of

. . . this Frenchman, who has so much order in his mind and so little in his acts, this logician who doubts everything, this lackadaisical hard worker, this stay-at-home coloniser, this enthusiast about alexandrines, tail-coats and public gardens, who, nevertheless, sings comic songs, goes about in sloppy clothes and strews the grass with litter, this Jacobin shouting 'Long live the Emperor!', this politician who forms the 'Union Sacrée', this man defeated at Charleroi who attacks on the Marne, in short, this fickle, uncertain, contradictory nation. . . .[105]

The name of a great military victory is the most powerful of all symbols at the politician's disposal; not only does it evoke images of pain and suffering, of grief and endurance, of appalling sacrifices of blood and treasure, it recalls a legendary time of simplicity, of a time when it was just us against them and nothing else mattered, a time when 'he that is not with me is against me'. Such a famous battle becomes myth when it is used not so much to define the cause for which it was fought as to define the nation which fought it. De Gaulle concentrates on France alone, the recurring drama of a nation saving her bacon at the last moment by heroic efforts. Hugh Gaitskell used the freshly remembered names of the first world war for a very different purpose. In his great speech to the 1962 Labour Party Conference at Brighton he buttressed a careful argument against Britain's entry into the Common Market with a reminder of what she owed to the 'old' Commonwealth countries: 'When people say, "what did we get out of New Zealand; what did we get out of Australia; what did we get out of Canada?", I remember that they came to our aid at once in two world wars. We, at least, do not intend to forget Vimy Ridge and Gallipoli.' Britain and France were fighting side by side in the first world war, both suffering by far the worst casualties in their history. Yet for de Gaulle the lesson was that France was responsible for looking after her own safety, alliances being useless; for Gaitskell, the lesson was that Britain's true friends were in the old Commonwealth. More remarkable still is that Gaitskell should have used these symbols at all; a purely military application of patriotism had been regarded as more characteristic of Conservative politicians. In fact, Gaitskell showed a sure grasp of his audience; he understood that he was speaking in essentially a conservative cause, the preservation of the *status quo*; it was therefore essential to give life and colour to that cause by the use of conservative symbols drawn from what he called 'a thousand years of history', in other words not social or economic history but the history of national independence, of Agincourt and Waterloo, of Vimy Ridge and Gallipoli. Gaitskell also knew that though these symbols, having little to do with the growth of social democracy, were not much mentioned at Labour Party Conferences, they appealed to Left and Right alike. They were the common heritage of the British people, landmarks on a well-loved and long-possessed landscape.

But the vast majority of peoples have not known until recent years what it is like to possess their landscape, even as insecurely as the French have possessed theirs. We come here to the specifically modern phenomenon of nationalism (superbly described by Elie Kedourie in his book *Nationalism*).[106] Patriotism is the rhetoric of possession and affection; nationalism the rhetoric of dispossession and hatred of the possessing usurpers; Gaullism represents a sort of half-way house in which the edge of enjoyment is sharpened by the perpetual threat of dispossession. Nationalism presupposes patriotism (there must be something worth fighting for) but it preys upon the memory of the lost love. Patriotism is transformed into nationalism at the moment when that loss is rendered conscious. In *Ai giovani d'Italia*, Mazzini rhapsodises over the beauties of the Alps and over the heights of Italian art and spirituality. But the dominant impression is of a grievance seeking its just remedy. He tells the youth of Italy: '*Vio cercate la Patria*'. And it is all the more unjust that they should have to *seek* their Fatherland, '*poveri Israeliti delle Nazioni*', because

La vita di Dio freme in seno alla vostra terra più che altrove potente. Immagini di bellezza e di forza s'avvicendano singolari su questo suolo, dove il Sole accende vulcani, e che gli uomini salutano del nome di Giardino d'Europa. La natura sorride per voi d'un sorriso di donna. I languenti per morbo vengono dalle brume settentrionali a ribever la vita nell'aure balsamiche de' vostri prati, sotto l'azzurro profondo de' vostri cieli.*[107]

The Italians are the children of Israel, the chosen people; their land flows with milk and honey, their air is balm for the consumptive northerners, yet they are deprived of their birthright.

The nationalist is defined by his sense of having suffered the harshest of all injustice, a sense far more immediate and primary than the affection for that which the injustice has stolen from him; what ought to be the purest moment of enjoyment – the contemplation of his native village, say – is tainted, for that moment is not *his*. The pain swallows up the pleasure. The tone of nationalism must always be radical and vehement, like the cry of a man in pain; any measures which can get rid of that pain may be worthwhile, even if those measures involve further pain. Nationalism is therefore a powerful booster rocket for redistributive movements. The notion of economic dispossession is a natural ally to the notion of being dispossessed of one's sense of identity, very nearly of life itself. Indeed, it is often felt that when 'we enter into our own again' we ought to be better off economically too; the right to choose our own government, to kick

* 'You seek a fatherland' . . . 'poor Israelites among nations' . . . 'In your country the divine life burns more strongly in the breast than anywhere else. Images of beauty and strength alternate in a remarkable way on this soil where the sun kindles volcanoes and which men hallow by the name of the Garden of Europe. Nature smiles on you with a woman's smile. Those who are ravaged by disease come from their northern mists to drink in once more the vitality in the balmy breezes of your meadows beneath the deep blue of your Italian sky.'

out foreigners or to worship our own gods may well be experienced as a disappointment, a hollow sham, if it is not accompanied by a satisfactory standard of living. Authoritarian nationalist regimes whose leaders, originally simple soldiers, may have had little initial interest in socialism, frequently introduce an increasingly socialist flavour into the nationalist brew as time goes by. Only thus can the inflamed, all-encompassing sense of grievance be assuaged.

Patriotism on the other hand predisposes its upholders towards conservatism, towards the politics of patching up, of make-do-and-mend, simply because they regard what they already possess as worth repairing rather than replacing. For that reason we must be careful when we place Burke as a forerunner of nineteenth-century nationalism, a theorist of the nation-state, 'to point out that it is of the nation-state *minus* the idea of sovereignty. To pass on to those who first recognised the fact of nationality any of the blame for the numerous excesses committed in its name would be patently unfair.'[108] Burke himself lived in a country where patriotism, despite all the Tom Paines and Dr Prices, was secured as the prevailing value, and when he had to deal with countries less happily placed (America, India, Ireland) he could not believe that sensible reform – the restitution of traditional rights and so on – was not capable of reconstituting a hearty and satisfying patriotism. He could not really imagine the total breakdown of a nation's political harmony, although he was ready intellectually to conceive of situations in which revolution might be justified. As a brilliant observer of men, Burke observed patriotism in action; but he did not observe anything more than the beginnings of nationalism (Paoli's Corsica and the France of the revolutionary wars) because this was all there was to observe at that time. He understood how the spirit of a nation was constituted and approved; he did not fully understand and strongly disapproved of the new, rancorous spirit of nationalism.

SCENE-SHIFTING

We have seen how Burke talks again and again of the difficulty and complexity of political activity. He stresses that this complexity stems from the need 'at once to preserve and reform'. He stresses also the importance of humdrum administrators, because by far the largest part of political activity consists in administering, maintaining and repairing existing institutions.

What is the use of discussing a man's abstract right to food or medicine? The question is upon the method of procuring and administering them. In that deliberation I shall always advise to call in the aid of the farmer and the physician, rather than the professor of metaphysics. . . . The science of government being therefore so practical in itself, and intended for such practical purposes, a matter which requires experience, and even more experience than any person can gain in his whole life, however sagacious and observing he may be, it is with infinite caution that any man ought to venture upon pulling down an edifice which has answered in any tolerable degree for ages the common purposes of society.[109]

Men of business, even solid men of 'inferior understanding' may be better suited to this humdrum activity than 'the aëronauts of France'.

This point has little to do with ideology or principle. It is merely a fact of life that the maintenance of existing social institutions is at least as important as the introduction of new ones. How many millions of pleasant and well-built houses in the western world have been allowed to decay into slums because government failed to alter the structure of housing finance? How many armies have lost crucial battles because their war offices had failed to keep up standards of training, discipline and equipment? And inside politics itself, how many regimes have fallen because they had not bothered to keep in touch with the people? Tocqueville's observations are telling:

I sometimes wonder what in the king's soul could have produced this unanticipated sudden collapse. Louis-Philippe's life had been passed amid revolutions, and he certainly lacked neither experience, nor courage, nor intelligence, although all those qualities deserted him on that day. I think his weakness was due to the intensity of his astonishment; he was knocked flat, unaware of what had hit him. The February Revolution was *unforeseen* by everybody, but by him most of all; no warning from the outside had prepared him for it, for his mind had retreated long ago into the sort of haughty loneliness inhabited by almost all kings whose long reigns have been prosperous, who mistake luck for genius, and who do not want to listen to anybody, because they think they have no more to learn.[110]

What Tocqueville describes is a classic failure in maintenance, a failure in the humdrum capacity to keep one's eyes and ears open.

It cannot be denied that this is a tedious and exhausting process, because it is so relentlessly continuous. There is no end to it, no moment at which the politician can say 'There, now it is finished'. It used to be said that the workmen never finished painting the Forth railway bridge; as soon as they had got to one end they had to start again at the other. They never finished, but equally they were never starting right from scratch; at all times by far the greater part of the bridge would have an adequate coat of paint, though that greater part would never be exactly the same stretch of the bridge. The maintenance of political institutions is a similar continuously flowing task within a hard, finite structure. As Burke says: 'Thus, by preserving the method of Nature in the conduct of the state, in what we improve we are never wholly new, in what we retain we are never wholly obsolete.'[111]

Here again it would seem that the duties of Burke's 'skilful workman' approach those of Popper's engineer. Are not both to adopt a piecemeal, pragmatic approach to the problems that confront them? But once again there is a great difference in the *attitude* in which workman and engineer start work, although in many instances the work done will take very much the same form because of the dictates of practical life. The workman is dedicated to maintenance and repair; the engineer to change and innovation. Only with the greatest reluctance will the workman conclude that a considerable portion of the fabric is rotten and must be torn out and rebuilt.

This difference in attitude has remarkable results. As soon as the innovation, the reform itself, becomes the centre of interest rather than the social area which is being reformed, it bulks larger than it should; exaggerated claims are made for it, while its opponents prophesy disaster if the reform is brought into operation. The whole public dialogue tends increasingly to be conducted on the premise that a constant procession of reforms is the mark of effective and responsive government; the public appetite for innovation is perpetually stimulated, in the same way that the popular press, by virtue of its format, has to 'create' a headline story every day.

The rule of traditional affection can be replaced only by the rule of novelty. For as we said earlier, the theatre lives by shock or novelty and by sentiment. And if we cannot have sentiment, then we must have shock. 'There must be a great change of scene; there must be a magnificent stage effect; there must be a grand spectacle to rouse the imagination, grown torpid with the lazy enjoyment of sixty years security and the still unanimating repose of public prosperity.'[112] The shifting of the scenes becomes an art in itself, regardless of the merit of the scenes presented. And as Burke points out, this makes for the worst theatre possible, so bad in fact that it would not be allowed on the stage. 'No theatric audience in Athens would bear what has been borne, in the midst of the real tragedy of this triumphal day; a principal actor weighing, as it were in scales hung in a shop of horrors – so much actual crime against so much contingent advantages – and after putting in and out weights, declaring that the balance was on the side of the advantages.'[113] Politics bears all too close a resemblance to bad theatre, as we said at the beginning of this work; and the closer politics approaches to melodrama, the worse for the audience; and the more the dramatist and the actors respect not only the classical unities but also the traditional virtues, of clarity, restraint and truth to life, the better. For once the professionals – actors, writers, producers – have started competing in melodrama, they will find it increasingly difficult to satisfy their audiences.

Mr Hume told me, that he had from Rousseau himself the secret of his principles of composition. That acute, though eccentric observer had perceived that to strike and interest the public, the marvellous must be produced; that the marvellous of the heathen mythology had long since lost its effect; that giants, magicians, fairies and heroes of romance which succeeded, had exhausted the portion of credulity which belonged to their age; that now nothing was left to a writer but that species of the marvellous, which might still be produced, and with great an effect as ever though in another way; that is, the marvellous in life, in manners, in characters and in extraordinary situations, giving rise to new and un-looked-for strokes in politics and morals.[114]

Burke himself was acutely sensitive to what he regarded as the perversion of the naturally theatrical element in politics, namely rhetoric, because it was liable to infect the whole body politic:

. . . a theatrical, bombastick, windy phraseology of heroick virtue, blended and mingled up with a worse dissoluteness, and joined to a murderous and savage ferocity, forms the tone and idiom of their language and their manners.[115]

Statesmen, like your present rulers, exist by every thing which is spurious, fictitious, and false; by everything which takes the man from his house, and sets him in a stage, which makes him up an artificial creature, with painted theatrick sentiments, fit to be seen by the glare of candle-light, and formed to be contemplated at a due distance. . . . If the system of institution recommended by the assembly is false and theatrick it is because their system of government is of the same character.[116]

Under the influence of Rousseau, the philosopher of vanity, the ordinary moral duties of life, the humble responsibilities of home and family, are neglected in favour of public posturing; 'thousands admire the sentimental writer; the affectionate father is hardly known in his parish'.[117] Political aims are now of interest not for their own sake but merely for the excitement they cause the political actor.

Guizot claimed that

> ... the French Revolution and the Emperor Napoleon I have thrown a certain number of minds, including some of the most distinguished, into a feverish excitement which becomes a moral and, I would almost say, a mental disease. They yearn for events, immense, sudden and strange; they busy themselves with making and unmaking governments, nations, religions, society, Europe, the world . . . they are intoxicated with the greatness of their design, and blind to the chances of success.[118]

It is this task of shifting the scenes which alone is studied by the modern revolutionary. One mechanical skill usurps the pride of place once jointly shared by actor, dramatist and producer. Burke saw 'a scene-shifter's theatre' as an inevitable consequence of an age obsessed by novelty.

In many respects Burke failed to grasp that this obsession was an inevitable response to major social changes: in Britain industrialisation, in France the decay of the old political structure. But he did grasp as nobody else did the consequences of that obsession. It is strange indeed that Professor Hampshire should assert that 'he saw less far into the future than the philosophical Radicals and the men of the Enlightenment, less far certainly than Condorcet.'[119] We leave aside the circumstance that Condorcet did not see far enough to prevent his own suicide in the shadow of the scaffold. But where in Condorcet is there an insight to match Burke's prediction of the coming of Napoleon?

> In the weakness of one kind of authority, and in the fluctuation of all, the officers of an army will remain for some time mutinous and full of faction, until some popular general, who understands the art of conciliating the soldiery, and who possesses the true spirit of command, shall draw the eyes of all men upon himself. Armies will obey him on his personal account. There is no other way of securing military obedience in this state of things. But the moment in which that event shall happen, the person who really commands the army is your master; the master (that is little) of your king, the master of your assembly, the master of your whole republic.[120]

And where do we find in the philosophical Radicals and the men of the Enlightenment so sharply conceived a picture of the tyranny of the majority, an adumbration of the Darkness at Noon which has so shadowed our century?

Of this I am certain, that in a democracy, the majority of the citizens is capable of exercising the most cruel oppressions upon the minority, whenever strong division prevail in that kind of polity, as they often must; and that oppression of the minority will extend to far greater numbers, and will be carried on with much greater fury, than can almost ever be apprehended from the domination of a single sceptre. In such a popular persecution, individual sufferers are in a much more deplorable condition than in any other. Under a cruel prince they have the balmy compassion of mankind to assuage the smart of their wounds; they have the plaudits of the people to animate their generous constancy under their sufferings: but those who are subjected to wrong under multitudes, are deprived of all external consolation. They seem deserted by mankind; overpowered by a conspiracy of their whole species.[121]

The man on the white horse, the division of a nation into black and white, into sheep and goats – these are the finales of a theatre of novelty. For the climax of such a theatre must be stark, awesome and above all *simple*. The spotlight plays on the lone, compact figure of Napoleon; Lenin's neat, round dome and trimmed beard stand out against the hubbub, blood and smoke.

By contrast, change in the theatre of sentiment occurs gradually. For the theatre of sentiment relies on a universe of discourse shared by both actors and audience. Indeed, without some notion of what that universe is or was we can hardly begin to understand a particular play. Here the distance between our theatrical terminology and the language of political history becomes minimal. Without understanding the concept of Divine Right the dramatic tension of Shakespeare's Richard II is no easier to appreciate than is the history of the Stuarts or of Richard II himself. The traditional theatres of Japan, the nationalist, propagandist theatre of Mao's China, the *bürgerliches Trauerspiel* of late eighteenth- and nineteenth-century Germany, the patriotism and obsession with honour of Cornelian tragedy, all rely for their effect on the understanding of a common language. This language may consist merely in the political slogans of the day, or it may reflect moral and spiritual norms of great power and antiquity; but it is essential that it be understood. And the more deeply this language expresses the prejudices of the audience, the more closely its syntax and vocabulary correspond to the audience's view of the world, the more powerful and lasting its effect. And by the same token, the deeper the language the more impossible it becomes to change it overnight.

New themes emerge slowly, reflecting but only rarely effecting gradual changes in the consciousness of the audience. The rise of nationalism and hence of patriotism as a great moral force, the increasing dominance of charity over chastity as a guide in human relationships, the decline of religion as a practical force in human affairs – all reflect when presented on the stage changes in social realities which have already taken place. The theatre interprets the way we live now; seldom does it tell us how we shall or should be living in the future. And when it does attempt to do so, its force is the force of shock and not sentiment; it therefore tends to terrify rather than to move us. In this sense the theatre is a reflector of social reality rather than a creator of new social reality even by comparison with other arts. The humanitarian themes of Shaw and Ibsen had already been developed throughout the nineteenth century in novels and social philosophy. Despair, alienation, the feeling of nullity – even when expressed with the greatest power by Beckett – have merely brought to the stage in the last thirty years one of the central themes of the Modern Movement in poetry and painting from the turn of the century onwards. The sources of the Theatre of Violence have an even longer history; interest in Sade is revived by the experience of violence in our time.

This very general point is not modified by the fact that some great artists have written for the theatre. Their work inside the medium tends either to be tame and ineffective compared with their work outside it (compare *The Cenci* with the rest of Shelley, *The Cocktail Party* with *The Waste Land*); or as in the case of Shakespeare and Goethe the aim is on the whole to deepen rather than to change the audience's consciousness. The great genius is still talking the familiar language.

It may further be remarked that any attempts to go even a little way beyond that language produce immediate shock and outrage in the audience. Witness the scandals created by the opening of *Ernani*, by Shaw's use of 'bloody' in *Pygmalion*, by Ibsen's use of hereditary syphilis, by the opacity of *Waiting for Godot*. Yet these techniques and references were already commonplace in other arts.

The audience exercises a strong and continuous pressure in favour of the familiar, the comprehensible and the conventional. Even such progressives as Senator Robert Kennedy, in their struggles 'to move a nation', are forced to admit that the nation is very conservative. The experimental theatre, as we said, usually has to receive a state subsidy.

By talking of the 'commercial pressures' on the playwright, we are merely indicating in a dry fashion this necessary relation between actor and audience.

II

The Language of Change

How then do we or should we innovate in politics? Let us consider Oakeshott's celebrated view:

> In political activity, then, men sail a boundless and bottomless sea: there is neither harbour for shelter nor floor for anchorage, neither starting-place nor appointed destination. The enterprise is to keep afloat on an even keel; the sea is both friend and enemy; and the seamanship consists in using the resources of a traditional manner of behaviour in order to make a friend of every hostile occasion.[1]

The Radical objections to such a view of politics as navigation may be subsumed under the heading of charges of 'opportunism'. R. H. S. Crossman raises this point typically in a critique of Oakeshott:

> A conservative political education, wedded to no principles and contemptuous of theory, is an essential element in a free society. It is right that the democrat should study its boneless anatomy and he can even admire the mystique which transforms opportunism into a political virtue. But it never seems to occur to Professor Oakeshott that this kind of politics ossifies into reaction unless it is constantly challenged by men who will fight for theories and movements that will fight for principles *before* they are accepted as respectable parts of our national tradition.[2]

The argument is informal and imprecise, but perhaps the more revealing for that reason. We may divide the general charge into three more precise (though not necessarily consistent) objections:

First – that politics-as-navigation is reactionary. It reacts against the tides of history and gives in only at the last possible moment. This objection is valid only for politics-as-bad-navigation. The good sailor makes the fullest possible use of winds and tides; no one is more alert than he for the slightest indications of the weather to come.

Second – very well then, if politics-as-navigation does not react *against* the tides of history (we mean circumstances and trends, not any Hegelian process), it only reacts *to* these tides. Conservatism is

199

unprincipled. Such an objection is not of course raised by Radicals alone; it is the substance of Disraeli's attack on Peel. We may well accept that bad navigation is likely to lack any clear grasp of principle. But good navigation is guided not by one but by several principles; and the art, if you like, of the business is to get the soundest balance between them when they conflict. The dichotomy between principle and expediency is, as we have said, falsely drawn. What is damned by its opponents as expediency may very well be a different kind of principle; for example, national reconciliation may be rated as a more desirable goal than free enterprise. Conservatism, therefore, is unprincipled only in the sense that its principles are not necessarily placed in the same order or pursued with equal vigour at different times. We may expect the rule of law, freedom of speech and private property to appear regularly at the top of the list; but all of them are capable of abatement, or even suspension, in time of national danger. National survival, national independence, national prosperity and national honour; the *relative* importance of even these principles also must vary with the exigencies of the times.

Third – even if it is conceded that the conservative is guided by a variety of principles whose relative prominence varies according to the situation, it may be claimed that the conservative is incapable of the building of theories and models which alone can stir change for the better in a stagnant or positively putrescent situation. There are, it is said, cases where only a leap of the imagination can bring us out of what seems a hopeless quagmire. So there are, though the Conservative would maintain that there are fewer of them than the Radical thinks. Most reforms are a long time in the making. Either matters are improved step by step whenever time, inclination and resources coincide: we may take the social services as an example. Or the reform is actually effected at one bound, after it has been elaborated, updated and popularised in debate over a period of years. (Examples: the abolition of slavery and capital punishment, votes for women, the abolition of resale price maintenance.) At what point then does the Radical maintain that the imaginative leap is taken? Certainly not at the point when a bill becomes law; long before that, the proposed reform has become part of the currency of debate and for its supporters may have even become part of the conventional wisdom.

Here we come to the crucial counter-objection to Mr Crossman – the question of *timing*. They sound admirable, these men 'who will fight for theories and movements that will fight for principles *before* they are accepted as respectable parts of our national tradition'. The picture conjured up is of a small handful of men with an eye for injustice and a passion for justice who, *from scratch*, discover something that is wrong, work out a way of putting it right, found a political movement to agitate for action and see that action through until it is incorporated into the legal and social framework. Yet is such a process typical? Surely in reality the righting of a major social ill (even one which can be righted by one legislative stroke, rather than by a hard-won increase in prosperity of the community) takes much longer and involves a very much larger cast of characters, which varies in numbers, energy and composition from decade to decade. The movement, say, for colonial independence can be traced back, in Britain's case at least, almost to the original setting up of the colonies. Crossman's repeated use of 'fight' in such a connection obscures more than it illuminates; the battle paradigm is hardly adequate to describe such a complex, shifting notion as the citizen's attitude towards his country's colonies, which may contain within it, for example, traces of all the following propositions:

– Colonies offer markets for our manufactures and hence increase our standard of living.

– Colonies provide opportunities for our restless young men.

– Colonies are a drain on our Exchequer.

– We should stop sending our young men overseas to die in native wars. The natives' quarrels are not ours.

– The welfare of native populations is the white man's burden. We have a duty to educate, civilise and industrialise them.

– The natives will get on better by themselves. We should leave them to pull themselves up by their own bootstraps.

– Every nation has a right to govern itself.

Each of these various propositions or questions is morally and practically tenable by itself; each has in fact been held by people of all kinds – politicians, economists, fishwives, steelworkers, filing clerks – at all times in every colonial power in the modern age. It is the *mixture* of prevailing propositions at any one time which determines the course of political events; the dialogue is structured by the language in which it is conducted.

The pamphleteers who are 'fighting' for one of these propositions – say, colonial independence – are certainly one element in that language. Anti-colonialism has always been 'a respectable part of our national tradition'. But circumstances such as the military and financial exhaustion of the colonial power have at least as important an effect on the final resolution of the colonial dialogue.

Crossman's implicit assumption is that a radical *invents* a language which he then teaches people to talk. Such indeed is the assumption, to a greater or lesser degree, of all Radicals. It is false in several ways.

(1) The new language will be derived both in syntax and vocabulary from previous languages. A totally new language which awakened no familiar echoes of previous linguistic experience would be that bizarre philosopher's construct, a private language. And nowhere is the notion of a private language more bizarre than in the public world of politics.

(2) In any case, the politician is not a teacher/lecturer. He is an actor. We can and do boo his new language off the stage if either he or it strikes us as foolish, outlandish, impractical or irrelevant.

(3) Even if we are willing in some degree to learn the new language, we may not be capable of doing so. The theatregoer may be avid for illumination but his existing language of experience may be unable to cope with the *avant-garde* play. With computers, for example, it has come to be seen that the real difficulty is not to invent a new language or to refine it to deal with the complexities of life but to make it a useful tool for laymen. The initial expense of installing computers is bad enough but the cost of training more and more programmers may make the whole operation uneconomic. We have now reached the stage where even enthusiasts for computers are beginning to doubt whether there are enough people capable of being trained to operate them. Is the pool of talent large enough to irrigate the garden of numeracy?

The language of change, like any other language, grows out of our experience. Just as it is not linguists but laymen who alter and develop our daily speech, so it is not ideologists but ordinary people 'who explore and pursue the intimations of a tradition of behaviour'.[3]

How then, for example, do Communists, who themselves glory in the task of restructuring our consciousness, gain power? By exaggerating and hence distorting a genuine intimation – the feeling that the existing political structure is rotten – by 'abridging a tradition of behaviour into a scheme of abstract ideas'.[4] The recollection of this genuine intimation helps to legitimise the distortion and engenders some degree of consent to its imposition by force. Without the use of force (which is to say, without the suppression of other intimations) the scheme of abstract ideas would remain merely an extreme linguistic hypothesis, an academic curiosity. It is as if the *Académie Française*, instead of just expressing a vague popular feeling against the dilution of the French language by Anglicisms, were not merely to proclaim that French national culture could be sustained only by a rigid exclusion of all foreign words but also to launch a mass crusade to bring this about, to seize power, and then to enforce laws forbidding the use of any word not in the *Académie*'s dictionary. This would be drastic medicine, but it would be the only way to prevent ordinary Frenchmen from developing their language to suit their own experience.

Politicians who renounce the use of force to impose a new language have to use the language of their own times even when they are claiming to be at their most original and unorthodox. This is largely true also of those who do not abjure the forcible restructuring of the public consciousness. Even so powerful and original a system as that of Marx derives most of its constituent elements – class warfare, the labour theory of value – from previous thinkers, such as Saint-Simon and the classical economists. The new thrust given to these elements by Marx's formidable capacity for intellectual organisation, combination and elaboration itself gained added momentum from the pace of the times; the Paris of the 1840s, the Paris of Bakunin, Proudhon, Heine and Herzen, added new phrases, whole sentences indeed to Marx's intellectual vocabulary, which had already been refitted with Hegelian jargon in Berlin.

Now if it is existing society which furnishes the intellectual vocabulary of a revolutionary who wishes to demolish the basis of that society, how much more is that vocabulary 'given' in the case of a gradualist reformer who respects the existing fabric and at least some of the already stated purposes of that society. This 'givenness' is made still more intense by the dictates of practical politics; that is to say, the more closely a reformer is concerned with the actual conduct of public affairs, the more completely and irresistibly his intellectual vocabulary is formed for him – by public opinion and debate, by incessant conversation with his colleagues and advisers, by the pressure of work which pushes him to choose always the ready-made solution; such originality as it is possible to achieve in the analysis of political problems demands a degree of detachment and of genuine leisure for thought which the practical politician is either loath or unable to secure.

This phenomenon of the givenness of a political language is nothing new, nor is it limited to a particular type of society; an articulate political community demands and develops such a language. Tocqueville describes brilliantly how

... When the peculiar language of Diderot and Rousseau had had time to spread and mingle with the vulgar tongue, the false sensibility, with which the works of those writers are filled, infected the administrators and reached even the financiers. The official style, usually so dry in its texture, has become more unctuous and even tender.[5]

Georgiana, Duchess of Devonshire, loved Rousseau's *Confessions*, their 'romantick sincerity and candour', 'their language and sentiments that inchant'. And she was not alone in her excited response. 'In Rome, everyone I saw was talking of it'.[6]

A change in language cannot be dismissed as a question of 'mere' fashion any more than, say, the fashion for nudity in the theatre could be dismissed as a trivial phenomenon of no more account than the refurbishing of a safety curtain; such a change both betokens and furthers a significant change in attitudes. Tocqueville notes that 'considerably before the Revolution, the edicts of Louis XVI frequently spoke of the law of nature and the rights of man'.[7] The revolution inside Versailles had been no less dramatic than the revolution outside; and the last few years before the Revolution saw a flood of social and constitutional changes which were initiated by the monarch and which, in shattering the last stable elements in the existing system, left that system defenceless.

In our own time, how far-reaching in their effects upon events have been the notions of 'growth', 'affluence', 'incomes policy', 'environmental pollution', and so on. Let us look more closely at one example of the influence of political language upon events.

FASHIONS IN PLANNING

In his books *Reconstruction*[8] and *The Middle Way*,[9] Harold Macmillan won a reputation as a Tory of fire, energy and independent judgment. He consolidated that reputation from the Conservative backbenches, launching vigorous assaults upon his party's leaders, describing them on one occasion as 'disused slag-heaps' – a phrase echoing Disraeli's 'exhausted volcanoes'. In his strong stand against 'appeasement' and his passionate denunciation of unemployment and industrial stagnation, Macmillan has come down to us as the epitome of the Good Thirties Tory. And indeed *Reconstruction* and *The Middle Way* do exhibit the characteristics which their author's admirers have claimed for them, in a way that, for example, Macmillan's own claims to have been one of the first to grasp the European vision after 1945 do not. Macmillan in the 1930s expresses genuine concern for the unemployed and the underemployed. He grasps the problems of the industrialists who are forced into suicidal price-cutting. He deplores the short-sightedness of the nations which compete in protecting their own industries. His writings are as much an exercise in the communication of sympathy as in the analysis of a crisis. They, like the writing of many politicians, read as a sustained and highly personalised speech to a very diverse audience. Let us briefly summarise his arguments.

In *Reconstruction* Macmillan says that the old economic system has failed. There is a disequilibrium in production. The only answer is planning, which he defines as 'the attempt to regulate production in accordance with effective demand'.[10] This entails protection from foreign competition and 'regulative powers amounting to monopoly' for efficiently organised and integrated national industries.[11] Each industry would thus be regulated by a council of wise men who would keep prices and profits steady by keeping production in step with demand and preventing excessive numbers of new firms entering the industry. Macmillan also includes a brief and vague section on the coordination of financial, industrial and political policy. And he does refer to an earlier proposal of his own for a brief monetary reflation through public works. But otherwise he seems unconcerned to demonstrate that his remedy will work; his only worry seems to be that he might be accused of advocating Socialism. This strikes us as strange, because what he describes seems to be government-approved cartelism. No question of responsibility either to the consumer or to Parliament and only token representation for the trade unions on industrial councils – this is hardly Socialism! It can of course be argued that a well-organised indolent cartel is riper for eventual nationalisation than a highly competitive and vociferous industry. But, as a matter of definition, cartelism is, to Socialists at least, the very antithesis of Socialism. To what most people would argue the greater danger – of exploitation by the cartel – Macmillan offers only a brief and blithe reply: 'It is unlikely that any industrial council would lightly incur the charge of being guilty in the suppression of inventions.'[12] Such phrases have a sinister ring today.

In *The Middle Way*, Macmillan offers a fuller exposition. We are not here concerned with his views about the welfare state, nor with his somewhat woolly efforts to define a middle way between collectivism and individualism. 'Economic reconstruction', Macmillan argues, 'is the only sound future basis of social reform.'[13] How is this to be done? First, through a modicum of protection. But much more importantly through the government-organised but industry-run cartels described in *Reconstruction*. Macmillan sees that the volume of credit and the quantity of money have something to do with the case, but he says they 'should be regulated in accordance with the needs of the productive system and not dominated by irrational and antisocial speculation in the fluctuating value of securities'.[14] Macmillan's answer to the latter problem is simple: set up a National Investment Board to rule the Bank of England and the Stock Exchange. The Board would deal only in the shares of *established* enterprises, leaving the private investor to finance new enterprise; the National Investment Board would in effect act as monopoly broker, jobber and issuing bank, a monster cartel of all the large companies in the city. In other words, the National Investment Board is simply an extension of the principle already laid down for industry. Macmillan offers no monetary or fiscal policy as such. Nor indeed does he offer any very clear explanation of why his cartelism should revive industry, let alone remedy the deficiencies in the fiscal and monetary fields. True, Macmillan believes that 'our problem . . . is primarily a production problem'.[15] But he does admit that 'there can be no general over-production until all the demands of man have been satisfied'.[16] Why then does he gloomily advocate a policy which would on balance reduce production? Because of a disequilibrium, because too much of commodity X is being produced, thus driving down the price and driving firms into bankruptcy and men into low wages and unemployment, while commodity Y is in short supply. Then, says Macmillan, the surviving firms put up their prices and profits again, thus attracting new entrants into the X industry and driving the price down again. This is what Macmillan describes as 'disorderly competition', with all the disapproval of a magistrate describing a disorderly house. It is, to present-day ears, also an extremely improbable form of competition. We are more accustomed to attribute the failure of a big firm to a failure in cost control (Rolls-Royce), a fall in demand for its product (ship yards) or as the consequence of a fall in the general level of demand (domestic appliances), not to this ruthless price war which Macmillan sees as paradigmatic. When a small firm fails we tend to blame either fiscal/monetary policy (the garage) or the greater efficiency of its bigger competitors (small shopkeepers). Such bankruptcies, whether big or small, eliminate the 'disequilibrium' with little or no resort to cutting of prices or wages; the quality of the articles produced and the efficiency of the producer are usually the determining factor. Nor is it likely that the prospect of bigger profits would induce enough new entrants into the industry to restore the disequilibrium. The market leverage of the established firms is enough to keep them out, unless of course the new entrants have some new or improved type of good or service to offer. We do not need to delve into the industrial history of the 1930s and argue to what extent there was a disequilibrium of production (if indeed this is a valid concept at all). It is sufficient merely to show that Macmillan's version of the self-defeating business cycle is not axiomatic, as he by virtue of his presentation seems to imagine it is.

We live in a different and, on the whole, more cheerful age. We are exercised by the dangers of going too fast – technological change, inflation – rather than by the dangers of social and economic stagnation. No doubt our problems give us an equally distorted vision in confronting reality. For example, our present worries about the monopoly bargaining power of the trade unions may seem quite ill-formulated to a later age. At the same time, we should be able to see with some clarity the fashionable fallacies of the 1930s. The possibility that we may not be able to learn from history because the same question never recurs in the same form does not prevent us from a proper analysis of past errors.

What is immediately striking is the way in which supposedly eccentric thinkers often appear to a later age to have been the very centrists of their time. Seen from a long way off, the big fish rising may scarcely seem to break the smooth surface. Macmillan's cartelism, though propounded by himself as a daring and dynamic breakaway from the ruling conventional thinkers, was in fact merely an energetically universalised version of what was happening gradually under the conventional leaders. 'Informed opinion' at the time was very largely in agreement with Macmillan, as Macmillan himself admits with charming *naïveté:*

The task of reconstruction is not one which is foreign to, or in conflict with, the opinion of the enlightened leaders of industry. It is a task which they have been attempting to perform themselves. The Amalgamations, Cartels, Producers' Agreements, Centralised Selling Agencies and the like, which have been formed in recent years, are evidence of the fact that industrialists recognise the need of integration, coordination, and regulation in the changed circumstances with which they are confronted.[17]

Exactly so. Huddle together, crowd out the small fry, keep up the prices and carve up the profits – just as Marx predicted. If industrialists themselves were arguing on these lines, surely that might induce Macmillan to take a more detached view of the situation and attempt a deeper analysis. But no. The truth is that monopolies were the fashion in the 1930s, either in the form of cartels (Macmillan and big business) Morrisonian state corporations (Social Democrats and Socialists) or producers' soviets (varying definitions from Trotskyists and other brands of Marxists). All were agreed that production – its ownership, control and organisation – was at the root of the problem and that the only solution was to rationalise production by eliminating 'disorderly' competition. Nobody liked competition. Everyone believed that it led to collective and individual impoverishment with only a few gainers at the expense of the many. Even those like Macmillan who were nominal defenders of private enterprise, though not necessarily of 'Capitalism', could murmur no more than a few embarrassed words in favour of competition's supposed merits – its promotion of innovation and choice and its spur to quality. Many indeed of these merits – price competition for example – were not regarded as merits in the 1930s.

To most people today the world looks very different. There has been such a tremendous upsurge in prosperity, which has coincided so strikingly with the return of peacetime competition and accelerated with its increasing intensity and diversity, that it is hard not to see some connection between the two. Social Democrats throughout Europe now accept a 'mixed economy' and expect the main thrust for improvement to come from the most competitive sector of private industry. Yet within this general tendency we have just witnessed the decline of a counter-tendency among public men, similar in direction to though far smaller in impact than the prevailing tendency of the 1930s. In Britain, Macmillan gave 'planning' renewed emphasis in the later years of his premiership; the concept was institutionalised in the National Economic Development Council, in the National Incomes

Commission and in Lord Hailsham's appointment as minister for the north-east, a run-down area with a persistently high level of unemployment. Harold Wilson retained the National Economic Development Council, inflated the National Incomes Commission into the Prices and Incomes Board, and founded an Industrial Reorganisation Corporation with large sums of public money at its disposal for the promotion of mergers. The founding of the Department of Economic Affairs and the National Plan which it produced were based on a similar belief in 'planning'. Most of these bodies are now either abolished or diminished in importance. Most of the proposals for the extension of 'planning' in current political debate relate to fields where it has not previously been tried: for example, the proposals in the Labour Party's Agenda for a Generation[18] for a National Investment Board to help 'public understanding and awareness of investment trends and patterns'; for 'the use of the Industrial Expansion Act to create New Industrial Boards, on the lines of the Shipbuilding Board, for other industries where crucial structural reform must come'; and 'for the establishment of a new State Holding Company as the base for seizing new economic opportunities, including those in the development areas.' Of these many bodies, Macmillan in *The Middle Way* thirty years ago urged in so many words the need for: NEDC, IRC, the National Plan, the Industrial Boards and the National Investment Board. In some cases, his blueprints for these bodies were rather different from their modern form; but the point is that they were covering the same ground.

Now the truth is that none of these bodies have had any marked success. Some have had no observable effect at all, such as NEDC and the DEA; others, such as the boards and public corporations set up to take over or reorganise various industries, have sometimes made the best of a bad job. But it would be a bold thesis to claim that, say, the cotton or the shipbuilding industry would be much worse off if the *government* had never attempted to rationalise it (we are not dealing here with the crucial question of protection against foreign competition). The search goes on for suitable new state schemes of 'coordination', 'regulation' or 'rationalisation', but with a good deal less enthusiasm than before. Yet the interesting question is why the search should go on at all. The experience of recent years would, one might think, lead to cries for sharper, more general competition. Naturally it would be the government's duty gently to pick up the casualties by means of welfare benefits and the luring of new factories to areas where the old ones had closed down. But in general the lesson of recent years would seem to be that it is best for governments to leave industries to find their own feet, giving them a nudge here and there and keeping a watchful eye on the social and financial aspects of industrial life. Why then does this enthusiasm for 'planning' persist?

One simple answer is that collectivism/Socialism/Marxism is such a powerful general idea that it is bound to leave a strong mark long after many of its original supporting arguments have faded away. It appeals most strongly in bad times, when a large number of people despair of righting the situation by mere tinkering. But it has also the general appeal of a system in a systemless age. We need not predicate any great natural human longing for a theology to account for this; the age-old instinct for novelty and for simplicity of thought will suffice. A system which is new, simple and all-explaining is hardly likely to fail to gain devotees.

But what has led Macmillan himself to accept this analysis which is ultimately incorrect? He was a man of his time, he talked the political language of the day, yes; yet he did not lack the courage to speak his own mind. And besides, if he was to be a rebel, he might as well have gone the whole hog. Moreover, this intelligent and cultivated man is aware of other possible remedies, fiscal and monetary policies, which were already being widely discussed. Why does he attach such a low priority to the latter and such a high one to the former? Why should he have chosen what would seem to us the less effective, if not positively ineffective, courses of action? Let us cast around for a few clues.

POLITICAL RELEVANCE

In the middle of an otherwise unremarkable argument in the writing of Macmillan (or of almost any other politician) the reader is liable to come across a forest of I's. 'It seems to me. . . . I have already said. . . . I have no doubt. . . . I believe. . . . When I was in X-land I found. . . . I think. . . .' This extraordinarily frequent use of the first person by politicians is particularly startling, not to say jarring, when it pops up in the sober pages of a treatise on economics, where we are accustomed to 'It seems. . . . It has already been stated. . . . There is no doubt that. . . . It is believed. . . . Research in X-land has shown. . . . It is widely held. . . .' This difference between the politician and the scholar is more than a question of manners or modesty. It is crucial.

The politician sits down to write a book which will win the applause of the scholars. He believes that to do this he must imitate their impersonal manner. Yet he is incapable of forgetting the audience who put him where he is. If he had never captured an audience of supporters, voters and people who at least know his name, who would bother to publish his book, which may well be of inferior quality, being rushed and based on but scanty research? The professor, on the other hand, has his professional title, the respect of his colleagues and the reflected glory of previous contributions to scholarship. The politician, having only his audience, may be a little excused for thinking of them occasionally, his irrepressible ego popping up to shout 'It's me! I'm here underneath all this stuff, the interpolations of my research assistant, the chunks quoted from ill-digested authority. It's me!' Of course, the politician believes that he is engaging in a thorough analysis of the problem in hand. But time and again he is constrained to 'make my own position clear'. He must strike a political posture. He must communicate with the audience.

It may be said that this pressure to communicate, to personalise, does not necessarily entail an acceptance of fashionable remedies, that, granted a certain oratorical top-dressing, what is in essence a political speech can contain a thorough analysis of a situation. This may on occasion be so.

But in the case of Macmillan it is not so. And it is not so in the case of most thinking politicians, still less so in the case of the unthinking. The political dialogue seems to impose extreme distortions upon analytical thought, even in activities where the dialogue is only, so to speak, a professional reflex. These distortions go deeper than the technical need to make one's voice carry to the top row of the gallery. That is mere elocution. Gielgud could make the gallery hear every syllable of *Principia Mathematica*, but he could not make them understand, let alone applaud it. Yet a successful political dialogue must do both. For political dialogue is persuasion. The thesis must be simple enough to be understood by a very large number of people whose knowledge of the topic may be minimal. It must also, to some extent, agree with or be made to seem to agree with the views that they already hold. If it does not, it will be booed off the stage.

Here we have already two potent distortions: the need to simplify matters which may not be at all simple and the need to make the proposed action in some way palatable. Even where the proposals are unpalatable – for example, proposals for economic stringency – they must be related to some deeper level of supposed agreement between speaker and audience: 'None of us likes having to tighten our belts, but we all know that in difficult times we have to accept austerity in order to build future prosperity. I do not believe that the British people will shirk their duty when the facts are placed in full before them.' It takes a master to present an analysis which survives such distortions. But there is another kind of distortion, more subtle and less often mentioned, but equally potent. It is the distortion engendered by the need to make an analysis seem 'relevant'. This epithet, much over-used in political discussion, is nevertheless precise. A 'relevant' plan is one which applies to the situation in its context. When a plan applies to all situations of a certain type, whatever the time and place, we would not think of calling it 'relevant'; we would be more likely to describe it as 'correct' or 'right'. As contemporaneity is what distinguishes relevance from other attributes of approval, it becomes bound up with fashion. We may become more interested in the connection between the proposal and our own times in general than in the connection between the proposal and the particular situation with which it purports to deal. For example, the case for sex education in schools at an early age is often supported by such statements as these:

One would have thought that now, as 1970 approaches, people would have woken up to the fact that we live in the twentieth century and that the days of Victorian prudery and hypocrisy are past. . . . Sex is as natural a part of life as drinking tea and going to work. And few things are more harmful to a developing child than a 'sweep-it-under the carpet' attitude.[19]

Such statements assume that the task is to make sex education relevant to existing society. They are to be distinguished from other statements which may be made in support of the same cause such as:
– Children should have proper scientific knowledge of the way their bodies work.
– Children should learn the facts before they are emotionally involved in the problems of puberty.
These latter propositions are of course also born of the age in which they are asserted. A society which did not believe in the freedom of scientific enquiry might find them puzzling or repellent. But those who assert them today would claim that their application was fairly general, in terms of both time and place; the two propositions

would be as true in Tasmania in 1790 as in London in 1969. But the *Sunday Mirror* propositions are localised, dated. This indeed is how their author attempts to give his case force and vitality. This idea that our times have or should have a certain harmony, that an anachronism is *ipso facto* a bad thing, is a powerful one, so powerful that it often breaks out of the shackles of common sense in which we imagined it to be confined. Relevance in psychological terms amounts to *interest*. A relevant argument sparks off the feeling of the times, a feeling not merely that the argument is right but that it shows what can and should be done *now*. It is the popular mood which decides whether an argument is relevant or not, not the politician. The politician merely trains himself to hunt for relevance, to find that remedy which is reasonably coherent, popular and practicable all at the same time. And on top of all this he hopes to give it a touch of drama, of novelty so that people will say, 'Ah, now *this* is what we have been waiting for all along.' Such a remedy must be both the child of fashion and its creator. The audience wait, relaxed and chattering, for their interest to be aroused. While he runs through his introductory patter, the politician is half-listening to catch the exact nuance of the public mood and half-riffling through his stock of ideas for the one which will evoke really thunderous applause. With such a nerve-racking task on hand, is it any wonder that the politician's attention strays from the slow, painstaking business of analysis?

In returning to Macmillan, we notice that he has tried to catch the interest straight away by calling his first work *Reconstruction* (the theme reappears unaltered in *The Middle Way*). An attempt to improve the state of the nation could equally be entitled *Revival, Change is Our Ally, Make Life Better, Onward to Prosperity*, or, in more overtly factional terms, *The Future Labour Offers You, Let's Go with Labour*. All such titles are vague, but only *Reconstruction* refers to what we intend to do. The others refer in one way or another to the desired result. With one word Macmillan has saddled himself with a commitment to rebuild the whole structure brick by brick.

This commitment undoubtedly catches the attention, but it allows of no backsliding. Macmillan cannot say halfway through, 'if we tinker a little with the South Front, the whole place will become much more stable' – and then a little later on still, 'If we run a new beam across the kitchen ceiling, we won't have to rebuild the walls at all'. Yet this is of course what Macmillan does. He is continually on the retreat from his initial premise of total reconstruction. Yet he never retreats far or fast enough to review the problem with incision and detachment. Too much has been invested in stocking up with new bricks. How does a man become entangled in such a botched job?

Macmillan argues that inaction is morally intolerable in a situation where men's lives are rotting away. At the same time he argues: 'Hysterical proposals of the "do something", "do anything" variety are extremely dangerous in a situation like that of this country at the present time. We have neither the time nor the resources for light-hearted experimentalism. If and when we start out on the road we must be clear as to our destination.'[20] Macmillan, then, realises that the pressure for action before analysis presents a danger, but he does not grasp exactly what type of danger. For the upshot of the political dialogue – namely that the politician must do something now – does not enjoin him just to 'do anything'. It enjoins him *to do something which we, the audience, can recognise as action.*

The political dialogue always pushes the political actor towards direct, tangible, concrete measures which are simple to understand and easy to dramatise. Naturally he may take complex and obscure actions as well; in a credit squeeze, a government will use complicated machinery to reduce the liquidity of the banks as well as simple machinery to restrict credit terms to the consumer. But the headlines will say 'H.P. terms tightest yet', and the government will spend far more public energy on justifying the H.P. measure than on knocking down the counter-arguments of the banks. The H.P. measures will be far more unpopular than the banking measures, about which the public knows little and cares less. But at least the former will be recognised as action. Now in this instance the direct action is effective; by demanding higher deposits it will force some people to postpone or abandon their plans for buying cars and washing-machines. Whether this will help to slow down the growth in wages, whether the money not spent on consumer durables will be saved, or spent on non-durables – these are different questions. By asking these questions, and the larger question of whether a credit squeeze is needed at all, we shall be able to decide whether hire purchase restrictions are the right policy. But that the restrictions have some effect we cannot doubt. Yet the relation between the directness and the effectiveness of a political action is only contingent.

The true criterion of the effectiveness of a political action is not whether it looks like action, nor whether it is backed by force ('given teeth' in the popular phrase), but simply whether it changes the behaviour of people in the required direction. For that reason it may well be essential that a policy should be visible and concrete to get the public into the right mood. A general feeling that 'they' are doing something about it may well help to produce the desired effect, may, but only may. For example, the Wilson government believed that the only chance of achieving some income restraint was to hold back increases in prices and dividends at the same time. This was no doubt correct; no wages policy could have succeeded without it. But it was clearly not enough. Some far more radical measure was needed to change the trade unions' traditional behaviour (or, as the unions themselves argued with some justice, their traditional and primary function).

Now many of Macmillan's proposals are of exactly this kind. Let us take just one example, his proposal for the establishment of a minimum wage. He works out with laudable care what the rates should be on the basis of the Rowntree studies. And he sketches a sensible scheme for the gradual introduction of the minimum wage. But, apart from its very obvious advantages, a minimum wage law has three great dangers:

(1) That higher wage costs will force marginal firms out of production. Macmillan answers this point thus:

> If it is an industry considered necessary to national well-being or safety, and if, on ordinary profit-making reckoning, it cannot pay a living wage, then we ought to subsidise it out of the earnings of more profitable enterprises. Whatever may be its circumstances, there is certainly no case to be made for subsidising it out of the undernourishment of the unfortunate workers forced to accept employment in it.[21]

Well, nobody *wants* sweated labour. But what if the alternative is unemployment? The industries which are considered necessary for our well-being or our safety will have plenty of jobs featherbedded by the state; and the 'candyfloss' industries will go broke, forcing their workers on to the dole. In both cases, the state will have to remedy the hardships created by the minimum wage laws. Would not family allowances/rent subsidies/free health foods be a better stop-gap answer to low wages? Perhaps, but such piecemeal remedies do not have the simple impact of the minimum wage law.

(2) That higher wage costs will induce all firms to economise on labour, discharging inessential, inefficient, frail or elderly workers.

This has proved in modern times, particularly in the United States, to be the commonest effect of minimum wage laws. Macmillan does not mention it.

(3) That firms will put up their prices to cover their increased wage costs. Macmillan points out that this would not only put up the cost of living, but would also as a result further increase the wage costs of other producers. 'One might expect, therefore, that the vigilance of the consumer would be reinforced by that of other producers and that the weight of this social condemnation would be enough to compel a worthier sense of social responsibility on the part of the offending industrial or commercial undertakings. . . .'[22] Yes, but we still wish to know how the firms are to cover their costs. 'If that did not suffice, then it would be the duty of the government to devise other means of ensuring that the minimum wage should be regarded as a first charge upon industry, and that it should be met out of increased productivity and greater efficiency, and not out of higher prices. . . .'[23] Yes, but where is an already productive and efficient firm to get the money from? 'An additional safeguard, not to be despised in modern conditions, is the power of Parliament to withdraw from an offending industry any of the advantages such as tariff protection, subsidy, or statutory approval of schemes under the [Industrial Reorganisation] enabling Act which it might be enjoying.'[24] In other words, bankrupt yourselves, or we will bankrupt you.

The truth is that nowhere does Macmillan solve the problem of how the firm with no spare cash is to pay the minimum wage, a wage which to the firm is uneconomic. A simpler solution would seem to be to leave it to the trade unions to extract all available cash out of the profitable employers and for the government to help those who were still low-paid, in spite of good trade union organisation, through the welfare state.

The minimum wage proposal does not change the actual behaviour of individuals and corporations, at least not in the direction desired. Like so many of Macmillan's proposals, it does not operate on reality but strikes a pose – a 'relevant' pose – in front of reality.

It is important to understand that Macmillan is by no means alone in this. His experience is typical of two generations of wishful thinking about the management of the economy. Samuel Brittan gives an admirably frank recantation of his own very similar beliefs in the latest edition of *Steering the Economy*:

Much more important than any possible underestimation of monetary policy in earlier editions is that I no longer believe that – irrespective of the instruments used – the Treasury and other monetary authorities have the power to determine the exact degree of full employment and capacity utilisation (or 'pressure of demand' as it is usually known) in the longer term. For a time they can push up economic activity. . . . But the ultimate effect of 'expansionist' demand policies is on the price level rather than on output and employment.[25]

And again:

My real policy error in 1964 was in the institutional sphere. I believed that the setting-up of the NEDC 'indicative-planning' machinery, and the nominal endorsement of that 4 per cent growth target, could have exercised valuable back-door pressures on official policy. On the contrary, the whole 'planning' movement was a bad tactical mistake which actively delayed the basic reappraisal of the exchange rate and of other priorities desired by its adherents. The moral* I would emphasise is that it is better for critics and reformers to argue for their beliefs directly and avoid getting caught up in fashionable causes of doubtful validity.[26]

Mr Brittan speaks for a whole generation of disappointed critics and reformers who believed that it was possible in a free society for the government of itself to bring about a higher rate of economic growth. The real 'pressures on official policy' come in through the front door, namely the financial circumstances of the nation and the desires and energies of its people. To 'plan' without taking these latter factors as central is to plan a theatre without taking thought of the audience on whose convenience and satisfaction depends the usefulness and indeed the very survival of that theatre.

THE VOCABULARY OF THE ELITE

The attitudes of the ruling elite towards 'planning' seem then to pass through a cycle which runs roughly: enthusiasm – disillusion – revulsion – indifference – enthusiasm. Running parallel with this cycle we find a similar cycle of attitudes towards technology. This is not surprising; if one believes that the economy is a machine whose design and performance can be perfected by the social engineer, one is likely also to see the perfecting of actual machines as an essential part of that social engineering. The five-year plans of highly collectivised

* A moral which Mr Brittan himself has taken to heart in his cogent, elegant exposition of economic liberalism, *Government & Market Economy* (IEA, London, 1971).

economies are built on a kind of reciprocal metaphor; the economy is a machine, but machines are also the determinants and hence the symbols of the economy. Hence the emphasis in such plans upon heavy industry; *large* machines are seen as the economic basis for development, the 'girders' or the 'chassis' of the whole structure. But as soon as public opinion forces the emphasis to be switched to consumer goods, the general attitude towards planning must also change; the wishes of the consumer, not the perfecting of the machine, now become the principal force. The consequence is, first, an increase in international or at least inter-bloc trade which serves the double purpose of increasing the range of goods available and of buying in the cheapest markets, and secondly, a diminution of autarkic policies which attempt to reproduce at home every element of an advanced industrial economy – steel mills, airlines and the building of aircraft, nuclear energy – regardless of the cost. This oscillation between planning and 'consumerism' is a familiar process in Communist countries; but it is to be observed also in a subtler, less extreme form in Britain.

Disillusion with Britain's economic performance in the late 1950s and early 1960s may have been confined to the elite. But the unpopularity of the increasingly weary Conservative government was a tangible fact. As soon as he became leader of the Labour Party in 1963, Harold Wilson made brilliant use of the technological theme both to increase that unpopularity and to smooth over the cracks in the unity of his own party which had been reopened by the disputes over public ownership. The Tories, Wilson claimed, had preferred the morality of the bucket shop, the candyfloss economy, to building the kind of modern industrial structure that Britain desperately needed. The distinction was constantly drawn between 'frivolous' consumer goods and serious goods – machine tools, computers, generating stations; another distinction was made between 'making' money in frivolous, if not dishonest pursuits, usually connected with finance, and 'earning' money in serious pursuits, usually connected with heavy industry. In his famous speech to the Labour Party Conference at Scarborough in 1963, Wilson reminded delegates of his statement there three years earlier that 'we must harness Socialism to science and science to Socialism'. He claimed now that

. . . if there had never been a case for Socialism before, automation would have created it. Because only if technological progress becomes part of our national planning can that progress be directed to national ends. . . . monetary planning is not enough. What is needed is structural changes in British industry, and we are not going to achieve those structural changes on the basis of pre-election spurts every four years in our industry, or in the hope of just selling the overspill of the affluent society in the highly developed markets of Western Europe. What we need is new industries and it will be the job of the next government to see that we get them. This means mobilising scientific research in this country in producing a new technological breakthrough . . . we are re-stating our Socialism in terms of the scientific revolution. But that revolution cannot become a reality unless we are prepared to make far-reaching changes in economic and social attitudes which permeate our whole system of society. The Britain that is going to be forged in the white heat of this revolution will be no place for restrictive practices or for outdated methods on either side of industry.

Perhaps the most remarkable single proposition advanced by Mr Wilson in this superbly constructed speech was that 'there is no room for Luddites in the Socialist Party'. The use of 'Socialist' tends to obscure the startling nature of this contention, for the tradition of Fabian Socialism has always welcomed the connection between the scientific organisation of society and the fostering of applied science, while the Marxist tradition has at least accepted this connection as an inescapable fact of development. But the *Labour* Party has always drawn the bulk of its strength from the trade unions; and in Britain the trade unions have always seen automation as the ally of the employers and a continual threat to the livelihood of the working man. Work-sharing and strict rules of manning and demarcation have been their weapons of defence against technological change. The Luddite strain – humane, fraternal, if short-sighted – is central to the trade union tradition. Harold Wilson was saying in effect: 'Your resistance is useless. You will never beat automation. You must therefore accept it, taking good care to control and plan its introduction.' And the argument was accepted, in theory at least, because its timing was right. To trade unions in declining industries which had suffered redundancies at an ever-increasing rate over the past twenty years this reversal of the traditional argument made sense and brought hope when it seemed lost.

The physical view of industry has a long history. We have seen how it permeated the elite's thinking in the 1930s. It is rooted in the Marxist belief that the forces of production are the dominant forces

in society. When the capitalist ceases to exercise his rights of ownership, managers who actually control industry move towards 'social
dominance', according to James Burnham in *The Managerial
Revolution*,[27] an influential book which, while purporting to show
Marxism as outdated, is in reality much influenced by Marxist
analysis; meanwhile the capitalists dwindle into a pampered leisure
class. Not only do the managers make sure that the state is run in a
way which suits their interests, their interests also become increasingly independent of the wishes of the consumer; to put it crudely,
they can produce what they like. The consumer has to dance to their
tune, either through the compulsion of the state (as in eastern Europe)
or through the manipulations of advertising (as argued by J. K.
Galbraith). If it is therefore in the managerial sphere that the 'real'
decisions are taken, the politician's task must be to control the
managers, to make them produce the articles that will benefit the
public, not those that merely add to the glory and financial gain of the
managers. This view was strengthened by the pace of technological
change in this century. The public, it was argued, had not *asked* for
hula-hoops or colour television; it therefore did not *need* them; the
large-scale production of such articles must then be due to the
frivolous pursuit of quick returns by the managers. This argument
could of course be applied to the introduction of almost any new
product; the public had not *asked* specifically for electric light, or
underground railways, or brandy snaps with cream in the middle, or
Hamlet, or motion pictures. But the introduction of so many new
products at an ever-increasing rate naturally led to a feeling of surfeit
among the austerer members of the elite, even if that feeling was not
shared by the poor, who had only just begun to be able to buy such
products.

By the 1960s the managerial view had become almost totally
detached from its Marxist roots. It could therefore be espoused by
those who had no sympathy with Marxism and who sought only an
explanation and a remedy for the shortcomings of Britain's economic
performance. The Conservatives took up the theme. After Macmillan's ventures into 'indicative planning', Sir Alec Douglas-Home
fought the 1964 general election almost exclusively on the theme of
'modernisation', which he seemed to embody somewhat less than
Harold Wilson. However, there was no doubt that the elites on both
sides took a highly physical view. The air hummed with talk of computers, new industries and re-tooling. It was explicitly on these

grounds that William Rees-Mogg, in the *Sunday Times,* campaigned for Sir Alec's resignation as party leader. He had claimed that Britain might 'sink or swim by the development of automation'. The developments of science and technology were 'changing the structure of political possibility, and of political necessity.' Liberalisation of trade and competition were in comparison of secondary importance.[28] Sir Alec was increasingly found wanting in this kind of world. And in a much-quoted phrase Mr Rees-Mogg delivered with regret the verdict that he could no longer think of any reason for voting Tory to give to a young scientist or engineer.

Sir Alec's resignation represented the high-water mark of the physical view. Thereafter its hold on the minds of the elite rapidly declined. Dissatisfaction with the tax-supported new industries, with the new groupings of established industries (groupings promoted by the government in the interests of modernisation), and with the subsidisation of unprofitable activities generally began to be voiced. But it was not until the devaluation of sterling in November 1967 that the physical view finally cracked publicly; old-fashioned 'monetary planning' seemed to be more important than had been supposed. Of course, the intoxication with 'technological breakthroughs' continued; witness the saga of carbon fibres, a potentially valuable synthetic material which had been prematurely pushed out of the laboratory into development, because it was believed that the root of Britain's problems was her notorious slowness to make industrial use of her inventive genius. The ill-fated use of carbon fibres in the RB-211 aero-engine added considerably to its cost and contributed towards the bankruptcy of Rolls-Royce.

Nevertheless the mechanical myth, as a general and sufficient explanation of Britain's difficulties, had lost its grip; it was therefore unhesitatingly replaced by another myth, the myth of business. Harold Wilson made speeches about 'merchant venturers'. New heroes – Arnold Weinstock of GEC, Frank Kearton of Courtaulds – arose; their legendary quality arose not from their technological brilliance but from their alleged wizardry with figures; they could 'read a balance sheet'. They had the incisive minds which could seek out waste and the ruthlessness to dispose of unprofitable activities. They were in fact the consumer's hatchet men – throwing out things he didn't want or was not prepared to pay for and supplying him with what he found acceptable. These new knights and barons were, indeed, as they proclaimed themselves with not wholly convincing modesty, just 'plain businessmen'. Yet they were worshipped by the same elite which had rhapsodised about new industries in spite of the fact that some of their most important and profitable decisions were to close down or dispose of new industries. In the 1960s attempts to diversify into new fields, to build a factory ten years ahead of its time, to start creating now the products of the 1980s, were regarded as laudable pioneering activities, regardless of their relevance to the balance sheet. It would have seemed impertinent then to ask drab accountant's questions about 'cash flow' – such a key phrase of the 1970s.

The change in myth is also to be observed in the changing attitude of the elite towards the justification of Britain's entry into the Common Market. At one point the great benefit was to be the formation of a European 'technological community'; the somewhat chequered career of joint European aerospace projects and the notable lack of any mergers for technological reasons across national boundaries discouraged this hope for the time being. The justification then switched to less elevated commercial ground.

Any government is bound to be concerned with both the technological and the commercial aspects of managing the economy. But what is so striking about the language of the elite is its extremism, its veering from an almost exclusively technological vocabulary to an almost exclusively commercial one. This veering is not a response to public pressure; the public wants success (a steadily rising standard of living), but there is no reason to attribute to it any strong views on the correct means of regenerating the economy, beyond a vague feeling that Britain ought to be up-to-date. It is the language itself which dictates this exclusion of qualification. For a century or more Britain's situation has been one of steady economic decline relative to other countries, though of enormous advance in absolute terms. In striving to find a solution to this seemingly inexorable trend, the active intelligence naturally seeks to establish the present as a turning point, a moment at which *if only* we do such-and-such the trend will be reversed. But why should we expect this to be a turning point? It feels just like last year; and, if we look at the world around us and at the statistics abstracted from that world, it looks just like last year. The active intelligence will not therefore be content to observe and interpret; it will attempt to force observable phenomena within the framework of a new language, a language of dynamism. To bring off this feat, the plainest, strongest language must be used; there can be no reference to weak points in the case. Only thus will the language make a real impact upon the audience.

The elite then generates this language. The language must also correspond to the mood of the general public. But even this is not enough. The language has to carry conviction in a more rigorous sense; the public must believe that the language has been created out of a sincere impulse for action, not for reasons of personal political advantage. The politician must have 'credibility'. This is a commonplace as applied to a politician who has made a string of statements which have turned out to be false and is therefore no longer believed, regardless of whether what he says seems likely to be true or not; the later years of Lyndon Johnson's presidency are the modern *locus classicus*; Johnson's unexceptionable statements about educational or economic progress were treated by many people with the same scepticism and scorn as his over-optimistic reports on the progress of the war in Vietnam. Yet the question whether this or that statement of Mr X's is true is only a part of the larger question which preoccupies the audience: is Mr X a *serious* man (*homme sérieux* is more precise), or is he a charlatan? Specifically, is he serious about this particular policy, or is it merely a piece of window-dressing which he has no intention of carrying through to the end?

The over-centralisation of France has been remarked on for at least two centuries, most memorably by Tocqueville in his aphorism that 'in France there is only one thing that we cannot make: a free government; and only one that we cannot destroy: centralisation'.[29] For twenty-five years the phrase 'Paris and the French desert' has been a vivid expression of provincial discontent and metropolitan guilt. French opinion polls showed a sturdy majority in favour of the regional reforms proposed by de Gaulle in 1969[30] (though not of the reforms of the Senate with which they were linked). De Gaulle made one or two speeches calling for a reversal of 'the centuries-old centralising effort'. The television service showed its usual zeal in promoting the government's cause. Yet the plebiscite which was to secure the general's authority only precipitated his departure. The reasons were manifold – the length of de Gaulle's rule and the emergence of Pompidou as an adequate successor being no doubt primary – but one reason was certainly that the public did not really believe de Gaulle's sincerity in pressing for regional reform. He was a recent convert to the cause; the reforms were patently only an administrative, not a political decentralisation; Paris did not dare, had never dared, to let go of either the apron or the purse strings. De Gaulle was at one with Louis XIV, the Jacobins and Napoleon. It was widely felt that the only effect of the reforms would be, in the words of François Mitterand, that: 'Instead of one Napoleon, we will have twenty-one.' The czars of the twenty-one regions would have considerable power, as does, for example, the first secretary of the party in the Ukraine, but that does not imply any increase in self-government for the people of the region. The reforms in fact had nothing to do with 'participation'; and it was as a measure of participation that they were presented. The result was that though the reforms were intended by de Gaulle himself primarily as an occasion for proving yet again his title to rule, they actually became a useful piece of evidence to disprove that title; their obvious inadequacy and the cynicism with which they had been cobbled together helped to destroy their author's credibility.

Comparable schemes for political reform have been put forward by the elite in other countries and aroused a similar lack of public interest: Senator Bayh's attempt to do away with the electoral college in American presidential elections; the oft-voiced proposal to introduce proportional representation in Northern Ireland elections; the plans for the reform of local government in Britain, advanced by the Redcliffe-Maud Commission and later in a somewhat different form by the Conservative government. The claims made on behalf of such proposals that they would increase the efficiency of government and/or public participation in government have been received with almost universal scepticism and indifference, so clear is it that the proposals measure up neither to the claims made for them nor to the desires of the people, but only to the need of politicians and administrators to appear busy.

How, then, does a political actor become credible in the first place? How does he convince his audience of his seriousness? One answer has been for the actor consciously and ostentatiously to detach himself from the elite and to declare that he speaks, not in the fashionable jargon of the metropolitan hothouse, but rather in the rough, clear, enduring accents of the people; he claims that it is not he but his audience who have generated this language.

'A TUNE THEY CAN WHISTLE'

In a recent newspaper interview Enoch Powell talked of the men and women who stopped him in the street to shake his hand.

They keep saying: 'Thank you for what you have done.' And I think to
myself: 'Done! What have I done?'
Then one understands that saying is doing.
One thing people want, which they feel they miss, is being spoken for.
They want to hear their hopes crystallised into words, dramatised, if you
like, made tangible.
They want to hear a tune they can whistle . . . a tune that makes sense
in their life, and the life of their country.[31]

This hits the essence of the actual relationship of the politician and his
audience. It is a demonstration of at least one side of that 'professional self-consciousness' to which we referred earlier. Mr Powell
clearly understands that the politician's first necessity is to gain an
audience and that his next task is to respect the autonomy of that
audience, to recognise that its support is voluntarily given and may be
equally voluntarily withdrawn and also that the politician cannot
forcibly seize or regain its attention.

Such an understanding has two main consequences. The first is
obvious. The actor who pays attention to the audience is more likely
to be able 'to crystallise their hopes' and to establish a rapport over a
period; he will develop a sensitivity to changes in the public mood
and, in most cases, a tendency to respond to such changes, as Powell
himself has done on the questions of coloured immigration and of
Britain's entry into the Common Market. The second consequence is
less often stressed: namely, that by constant attention to the actual
desires and affections of the audience, the actor may improve his
powers of *analysis*. People, not demand curves, are the raw material
of sociology. And only by examining what people actually want can
we make rational forecasts about the likely effect of a particular
governmental action upon their behaviour. For example, British
governments have for many years attempted to increase the total
volume of saving by offering more attractive rates of interest on
National Savings and also new forms of saving such as Premium
Bonds, Save As You Earn. Mr Powell argues in his essay *Saving in a
Free Society* that these conventional methods do not work. New
schemes and higher rates of interest merely induce a diversion of
savings from other channels; they increase neither the propensity to
save nor the total volume of saving. The distribution of that volume
may vary with the rate of interest or with people's expectations of a
greater or lesser fall in the value of money; but total savings will,
broadly speaking, increase only when people have the money to save.

This suggests to Powell 'a method [of increasing personal savings] as obvious as it is difficult: to increase the proportion of net to gross personal incomes, or in other words, to reduce the proportion of personal incomes collected in direct taxation.'[32]

The more we examine Mr Powell's work, the more we shall find that his arguments follow a pattern similar to the above, that is: it is generally believed that doing x is the way to bring about y; this is a myth having no basis in reality, for the truth is that public opinion will not tolerate x or its consequences, and since it is the feelings and actions of the public which dictate the course of events, the result of x will be to bring about not the desirable y but the catastrophic z. Thus all attempts to integrate the coloured immigrants into the general community are worse than futile: for the immigrants regard themselves and are regarded by the natives as irremediably 'alien'; attempts to disregard this social fact can only exacerbate it. Similarly with Britain's attempt to join the European Economic Communities; the consequence of entry would be to draw Britain into a federal community and so to take away much of her political independence; the British people, still only half-conscious of this danger, will be outraged when they become fully conscious of it; and a bitter upheaval is bound to follow. It is not our intention here to discuss the truth of these various propositions. We merely wish to indicate the particular type of Enoch Powell's argument.

On the face of it, he would appear to be practising or attempting to practise a value-free science of politics, though he would no doubt deplore such dry language. His typical argument runs: this is the way people behave and feel; you and I may or may not like it; that is irrelevant; it is our task as politicians and as citizens to achieve the best possible solution, that is to say, the optimal blend of peace, prosperity and national harmony, and we can do this only by working within the limits laid down by popular feeling and behaviour; furthermore, we cannot and should not try to use moral persuasion to alter these limits to suit our own individual purposes and beliefs.

It is in this last proposition that Powell clearly goes beyond traditional Toryism. Instead of Burke's free-ranging dialogue between actor and audience, Powell lays down a rigid system in which the actor's duties and the audience's rights are fixed. He describes a political contract rather than an open-ended drama, though of course he differs from the Contract philosophers in that the Powellite contract is not a compact between the members of society but the contract of employment that the politician receives from the people.

This view of politics is frequently dismissed as 'populist', though we may well come to suspect the motives of those who use this term with an unthinkingly pejorative inflection; for a populist movement can be sparked off only by a regime which is in some respect 'anti-populist'; if the regime were responding quickly and sensitively to public opinion, why should the grass-roots catch fire? And if populism is a defective political science, anti-populism hardly has a more sympathetic ring.

Yet the defects of populism/Powellism are worth looking at. First, it has to insist that human behaviour and feeling are relatively static and immutable. We have to assume that people will always save only when they have more money to save, that black people and white people will never want to live at close quarters with one another, that British citizens will never accept any limit on their right to run their own affairs. Why must we assume these things? Because if we do not, if we accept that popular attitudes may change according to the season and the circumstances, it follows that we politicians might play our part in changing these attitudes; indeed, if these attitudes are in some sense to be deplored, we might have a moral duty to try to change them. The politician who accepts the flexibility of 'human nature' accepts also a certain burden of moral responsibility.

Now it seems plain that to a very large degree what Mr Powell uses as immutable facts of human nature are no more than passing abstractions from social reality. Indeed he himself has to recognise that many black and white people do already live together amicably; he has therefore to insist that friction is caused by *large-scale* immigration; that 'it is a question of numbers'. But if new immigration is reduced to a trickle as it has been, why should not the immigrants already here become a familiar and therefore tolerated part of the scene? Why, similarly, should not the British accept the limitations of further international treaties when they have already accepted without complaint the extremely important limitations and responsibilities of GATT, NATO and the UN? Public opinion may have turned temporarily against entry into the Common Market; but that is surely more likely to have been the result of previous diplomatic rebuffs – and the fear of a further rebuff – than of a gradual awakening to the supposed dangers of loss of national identity – a peril likely to make an *immediate* impact upon the patriot. The change in public opinion after the negotiations would seem to support this.

The paradox is that Powellite sociology, although claiming to study the realities, to build its conclusions strictly from the evidence rather than from wishful thinking, comes to share the faults of the methods which it criticises, that is to say, the tendency to select and abstract evidence to suit an *a priori* case. The difference between the Powellite and the Radical lies of course in what is selected, between the static and dynamic. Mr Powell concentrates on indications that 'you cannot change human nature' because on the whole he does not seem to want to. The Radical will seize on evidence of shifts in social attitudes which will back his contention that further shifts are not only desirable but possible. In both schools, fact and value are absurdly intertwined in spite of all claims to be finally rid of the latter.

There is something decidedly bizarre about the attempt to deal in an entirely value-free way with a universe of which you yourself are a part; the sociologist may excuse such putative impartiality on the grounds of his devotion to knowledge, but the politician has no such excuse. Nor indeed does Mr Powell consistently reject value, any more than Montesquieu was able to give a totally value-free account of the climatic origins of slavery. For example, Mr Powell says of the National Health Service:

A great part of the efforts of a civilised community are devoted to purposes which are not economic at all, but humane and human, altruistic if you please. Look at our vast expenditure, £1,000 million a year and more, upon the National Health Service. I would scorn to justify it – even if the assertion were true – on the basis that somehow it promoted economic and productive efficiency. It is completely, triumphantly, justified on the simple ground that a civilised, compassionate nation can do no other. It, and all the other social services, is the corporate recognition by the community of its common obligation to its individual members.[33]

Yes, but how did that obligation come to be generally recognised in Britain? It has not yet been so recognised in the United States; the arguments there still advanced against 'socialised medicine' were put forward in Britain within living memory. They were overcome by a combination of circumstances, in particular the increased expectations aroused by the deprivations of the war and by the coming to power of a Labour government in 1945. But that coming to power was itself only symptomatic of a great change in public feeling which had already taken place. The scheme for a National Health Service had already been outlined in a White Paper by a Conservative minister in the wartime coalition. The ground had been well prepared by assertions of value.

The politician's task is to establish a *modus vivendi* between fact and value. He cannot suspend all judgments of value save the judgment that whatever a majority of the people will is in itself good; to do so may legitimise the worst deeds of a Hitler or a Stalin. Equally, he cannot expect to be able to act at all times, and act effectively, in a manner which is totally in accord with his moral preferences. This last statement may sound equivocal; let us take an example. A moral politician will no doubt wish that all men should love each other. But can he expect to bring about this desirable state of affairs? If A comes to his door with a gun asking for his enemy B whom the politician is sheltering, the politician might be unwise to show A in and ask him to shake hands and make friends with B. He might be well advised to say falsely that B was elsewhere. He may even have to pay A to go away, or agree hypocritically to A's complaints that B has wronged him in order to calm A down. Evasion, falsehood, bribery, betrayal – all morally inelegant but justifiable in such circumstances.

Equally, sometimes morally elegant assertions can be justified although they may be of no immediate practical effect. It may seem to A that his fellow-countrymen are resolutely determined upon some ignoble act, for example, persecution of the Jews. It may be that by rebuking the persecutors he will only make them angry and so more cruel. It is very likely to be the case that A's own career, if not his life, will be endangered. He is unlikely to help the Jews much. And yet most of us would feel that it was A's duty to speak out boldly. After all, he *might* do some practical good; but in any case there are times when we believe it to be essential that moral truths be clearly enunciated. It is on this latter point, not on his relative failure to be of practical assistance to the Jews, that Pope Pius XII is most fiercely condemned today.

Moreover, we may question to what extent assertions of value by a politician are of importance or interest if it is laid down that such assertions may only reflect an already existing popular feeling; or, more precisely, of what use is it to describe them as assertions of value rather than simply as echoes of the general will? The test of a freedom is whether one may exercise that freedom in a way which is unwelcome to others. Similarly, it is reasonable to say that the test of whether the politician is to be regarded as a moral being or not is whether it is his duty to make moral statements which are repugnant to his audience. If not, he is no more than a messenger boy and cheer-leader.

Whether tenable or not, such a limitation of function does not appeal to politicians. Yet not a few politicians are capable of just such a limitation when it suits them. On some occasions the politician may claim that his function is merely to interpret and implement the wishes of his constituents; on others (where the assertion of moral values is more attractive to him) he claims the prerogative not merely of a rational moral being but of a pastor and preacher.

The conflict between fact and value leads to two conflicting views of the politician's function: first, the politician as exponent of socio-logical facts (in particular the wishes of his constituents); second, the politician as exponent of moral values. On the first view, even the elaboration of moral values is merely part of his appeal to his audi-ence; his success is to be measured solely by the volume of applause he receives; and his declarations in favour of chastity, the family and so on have no more real moral content than a comedian's red nose.

On the second view, the politician is at all times to be judged as a rational moral being. We must take his assertions of value seriously. Moreover, when he makes no explicit assertion of value but simply carries out a popular wish, we may legitimately assume that he shares that wish and accepts the values which have prompted it. For if he did not, it would presumably have been his duty as a rational moral being publicly to argue against that popular wish, and, if unsuccessful in his argument, to resign or at least abstain if he thought the issue trivial. When a man has chosen the public stage, we may regard not only his words as actions but also his silences. In the case of a private citizen it is debatable whether he may be said to have 'consented' to a par-ticular form of government or to government by a particular party unless he actually voted for or spoke up for that form of government or that party. We may argue about the degree of explicitness required before a person may be said to have consented. The criteria are further complicated by ignorance, apathy or the relative difficulties experi-enced by citizens in making their views known. None of these problems affects our consideration of the political actor. The supreme characteristic of his position is that he is 'to be held responsible'. And only a rational moral being can be held responsible for his actions. The functioning of a machine, for example, is the joint responsibility of its designer and its minder. Equally, the typical definition of a lunatic offered both by everyday speech and by the law is that he is not responsible for his actions.

There can be no question of choice between these two views. The politician must not pretend, as he is all too prone to do, that he can sometimes take one, and sometimes take the other. He has to exercise the two functions concurrently and try to reconcile them. As an exponent of sociological facts he must use the language of his time; as an exponent of moral values it will often be his duty sharply to question the implications of that language. The political dialogue is simply the expression of this conflict. Enoch Powell in his role as populist is no more a complete political actor than the dogmatic Marxist as preacher.

When a specific political dialogue implies the acceptance of certain values, the participant who does not assert contrary values may legitimately be assumed to share in that acceptance; may be assumed, that is, unless he denies such acceptance either by the irony of his tone of voice or by our memory of previous conversations with him on the same topic. A man who does not make his position clear is likely to be misunderstood.

Like many another politician, Mr Powell complains of being misreported and misunderstood, sometimes wilfully so. Such complaints may well be justified literally; inaccuracy and ill-will are a constant threat to the transmission of truth. But is there not a sense in which such complaints must be ill-founded? The politician operates in a world that is, so to speak, saturated with assertions of value; it is indeed for the soundness of his beliefs as much as for his skill as a 'social technologist' that he was elected. He is well aware that his selection of *this* topic at *this* moment in time, his choice of *this* piece of evidence and *those* friends to support his case, even his preference for *this* kind of suit or hat – all are proclamations of the kind of person he is and of the kind of values he wishes to promote. The octave of public behaviour which he has selected (or which temperament and environment have thrust upon him) has already limited him to a certain *range* of values. It is up to him to make articulate the precise composition of his beliefs within that range.

Finale

THE PLOT SO FAR

We have attempted to isolate and analyse the theatrical element running through all political activity. There is a fine distinction to be drawn between the necessary and syntactical aspect and the sociological aspect, between the timeless and the timebound. It is hard to conceive of any political structure being able to remain healthy without a lively and continuing dialogue between governors and governed. Almost all political theorists and framers of constitution have sought the establishment of such a dialogue, although few have put it in the kind of language we have used in this essay. In practical terms, where freedom in the western democratic sense is absent, even the semblance of dialogue may make life easier. Cuban jails may contain as many political prisoners in proportion to the population as Russian jails do; state control in both countries may have done as little to increase prosperity as it has done much to improve social services; yet observers concur that Cuba is a more cheerful place to live; and the reason generally and plausibly given is that Castro's 'road-show' – his spot-lighted conversations with peasants, his public talk-ins, his unheralded visits to the provinces, in short, his political theatre – manages to keep alive both the feeling of contact between governor and governed and also the fading romance of the historical revolutionary drama. And this is not just a Machiavellian observation, not merely a question of 'how the prince may maintain himself in power'; a political dialogue must mesh with reality if it is to satisfy the audience. Talk of liberty must reflect or eventually lead to specific liberties: the freedom to travel abroad, to publish newspapers, to change one's job or residence. The Russians appear to have been startled by the speed and extent to which the Czechoslovak reformers introduced such specific liberties in the 'Prague spring' of 1968; but there was no alternative, for the continued denial of such liberties would have rendered the dialogue a sham. Only in a country where the dialogue

232

had been a sham for forty years could this elementary point have been even partially overlooked.

Yet if theatricality is always present, its nature changes with the size and social structure of the polity. We have argued that in large, complex, modern societies which can function only by representative government the dialogue is under particular strain. The sense of distance lends awkwardness to the expression of familiar sentiments and everyday requests. The political actor's task is to diminish this sense of distance, to shorten the lines of communication, both literally by talking directly to as many of his constituents as he can, and figuratively by creating a sense of intimacy. This art is far finer than that of the social technologist; it requires an acute professional consciousness of the political actor's role; in particular of its split nature. The political actor is both interpreter and protagonist, both observer and participant. He has a duty to the public and a duty to his own conscience, mirroring the antinomy between sociological fact and value. There is a further duality in his role: the disproportion between the banal business of politics – the conciliation of interests and passions, the bargaining and broking – and the precious hopes and fears, the elevated moral and spiritual principles which are at stake.

This disproportion is most easily seen in the commercial theatre. Its form is conventional, its language unambiguous and well-worn, its sentiments familiar; it is indeed the very familiarity of these sentiments which woos the audience. There is no attempt to shock the audience out of its preconceptions. According to Samuel Beckett, 'The fundamental duty of habit . . . consists in a perpetual adjustment and readjustment of our organic sensibility to the conditions of its worlds'.[1] And the task of the commercial theatre is to reinforce our habits, our mores – also to illuminate them and lighten the task of complying with them, but basically to strengthen them. So it has been from Aristophanes to Molière and even to Terence Rattigan. The commercial theatre is a *moral* theatre dealing with intellect, self-control, moral choice, the impact of means upon ends, the impact of our own actions upon the lives of others.

The *avant-garde* theatre, at least in the characteristically modern form it has assumed since Kant, Byron, Rousseau, Sade (the exact starting point and the emphasis are matters of taste, the general direction is a matter of observation), deals with quite other material. It is an exploration of sensation, a beating of the bounds of human experience and feeling. But surely, it may be objected, this cannot be said of, say, Shaw and Ibsen, trail-blazers in their time. No, it cannot and precisely because Shaw and Ibsen were modern only in the sense that they dealt with modern conditions and modern attitudes; theirs was a kind of secondary reaction to the impact of the real *avant garde* upon the way people thought and felt. They confront new problems but in a classical manner. This breaking of fresh ground with old spades is characteristic of good commercial theatre. Fresh ground has to be broken if the play is not to lose its grip on the public, particularly in a society which is increasingly habituated to an accelerating flow of novelties; this habituation, together with the novelties themselves, creates a constantly changing field of experience which the commercial theatre is, so to speak, under contract to harvest.

By contrast, the pure *avant-gardiste* refuses to accept what is in essence an *assimilation* of novelties. He cannot tolerate that the novelty should be turned into a habit, that an experience which was so fresh, which gave him the feeling of being so much *alive*, should be dulled by what Beckett calls the 'narcosis' of habit. Therefore he cannot accept politics; for the call for a perpetual revolution is nothing less than a rejection of politics. Politics is a practical mode of experience; its task is to reconcile habits, not to intensify and explore sensation. The politician has to make friends not only of occasions but of individuals and groups to whom his heart may be hostile or indifferent. But, in Beckett's words, 'for the artist, who does not deal in surfaces, the rejection of friendship is not only reasonable but a necessity. Because the only possible spiritual development is in the sense of depth. The artistic tendency is not expansive but a contraction. And art is the apotheosis of solitude.'[2] Such an intense vision of the artist's life may seem far removed from the gimcrack romance which so appeals to the intellectual in politics. We may at first find it odd to see sensitive and skilled literary craftsmen or careful and industrious scholars giving enthusiastic assent to the wildest, most incoherent political gestures. Yet the chain linking the Lamartines and Büchners to the Marcuses and the Sartres is strong and uniform. The intellectual in politics shares with the intellectual as artist an obsession with his own authentic and intense sensation rather than with what Beckett calls the 'social expedient' of friendship. It is in fact this overweening self-obsession, this violent, blundering search for ultimate experience which renders the intellectual such a hazard to the theatre of politics. As actor-manager Philinte is doing his best to satisfy the public, but Alceste keeps breaking into his office with wild schemes and furious accusations. Worst of all, Alceste sometimes forces his way on to the stage.

THE THEATRE TODAY

But if the conventional theatre of sentiment has as its primary task to satisfy the public, it also has a duty to the pursuit of excellence in its own terms, to raise the quality of expression to the highest possible pitch. Only thus can it avoid staleness and eventual decay; it is in this sense that relevance is a political good, that is, not in the sense of blindly following fashion but in the sense of responding to actual social conditions and reflecting actual hopes and fears. How far are politicians today succeeding in this pursuit of excellence?

If we take a broad look at political life in western Europe and the United States, we may note several decisive gains: the decline in corruption, the improvement in the administration of justice, and on balance an increase in the volume of information made available to the public. Also, while we may be dubious about the increasing activism of governments, the increasing alertness to the existence of previously unnoticed problems or to the emergence of new ones signals without doubt a *refinement* of political activity. For example, a Burke today could not remain unaware of the significance of an upheaval such as the Enclosures. The greatest gain of all is the vast enlargement of the political audience or, as nineteenth-century observers would have called it, 'the political nation'. Conservative criticism of mass or popular democracy tends to miss the point. There is plenty of scope for argument about the right balance between representation and participation. It cannot be said that the fears of Sir Henry Maine have been completely fulfilled when a British prime minister in 1971 could still appeal to Burke's Bristol doctrine of representation as a justification for taking Britain into the Common Market against the wishes of what was at that time a majority of the public. No, the change is more general and more interesting. Obviously the politician has always had to appeal to the citizenry as a whole, but until the present age he has been required to appeal to the poor only in a crude or indirect way; it was a question either of preventing a rebellion or of soothing the social consciences of himself and those of his supporters who did form part of the political nation. Now he must converse with the same directness and sensitivity to everyone. Naturally he will listen with greater sympathy to certain groups – his fellow party members, his constituents, floating voters. But everyone comes into the political equation. And this is a clear gain, because social harmony is more likely to be promoted by inclusion rather than exclusion.

The material comfort of our times has given these new political modes plenty of room to operate in. Governments are less loath to pass out information which shows them in a bad light as long as they have plenty of other things to boast about. Universal suffrage holds no terrors for the rulers if the general standard of living is improving steadily. Technological advance and a less certain, but undeniable, improvement in techniques of economic management have created a growing prosperity and a concomitant confidence in the stability of the polity that makes it far easier to push through reforms both wise and foolish.

These advances in honesty, flexibility, refinement and scope are worth noting, because they make the shortcomings of modern political life all the more remarkable. We have sketched (in Act I, iii) the reasons inherent in the syntax of politics why politicians are likely to be unpopular. The complex structure of modern society and the still growing critical tradition (embodied in the fashionable notions of 'alienation' and 'healthy scepticism') tend to increase this unpopularity. But to mention these factors is not to give a complete picture of the politician's place in modern society. For to the loss of affection for and the loss of a sense of intimacy with the political actor we must add two other characteristics of his position: a loss of centrality and a decline in authority.

Lionel Trilling says:

> The literature of the modern period of the last century and a half has been characteristically political. Of the writers of the last hundred and fifty years who command our continuing attention, the very large majority have in one way or another turned their passions, their adverse, critical and very intense passions, upon the condition of the polity.[3]

Yes, the characteristic concerns of the intellectual world have been this–worldly, materialist, social. Yet while the intellectual dialogue has been increasingly concentrated upon the politician's sphere of activity, the political actor himself has played an increasingly undistinguished part in that dialogue. From, say, 1850 to 1900 the leading strains of political thought were most vividly and cogently expressed by political actors – Lincoln, Gladstone, Disraeli, Mazzini, Cavour, Bakunin, Blanqui, Kautsky, Lord Randolph Churchill, Lord Salisbury, Tocqueville. Marx and Engels took a hand in political activity. In the twentieth century we find the same leading intellectual role only among revolutionaries in poor countries – Lenin, Gandhi, Fanon, Mao. Among politicians in western Europe and the United States we find little or no political thought of any real substance and energy. Political life in these two areas of the world is thriving and, by and large, fruitful. Yet its politicians have accepted almost entirely a Martha-role; and those, like Churchill, de Gaulle, Roosevelt, who do take on a Marian challenge in time of crisis do so (often very successfully) with well-worn, traditional weapons. Since the death of these giants of action if not of intellect, the Marthas have reigned supreme.

Now it may be of little concern whether our rulers are protagonists in the intellectual as well as in the political debates of our time. Provided that we are reasonably well governed, why should we worry that our governors have limited, provincial minds? In Walpolean times who could govern better than Sir Robert Walpole? This argument is most· memorably summarised in Harold Macmillan's rejoinder: 'If people want a sense of purpose, they should get it from their archbishops. They should not hope to receive it from their politicians.'[4] If the basic questions have been settled, surely we may leave the complex details to the formidable skills of the negotiators.

Over a limited period this argument – that the political actor does not *need* to be a central figure in the intellectual life of his time – is pleasantly tenable. But those who accept the argument do not take full account of its inescapable implication, namely that the political actor has then to derive his authority solely from the existing political framework (the 'system'), not from the strength of his own intellectual position. It is significant that the most frequently quoted tag during the American political crisis of the late 1960s was Yeats's:

> Things fall apart; the centre cannot hold;
> Mere anarchy is loosed upon the world.[5]

The centre would not hold, it was felt, because there was nothing there, no lynch-pin, no keystone, no main beam. The politician could not maintain his authority when the system was under attack because he was not sufficiently central. Senator Eugene McCarthy's campaign for the presidency was an interesting attempt to gain authority through centrality; neither his intellectual nor his political energy was strong enough to maintain the attempt, but he showed what could be done. The fact that the system so brilliantly elaborated by the fortuitous conjunction of some of the strongest political minds in history one hundred and seventy years earlier proved tough enough for the time being to endure the shocks does not mean that the attempt was not worth making; nor that it will not have to be made again when the shocks recur.

One simple if superficial explanation of the phenomenon we have just been describing is that there is a dearth of distinguished men suited or eager for a political career. There is no doubt that the lack of distinction among political leaders does give a listless tone to public life. Henry Adams describes the United States as being in just such a listless condition under President Cleveland. Democrat observers considered the same to be true of the Eisenhower presidency. Tocqueville saw the era of Louis-Philippe in the same light. British commentators have described the Baldwin Age[6] and the later years of Harold Macmillan's second ministry in analogous terms. This listlessness is not to be equated with crassness, Philistinism or even inertia – although these may well be characteristic of such periods – but rather by more intangible feelings: that the government 'has lost its way', 'has lost the will to govern', 'has run out of steam', 'is failing to give a lead', 'is no longer the master of events'. These vague phrases do more than record the plain fact of a loss of public confidence; they are firmly based on the implicit premise that the decay is internal, not forced by external events. That is, a different ministry led by a different man would have been able to cope with the problems of the day, would have been able to rally public support, would have been able to provide fresh talent and energy from within its own ranks.

Such an explanation, though according with the observed facts, is really no explanation; it records the symptoms, not the cause. To ask what started the internal rot we must refer back to the factors which gave the government its energy in its healthier days. To discover the cause of cancer, we must understand how healthy cells are formed.

The consciousness of modern politicians in the west, whether they be assigned to the Right or to the Left, has been predominantly influenced by the three paradigms discussed in Act I, i.: politics as battle, politics as progress, politics as science. We attempted to show earlier that these paradigms, both singly and collectively, are partial and even misleading guides to an understanding of the political process. Yet of course each has produced certain practical benefits when used as a guide to political action: the theory of politics-as-science has led to an increasing use of science-in-politics, such as the use of social statistics for the identification of problems of poverty; the theory of politics-as-progress has induced in politicians a hopeful, alert and energetic posture which, for all its faults, often stands in welcome contrast (at least in our own Faustian eyes) to the lethargy and callousness of governments which accept a sharply diminished view of what is possible and of peoples who expect and demand less of their governments; and the theory of politics-as-battle has at its best given the political actor a bleakly realistic view of the world and a clear understanding of how to maintain his own position in it, both of which may well improve the security of his audience. When dealing with specific challenges – some neglected area of social collapse, some gathering danger to the nation – these paradigms may still be vital spurs to action.

Yet a majority is emerging in the western industrial world with whose direct and predominating experience the old paradigms are powerless to deal. This statement should be carefully distinguished from the anxious apprehension of the fact that we are moving towards a period in which half the world's population will be under the age of twenty-five; for the great preponderance of this increase will take place in poor countries beset by disease, illiteracy and injustice of the most glaring sort. The problems of such countries are horrifying, but at least they are readily identifiable and the old paradigms are capable of providing the energy to solve them.

In western industrial countries, on the other hand, the emerging majority has known only individual and national security and an unprecedented and continuing growth in prosperity. The maintenance of this enviable situation naturally demands political skill and application. And yet, as Burke made clear, the rhetoric of repair has little appeal to those who *expect* their social equipment to be kept in good running order. *The notion of 'a revolution of rising expectations' is even more aptly applied to our expectations of government than to our expectations of prosperity.* Not only do we expect government to perform its traditional tasks of keeping the peace and maintaining public order; we expect it to be unfailingly alert to the existence or emergence of social or economic problems and unfailingly resourceful and energetic in the resolution of those problems. It is in this sense that the old paradigms have lost their power. It is as if the politicians were talking a dead language like ancient Greek, a large number of whose words, grammatical structures and concepts have been absorbed into modern English but the speaking of which must now be a scholarly pursuit. Progress? Naturally we expect governments to make progress. Science? Naturally we expect governments to use the most exact methods and to collect the most accurate evidence. Battle? Of course we must defend ourself against external threat or internal disorder, but these disagreeable necessities are not exactly *interesting*.

What have the politicians to say about such things as the enjoyment of the present, the good life, national and communal harmony, morality and the family, the purpose of education, liberty and responsibility? Very little, or at any rate nothing to seize our sympathies or fire the informed imagination. Yet these things, vague and ill-defined as they may seem, are the 'human' side of politics. And a time of peace and growing prosperity gives us more leisure to think about that human side; the mechanistic notions of politics which have culminated in the international contest for the highest rate of economic growth comes to seem pitifully inadequate. We are all well aware that, as Anthony Crosland has so cogently argued, many less 'materialist' achievements (the care of the sick and the poor, clean air and the preservation of open country and fine buildings, the education of the disadvantaged child) depend directly upon the achievement of economic growth. Galbraith's abstraction of 'private affluence and public squalor' reflects only a transient reality. Private affluence eventually calls forth public affluence; for example, the private elegance of the Georgians is succeeded by the public munificence of the Victorians. When Number One has been looked after, people in general are quite ready to look after Number Two.

But the fact that economic growth is now, as it has always been, one of the prime aims of any government which hopes to stay in power and to be remembered with respect by posterity, this fact does not mean that political actors should talk only about economic growth any more than the fact of a long and arduous journey to visit an old friend means that the visitor should talk of nothing but the hardships of the journey when he reaches his destination.

IN DEFENCE OF ELOQUENCE

The decay of a tradition of active political thought may seem strange in an era which is so highly politicised. Yet it is true that, to the majority of young people at least, political actors appear to be mysterious, lumbering survivals of another age, unable to converse with the modern inhabitants. The hysterical nationalist outpourings at the United Nations, the empty sonorities of Kennedy–Sorensen prose, the short verbless sentences of Edward Heath (the grammar or lack of it being intended to convey dynamism and streamlining), all these attempts, so different from each other, fail equally lamentably to provide a working political language. So do attempts to liven up stale arguments with modish or fashionable references; there is nothing more embarrassing than the politician who makes matey allusions to last year's pop star.

But in pointing out that political rhetoric is tarnished, we should not forget that we live in generally anti-rhetorical times. As George Steiner remarks, 'Rhetoric and the arts of conviction which it disciplines are in almost total disrepute.'[7] Political rhetoric is only the most extreme example, evoking our most intense distaste for lies and half-truths, clichés and evasions. An intelligent person today would not dream of expecting a politician to provide serious insight into the way we live now; a statistician, a psychologist, a poet or novelist, even a theologian perhaps, but not a politician.

Dr Steiner contends that we are living through a decline from our verbal culture which is expressed in a general 'retreat from the word'. He says that 'words are corroded by the false hopes and lies they have voiced'.[8] Auditory, tactile and pictorial means of communication have taken over from the lying word (though, oddly, neither for Dr Steiner nor for the other members of his school does the olfactory sense appear to play much part). Music, in Dr Steiner's case, is a particular stimulant and solace. 'At every knot, from the voices of public men to the vocabulary of dreams, language is close-woven with lies. Falsehood is inseparable from its generative life. Music can boast, it can sentimentalise, it can release springs of cruelty. But it does not lie.'[9] The same sort of thing is widely voiced, though with much less sophistication and articulateness, throughout the whole 'counter culture', 'alternative society' or 'underground' (the various names assumed by groups given to a bohemian, anarchic life in which

241

the unmediated enjoyment of the moment is the supreme value). Those like Dr Steiner and, in a not dissimilar fashion, Marshall McLuhan, who believe that this analysis is accurate also seem to give a measure of unstated approval to this new way of life. And indeed the terms in which Dr Steiner makes his point indicate the bias: 'from the voices of public men . . . language . . . lies.' The implication is: well, we can start by agreeing that all politicians are liars, that political debate is a *reductio ad absurdum* of language. A commonplace statement indeed and yet one which if taken at its face value immediately misleads the reader into a totally false picture of politics, for a political speech, as we have explained, does not consist in a series of propositions to be verified. True, the politician's task of persuasion often needs the support of factual propositions whose truth can be tested. Here indeed plain lies may be and are told; a statistic may be falsified, a piece of evidence may be taken out of context. We may assume, however, that it is not of such lies that Dr Steiner is thinking, but rather of 'the lie in the soul'; Hitler's wickedness was not merely to feed out misleading statistics about the Sudetendeutschen. And the trouble about the lie in the soul is that it cannot be cut out by the paring away of language; it is in fact in the soul and not in the tongue. To say that music does not lie is trivial; only persons using words can lie. But to admit that 'music . . . can release springs of cruelty' is to admit something fascinating and terrible (a theme superbly played by Thomas Mann in *Buddenbrooks* – finished in 1901 – long before Wagner had been tainted by Hitler).

The retreat from the word does not then for Steiner betoken a long march towards *innocence*, as the hippies might hope; it merely pares away the opportunities for the essentially verbal sins of deception and falsehood. So far so good, if it were not for the fact that it also removes the opportunities for moral analysis. A wordless culture has no machinery for developing traditions of moral choice; the instinctual, inarticulate man, for all his fresh, tingling enjoyment of immanence is deprived of the opportunity of exercising his humanity.

For the twentieth century, to be anti-political has meant to be also anti-rhetorical. Unfortunately, both characteristics represent an impoverishment, not an enrichment, of the moral life, perhaps even of the sensual life as well. After all, who is to say whether the febrile examination of sensual experience is not more truly felt, more 'real', than the unthinking acceptance of that experience? To claim that Proust's love for Albertine is inferior to a cowman's love for his girl rather than *vice versa* is merely to prefer one kind of snobbery to another. But if the right way to enrich sensual experience is a matter of taste, the way to enrich moral experience is not. This is not to say that moral norms may not obtain greater authority if they are learnt without intellection in childhood. Nothing could be more powerful than the fervour of the *Chanson de Roland*: 'Pagans are wrong and Christians are right.' That great epic has moving moments; its overall moral effect is nevertheless one of thugs slugging each other for the hell of it. The concern for the conflicting wishes of others, the conflict between equally valid principles, the conflict between the private and the general good; these subtle, complex conflicts cannot be resolved without the most serious and patient intellection. The moral world of Henry James is richer than that of *Roland*. And it is this complex, awkward world which is the stuff of politics.

Yet the virtue of language is not simply that it serves as a tool for painstaking analysis but also that from it we can seize upon patterns, we can abstract paradigms. The first vague stirrings of dissatisfaction with the existing conventional wisdom; the first attacks upon that wisdom; the formulation of the rebel doctrine; the incapsulation of the rebel doctrine in a book, a phrase, a word – we are accustomed to report this typical sequence in the terms of the dialectic: thesis, antithesis, synthesis. But the brilliant notion of the dialectic (itself an abstraction) tempts us to regard its terms as being substantial objects instead of verbal abstractions. This brilliance of the abstraction is dazzling; we do not for the moment fully perceive the daring way in which its few simple lines overlay a vague, irregular, inconstant reality.

Indeed when a thorough, energetic scholar has elaborated his abstraction into a personal monument, as Marx pre-eminently did, his admirers may take centuries to realise that they are looking not at the whole truth but at an abstraction. By contrast, it is in the nature of the politician's abstraction that it should be flung together to meet the exigencies of the moment. As soon as the stage lights are switched off and its usefulness is at an end, we see the flimsy struts, the cheap canvas, the coarse application of the paint. The shortcomings in, say, Marxism or classical economics may be no less substantial than those in the ideas put forward by, say, Young England, the Fabian Society, Americans for Democratic Action, One World, Students for a Democratic Society, Campaign for Democratic Socialism, One Nation, and so on. All the same, the latter being dedicated to immediate, practical ends have in retrospect an irretrievably gimcrack, shoddy air about them. Yet their effect reaches far beyond immediate events. They change the language and attitudes of millions of people who may regard themselves as 'non-political'. They teach people to accept new responsibilities, to demand new rights, form fresh expectations of life in general and of government in particular.

The politician has to catch his audience on the wing or not at all. His speech must therefore have all the impact and all the ephemerality of this morning's newspaper. Yet the perpetual 'liveliness' of journalism brings its own staleness. Only when the politician is master of a rhetoric which strikes us as being both fresh and relevant to our situation are we likely to grant him the quality of *eloquence*. The content must be as applicable to reality as the form is appropriate and stimulating. It is in this eloquence that the commercial theatre reaches its high point.

Political eloquence lays no claim to intellectual originality. Its originality lies in its unique attempt to *embody* the consciousness of its time. This consciousness may be suddenly thrown up by great events; it may have been slowly brought into being over a long period of social change; it may even express a waning tradition, such a consciousness being a sudden collection and recollection of old values and dying ways of life, the threat to which has been gradually growing and now out of its very fearfulness evokes a momentous reaction.

We are familiar, for example, with the complexities of the new consciousness created by the Industrial Revolution. From Southey and Cobbett to Dickens, Ruskin and Marx, the cry of indignation becomes louder and fiercer. From the beginning, observers were alert to the spiritual as well as the material deprivations to which their fellow-men were being subjected. Romanticism, even in its most naïve, lyrical moods, did represent a revulsion against the inhumanity of modern technology. At first the horror is vague, undifferentiated. John Sell Cotman's *Bedlam Furnace* of 1802[10] contrasts the gentle, feathery outlines of the trees, all green and brown, with the explosive orange and ultramarine and the sharp lines of the furnace, or 'hellmouth' as such furnaces were dubbed at the time. The whole is both an exercise in the picturesque and the presentation of a threat to the harmony which should link man and nature. Southey's *Colloquies* are a full-scale indictment of the human consequences of industrialisation. Men are being reduced to machines and 'he who, at the beginning of his career, uses his fellow-creatures as bodily machines for producing wealth, ends not infrequently in becoming an intellectual one himself, employed in continually increasing what it is impossible for him to enjoy'.[11] The notion of alienation is, then, not Marx's personal discovery, though this is hardly surprising as in one form or another it is one of the oldest notions in human thought. St Paul spoke of 'aliens from the Commonwealth of Israel and strangers from the covenants of promise, having no hope and without God in the world'.[12] And Disraeli puts the notion into the mouth of the Chartist Stephen Morley in *Sybil*: 'There is no community in England; there is aggregation, but aggregation under circumstances which make it rather a dissociating than a uniting principle. . . . Christianity teaches us to love our neighbour as ourself; modern society acknowledges no neighbour.'[13] Critics and historians may seek to establish a diagram of influences; but the natural response of the sensitive intelligence to remarkable changes in society is enough to explain most coincidences of viewpoint. Such an intelligence cannot honestly avoid dealing with the glaring tendencies of the times; those tendencies do not necessarily determine what the intelligence makes of them; but, naturally enough, observers of the same event quite often produce the same answer.

But what determines the relation between the individual response of the sensitivity and the collective response of the polity ('individual' not in the sense of being felt by one man only, but as being experienced individually)? Between, if we can put it so crudely, a culture and its politics?

Many, varied and weird have been the efforts to establish some all-answering pattern which takes account of the irregularities and incongruities of history; Marx's dialectic, Vico's cycles, Condorcet's linear progress, Toynbee's parabola of each civilisation's rise and decline – almost every geometrical and syntactical metaphor has been employed to give some shape – therefore some meaning – therefore some hope – to this monster, as 'loose and baggy' as Henry James's characterisation of the novel. Even those who regard such theories as high-flown nonsense may not be free from it themselves when they describe politics in terms of a system of forces; if we are to say, as the practical man will, that the success or failure of a revolution depends not on 'the ripeness' of the country concerned but on a combination of chance and of the relative strengths of the existing regime and of the revolutionaries, what determines these relative strengths? Clearly, Marx's productive forces are not a sufficient explanation of the disparities which history shows. The practical man will say that, yes, remarkable individuals have a great deal to do with it: if the czar had had better advisers, if Kerensky had been tougher, the whole process of 'democratisation' might have been very much better managed and the Bolsheviks might never have been able to seize their chance in the midst of war and chaos. Yes, but why was the czarist elite so rotten, why were the Liberals and Social Democrats so comparatively feeble? And the only answer can be that they had lost the debate years before; that in czarist Russia never had the notion of gradual humanitarian reform, the hope of shared prosperity through technological advance, been embodied with anything like enough force and energy. With hindsight it now appears that never before had the social condition of Russia improved so fast as it did between, say, 1880 and 1914. But the governing group never developed a rhetoric of sufficient eloquence to convey the requisite impression of dynamism and optimism. The rebelling groups, on the other hand, not only benefited from their own superb rhetoricians but were strengthened by the voices of sympathetic rhetoricians in other countries.

Let us be more precise about our use of 'embodiment'. We do not mean a simple personal or collective commitment to embody the promptings of our consciousness in practical political action. Still less do we mean to imply any notion of the maturation of a consciousness, the concept of 'an idea whose time has come'. We mean very simply that at certain moments in history it is essential, if a new consciousness is to have an effect upon the social framework, that it be translated by means of rhetoric into a political programme. This is a translation from statements of facts to statements of purpose, a translation from the contemplative to the active. The effectiveness of such a translation is to be judged by its success in wooing its intended audience, not by the historical or sociological accuracy and comprehensiveness of its supporting arguments.

Such a translation is the Communist Manifesto. Historical narration, sociological observation and analysis are all absorbed into a dynamic call to arms. The lightning of its celebrated beginning is logically and inevitably echoed by the thunder of its still more celebrated finale.

A spectre is haunting Europe – the spectre of Communism. All the powers of old Europe have entered into a holy alliance to exorcise this spectre: Pope and Czar, Metternich and Guizot, French Radicals and German police spies.

Where is the party in opposition that has not been decried as Communistic by its opponents in power? Where the Opposition that has not hurled back the branding reproach of Communism, against the more advanced opposition parties, as well as against its reactionary adversaries?[14]

In the seconds intervening between the lightning and the thunder we have the justification, the argument – all of which merely mark time for the conclusion that the moment for action is at hand:

The Communists disdain to conceal their views and aims. They openly declare that their ends can be attained only by the forcible overthrow of all existing social conditions. Let the ruling classes tremble at a Communistic revolution. The proletarians have nothing to lose but their chains. They have a world to win.

WORKING MEN OF ALL COUNTRIES, UNITE![15]

Seventy years later, the vigour of that invocation had not faded from men's minds. On the contrary, the ferocity was even more intense, as witness the conclusion of *What Does Spartacus Want?*, the draft programme of the German Communist Party in December 1918:

Arise, proletarians! To the battle! We have to struggle against a world, to conquer a world.
In this last class struggle of history for the highest aims of humanity our motto towards the enemy is: 'Hand on throat and knee on the chest!'[16]

Such rhetoric absorbs and dynamises the whole consciousness which was the human response to the Industrial Revolution and its consequences. This is not to say that the analysis of history and society on which it rests is necessarily correct. But it does mean that the translation from the contemplative to the active has been effectively carried out.

It is possible to use exactly the same data of consciousness and translate them into a totally different statement of purpose. Three years before the Manifesto was written, Disraeli's *Sybil* was published. This highly coloured, romantic novel may seem worlds away from the rough, vigorous journalism of Marx (and Engels). Yet there are close parallels between the attempts of these two Christianised Jews to find an effective translation of the *Zeitgeist*. There is the devotion to sociological description, the use of government blue books; there is the creation of the mythic past, in particular of the Middle Ages. Each ascribes to his own group far greater influence than it actually possessed at the time; the Communist League barely existed, Young England was no more than a convenient vehicle for young bloods to harry the old gang. The Manifesto itself robustly dismisses the pretensions of 'Feudal Socialism': 'The aristocracy, in order to rally the people to them, waved the proletarian alms-bag in front for a banner. But the people, so often as it joined them, saw on their hindquarters the old feudal coats of arms and deserted with loud and irreverent laughter.'[17] Subsequent history has not confirmed this; for 'feudal Socialism' has proved a highly popular and often effective way of governing, as the examples of Roosevelt, Kennedy, Salisbury and Macmillan all attest in some degree. Even when pursued for opportunist reasons, the notions of Lord Randolph Churchill and the Fourth Party have turned out to be a means both of gathering working-class support and of regenerating Conservative parties which had become either sunk in sloth or the prisoners of limited vested interests. Though we are hard put to define the exact creed of Young England, its general ideas of national harmony and of moral duty remain obstinately alive – as of course do those of the Communist Manifesto, for all the evil that has been done in its name.

It is not hard to find examples of the following sort:

[William] Whitelaw [Leader of the House of Commons and later Secretary of State for Northern Ireland] made the decision to become a politician in 1944. He was serving in Normandy. Two-thirds of the ranks he commanded were blown up. He had the task of writing to the relatives of the dead men. So moved was he by the replies that he decided to 'do something'. Therefore he would become a politician.[18]

From Plato onwards political thinkers have debated how to ensure high standards of probity in our masters. One simple answer is to encourage a tradition of regarding politics as an honourable profession and thereby hope to attract to it honourable men.

It is easy to concentrate too dully upon the defects both of history and of tone in such memorable utterances as those of Marx and Disraeli – and so forget the intentions behind them, a precisely calculated intention which had precisely calculated effects upon the minds of their respective audiences. It is particularly easy because the defects are so firmly embedded even in the most central passages, the appeals to action. The most passionate moments in *Sybil* are shot through with a gimcrack romanticism. Witness the two famous passages that correspond to the opening and closing words of the Manifesto which we have just quoted:

In a parliamentary sense, that great party has ceased to exist; but I will believe that it still lives in the thought and sentiment and consecrated memory of the English nation. It has origin in great principles and in noble instincts; it sympathises with the lowly, it looks up to the Most High; it can count its heroes and its martyrs; they have met in its behalf plunder, proscription, and death. Nor, when it finally yielded to the iron progress of oligarchical supremacy, was its catastrophe inglorious. Its genius was vindicated in golden sentences and with fervent arguments of impassioned logic by St John; and breathed in the intrepid eloquence and patriot soul of William Wyndham. Even now it is not dead, but sleepeth; and, in an age of political materialism, of confused purposes and perplexed intelligence, that aspires only to wealth because it has faith in no other accomplishment, as men rifle cargoes on the verge of shipwreck, Toryism will yet rise from the tomb over which Bolingbroke shed his last tear, to bring back strength to the Crown, liberty to the Subject, and to announce that power has only one duty: to secure the social welfare of the people.[19]

And:

There is a whisper rising in this country that Loyalty is not a phrase, Faith not a delusion, and Popular Liberty something more diffusive and substantial than the profane exercise of the sacred rights of sovereignty by political classes.

That we may live to see England once more possess a free Monarchy, and a privileged and prosperous People, is my prayer; that these great consequences can only be brought about by the energy and devotion of our Youth is my persuasion. We live in an age when to be young and to be indifferent can be no longer synonymous. We must prepare for the coming hour. The claims of the Future are represented by suffering millions; and the Youth of a Nation are the trustees of Posterity.[20]

Florid, overblown, unhistorical – yet these two passages, like their counterparts in the Manifesto, remain famous because the rhetoric imbues them with a fascinating sense of movement. Such rhetoric forcibly confronts all those who are troubled by their times with a possibility of action. That possibility both demands and provides energy; it removes the excuses of lethargy and impotence, the reasons for doing nothing. And it does so by setting our present consciousness within a historical continuity. Look, the orator says, how low we are sunk now; but look at what we have been; so conclude that our present state or tendency is not fixed or immutable; history is on the move and we must be on the march. We may note in passing that the alleged nature of 'what we have been' varies: for a moderate progressive of the type of Bertrand Russell or Karl Popper the past represents squalor, disease and superstition; for Burke or Disraeli it means the harmony of an organic community, the peace of the cloister; for Marx, primarily just another stage in the development of the forces of production. The importance of the past lies simply in its *difference* from the present, thus providing grounds for imagining that the future in its turn will be very different from the present.

We have described the *effect* of rhetoric; we have not justified it. Is it possible to do so? Political rhetoric invites us to share a moral and practical risk, both with one another and with the rhetorician. That risk is formidable. At best, we may find ourselves committed to a wild goose chase, an impracticable project supported only by fine words. Both speaker and audience run the constant risk of suspending both their moral and intellectual judgment in the shared verbal delirium. *Have we the right to allow ourselves to indulge in political rhetoric, when the consequence may be a Hitler?* Can we be so sure of keeping a level head when history is littered with cases of supposedly intelligent and worldly-wise characters who have lost theirs? Albert Speer's account of Hitler's wooing of the gentle students and professors at Speer's university with their irreproachable folkloric interests is a cautionary tale.

Dr Steiner stands thunderstruck before the appalling fact that language which 'so far in history . . . has been the vessel of human grace and the prime carrier of civilisation'[21] should have been perverted to serve the bestiality of Nazism; or rather that 'Nazism found in the language precisely what it needed to give voice to its savagery'. He concludes that in postwar Germany language has 'gone dead' and that in the world at large modern barbarism has driven the moral intelligence into a retreat from the word; therefore:

> Let the scholar cease from editing the classics a few miles down the road from the death camp. . . . Precisely because it is the signature of his humanity, because it is that which makes of man a being of striving unrest, the word should have no natural life, no neutral sanctuary, in the places and season of bestiality. Silence *is* an alternative. When the words in the city are full of savagery and lies, nothing speaks louder than the unwritten poem.[22]

This reluctant quietism has its appealing side; but its bottom is hollow, for it refuses to accept the reality of moral choice. Silence is not enough. The risks of rhetoric are simply the risks of moral choice writ large. Dr Steiner rightly attacks the failure of leading politicians outside Germany to speak out against the murder of the Jews. Why should men be silent now, thirty years later, because of the horror, when it was silence then that gave consent to that horror? Language does not go dead, only the moral faculties of those who use it.

Silence gives consent; that is the dictator's crude solution to the problem which has exercised the minds of the subtlest political thinkers for centuries, namely, what is the nature of consent? The problem today is not, as Dr Steiner claims, that politicians have perverted language so much that it has become unusable, but rather that the dialogue between politicians and their audience threatens to dry up; and the mantle of silence which the 'alternative society' regards as the only fit garb for an honest man is for politics the pall of death. Moreover, the reason for this is not so much the moral failures of politicians past and present, as the size and complexity of modern political communities, which demand that the rulers concentrate upon administration instead of communication.

One symptom of growing disquiet is the cry for more public decision-making; throw open the doors of the smoke-filled room, the caucus chamber or the cabinet and let the public join in. Alas, this cannot be done, at least in the literal sense. Most decisions always have been and always will be *taken* in private – inside one man's brain, in a whispered negotiation between two or three key members of a key body. This kind of process cannot be shown in public. One can watch a Michelangelo painting a ceiling; one cannot see into his brain. But the actual taking of a decision is only an abstract point, an imagined fulcrum; it is the wider and richer context of that decision which is the stuff of public politics. *Before* the point of decision is reached, the audience must make its own views known, articulate its power: 'If you vote for this, we may be compelled to withdraw our support for you', or 'We feel very strongly that. . . .'. Factions and wings of factions must apply what leverage they can. The decision-takers themselves must test the water – drop hints, try out arguments, listen to reactions, talk to station-masters, taxi-drivers and local party leaders, take opinion polls. *After* the decision is taken, it must be announced and defended; the public cheer or boo, sometimes so loudly that the decision has to be revised or retracted. All this is decision-*making* in the broadest and most important sense – a process which includes all the determinants of decision. This is what we have called the theatrical element; it is the sign of a responsive life in politics; in traditional terms, its scope corresponds to the varying relationships between rulers and ruled which are grouped together under the general heading of democracy.

It is only when we examine societies which have no such political theatre that we see the value of what we may be in danger of losing. Soviet Russia possesses a few mythic props – military pageants, Lenin's tomb, the symbolic glory of her achievements in space – but there is no common language to animate those myths, no public debate. K. S. Karol recounts a poignant description given to him in Moscow by a senior party official:

> Beneath the flat surface of society in Russia, as presented by *Pravda*, a rich and complex life abounds but it totally lacks any means of expression or communication. We are not a 'one-dimensional society', as westerners believe; on the contrary, we are a fragmented society. Prevented from communicating with each other, we have almost no common criteria. Everyone takes hold of a piece of the truth from his daily experience and interprets it according to his own lights. The same words have a different meaning for each social group, almost for each individual. In such conditions we just cannot make a serious analysis of the real state of affairs; so we try to tackle the problem in a pragmatic manner by studying what happens at the different levels of this closed and, up till now, inexplicable society. . . .
>
> Our country has no civil tradition. The taste for association, for organising communal life together, for getting to know each other and taking decisions together, never really existed in Russia. Between the czar and the moujik there was nothing; equally, between one moujik and another there was nothing except for essential personal relationships. We were and we remain a huge body, colossal even, but shapeless and deprived of articulation, of that political fabric on which the modern states of Europe were built. The Revolution failed to make the Russian masses articulate because the experiments of Lenin's soviets were quickly stifled. . . .[23]

Slowly and painfully, the Sakharovs, Amalriks and Marchenkos are trying to stitch together a political fabric. Already the underground literature is revealing two distinct groups, the pure Marxists and the Liberal Democrats; the first phrases of the long buried language of free debate are tentatively mouthed; their long immersion in the solitude of individual minds has given them a haunting freshness, reminiscent of the freshness of the great nineteenth-century Russian writers. How far the debate will be allowed to develop only time can tell. But its natural, spontaneous upsurge makes a fascinating contrast with the example of China, where Mao Tse-tung has attempted not merely to suppress the growth of a popular language (in his view, a slack bourgeois revisionism) but also to *impose* a new political Esperanto – the language of the Red Guards. Mao believes the Chinese people to be 'poor and blank'; and on a blank sheet of paper 'the freshest and most beautiful characters can be written'. Can such an artificial language in fact ever develop into a real language in daily use? Or must public languages grow spontaneously from the grass roots if they are to endure? In time, no doubt, the grass does force its way up through the cracks in the paving stones; that is precisely Mao's reason for laying down new paving stones. For an imposed language needs to be renewed and reinvigorated just as much as one which has grown naturally out of the common conversation of the people.

But when silence has once fallen upon a political community, it takes time to re-learn the necessary skills, to pick up the threads of the conversation. In the case of Soviet Russia, the old Marxist–Leninist rhetoric is still enthroned as the official language, but it is used only by party officials on ceremonial occasions. It has long ceased to answer the needs of the people, if it ever did, because the party has never allowed it to grow and change with the times.

The lesson to be learnt from the great moral failures of history, the global cautionary tales, is that we should subject all rhetoric to thorough and continuing criticism, not that we should try to avoid rhetoric altogether. The antithesis between doctrine and practice, between ideology and problem-solving, is basically a false one. This is the point which, for example, Noam Chomsky struggles to make in *American Power and the New Mandarins.*[24] The New Deal Liberals who have largely controlled American foreign policy since the war proclaimed themselves as pragmatists operating in a post-ideological framework. Yet in fact they were living on a powerful ideological tradition which appeared to be dead only because it was neither openly expounded nor openly criticised. Chomsky's attack on that tradition and the policies which it inspired may be shallow and distorted; yet the counter-rhetoric to which his criticism amounts has had a considerable influence because it attacks largely undefended positions. He has had the advantage of surprise.

The choice is not between rhetoric – with all that word's connotations of exaggeration, sentimentality and outright falsification – and a calm, businesslike attention to political arrangements. The choice is between a new rhetoric and the revival or reassertion of an old rhetoric. When Baldwin claimed that he disliked rhetoric and preferred 'plain, unadorned statements of cases', he was merely expressing a preference for his own brand of rhetoric – an intimate, unbuttoned manner which, along with Roosevelt's fireside chats, has developed into the prevailing political style of the age of radio and television. The politician who fails to understand this point will sooner or later be deprived of the authority to attend to his nation's political arrangements, calmly or otherwise. It is for this reason that the greatest politicians have always striven to master the craft of self-projection, as an actor strives to learn how to throw his voice to the gallery. These men, so unalike in everything but energy and ambition, have often been conspicuously lacking in natural talent for the task; we recall Churchill's speech impediment, the squeaky voices of Lincoln and Bismarck, the absurd grandiloquence of Disraeli's maiden speech, the shy manner and stilted delivery of the Kennedy brothers when young. In contrast, many others have possessed a superlative natural eloquence – Chatham, Clemenceau, Trotsky, Lenin, Stevenson, Lloyd George, Bevan, Iain Macleod. Yet all have realised the essential part played by rhetoric in the accomplishment of great political enterprises.

The mention of Lincoln's speeches may today evoke the image of a highflown biblical tone, abstract both in style and content. In fact, this biblical tone was much more familiar to his audience than it would be today, certainly more familiar then than the classical rhetoric of Calhoun or the close-knit political argument of the Federalist Papers. Moreover, Lincoln *achieved* his audience by his direct, colloquial style. In his early days on the stump in Illinois he had a name for homely, even bawdy parables. When he came to handle abstract ideas – slavery, state rights, the indissolubility of the union – he did so in an easy, down-to-earth fashion; there was no attempt at elegant synthesis, no straining for conclusions. He laid out ideas and emotions, both complementary and opposed, with the simplicity of a man laying bricks. Lincoln would say in effect: 'This is what you feel. You feel it very strongly. So do I. But this is what the other side feel.

They feel as strongly as we do. We believe that they are wrong for this and this reason. But we must respect them. We must listen to them. And they must listen to us.' In his great speech at the Cooper Institute[25] Lincoln attains a magnificent reasonableness, so cogent, so attentive, that one feels that the opinion of everyone, not only in the hall but in the entire political community, has been considered, respected and answered. This handling, with all its delicacy and dignity, is essentially conversational. As Carl Sandburg puts it: 'He talked to thousands of people as if he and another man were driving in a buggy across the prairie, exchanging their thoughts.'

Lincoln never lost his grip on this conversational tone; to the end of his life his speeches set out the various political considerations, granting full weight to his opponents' views, sharing his perplexities with his audience. Yet as the years went by, the moral imperative became stronger, more concrete; the sight of 'ten or a dozen slaves shackled together with irons' is 'a continued torment to me'.[26] He had always believed that 'if slavery is not wrong, nothing is wrong'.[27] But there was an increasing weight in his statements of that belief, as if he thought it necessary not merely to make his own position clear but to make a monumental gesture for the health of the polity. The day after Richmond was taken, Lincoln walked in triumph through the streets, surrounded by a great crowd of cheering Negroes, waving bonnets and handkerchiefs, and singing 'Glory to God! glory! glory!' in honour of the man who had set them free. According to the *Atlantic Monthly* of the time:

> The walk was long, and the President halted a moment to rest. 'May de good Lord bless you, President Linkum!' said an old Negro, removing his hat and bowing, with tears of joy rolling down his cheeks. The President removed his own hat and bowed in silence; but it was a bow which upset the forms, laws, customs and ceremonies of centuries. It was a death-shock to chivalry and a mortal wound to caste. 'Recognise a nigger! Fough!' A woman in an adjoining house beheld it, and turned from the scene in unspeakable disgust.[28]

Coming from a man of Lincoln's caution and experience, this gesture could only be a deliberate one; a gesture made in the most public circumstances possible at a dramatic moment of history and therefore intended to be seen, remembered and imitated. It is in this sense the gesture of an actor; and it must have helped to provoke the response only a few months later of the half-crazed John Wilkes Booth, that other actor who thought he was avenging the south. In fact Lincoln's murder brings home to us the full daring of that gesture in Richmond; for nobody knew better than Lincoln himself the depth of the feelings which the gesture embodied, the bitterness of the hatred which it was bound to inflame. For thirty years he had carefully husbanded the trust of many people whose views were basically opposed to his, not by concealing his own views but by granting public audience and respect to theirs. Now with this single gesture he expends that trust and the authority which it gave him; he comes out into the open, he makes it clear that his policy will at last give full expression to those of his feelings which have for so long been kept in check by political compromise. In short, he makes a moral gesture. This gesture is not merely a reassertion of the axiom in the Declaration of Independence that *all* men are created equal, and an assertion that the United States can survive as a nation only upon that principle; it is also a recognition that, while political activity may be, must be, a business of reconciling and balancing, the politician is still a man and not a computer. The politician cannot in the last resort pretend neutrality towards moral issues. Nor can he pretend that his own character and bearing are irrelevant to the business. He cannot ignore the spotlight. When he takes off his hat, it is a political event, but when he makes a political decision he may also be making a personal moral choice. It is the peculiarity of his trade that it allows him no real distinction between public and private life. His is a world of words and gestures which have to stand for real facts and feelings; and he consciously puts these words into his own mouth, like a ventriloquist with a dummy. He is an actor. 'Though I sit down now, the time will come when you will hear me.'[29] To be heard, that is the politician's task; and political history is a story of the gaining and losing of audiences. It is the story of a theatre.

Epilogue

THE MORAL RISKS OF LIFE ON THE STAGE

It was Thespis, first of a long line, who broke away one fine day during the feasts of Bacchus from out of the ranks of the austerely chanting chorus, in order to mime and to declaim with real gestures and real cries the anguish of the protagonist. (What an evening: I am shaking as I tell you all this. How I should love to have been there!)

That was a true first night. The only one, in fact.

Venerable Solon, Master of the City, bearded and leaning on his staff, came to see him after the performance, to what corresponded to back-stage at the time. He studied the monster with silent curiosity, suspiciously, and then cried out, striking the ground with his stick:

'But if you can lie like that and arouse our pity for no reason, will not our magistrates (he meant the politicians) and our merchants learn to do it too?'

Worthy Solon! How ingenuous he was! (Or how well he pretended to be, you can never tell with Greeks.) It was many a day – long before the first actor – since politicians and businessmen had first learnt to sing that tune. . . .

Jean Anouilh: *Letter to a young girl*

Notes

PROLOGUE

1 Raymond Aron, *La Révolution Introuvable*, Paris, 1968 (translated in *Encounter*, December 1968).
2 *ibid*.
3 Alexis de Tocqueville (Eds J. P. Mayer and A. P. Ker), *Recollections*, London and New York, 1970, p. 53.
4 Robert Brustein, 'A Night at the Symposium', in *Revolution as Theatre*, New York, 1971.
5 Profile of Roel van Duyn, *The Observer*, 16 May 1971.
6 Brustein, 'A Night at the Symposium', p. 18.
7 Walter Bagehot, *The English Constitution*, London (World's Classics Edition) 1928, p. 7.
8 J. McGinniss, *The Selling of the President*, New York, 1968/ London 1970.
9 Lord Halifax, *Works*, Oxford, 1912, p. 54.
10 Edmund Burke, First Letter on a Regicide Peace, *Works*, London, 1808–13, vol. 8, p. 80.

ACT I

i. Towards a New Theory
1 Alexis de Tocqueville, *Séances et Travaux de l'Académie des Sciences Morales et Politiques*, March–April 1852 (translated in *Encounter*, January 1971).
2 Lord Acton, *The History of Freedom and Other Essays*, London, 1907, p. 3.
3 James Mill, *Fragment on Mackintosh*, London, 1870, p. 25.
4 Karl Popper, *The Open Society* (4th ed.), London and New York, 1962, vol. 2, ch. 20(ii).
5 Thomas Kuhn, *The Structure of Scientific Revolutions* (2nd ed.), Chicago, 1970.
6 F. A. Hayek, 'The Primacy of the Abstract', in Arthur Koestler

(Ed.), *Beyond Reductionism*, London and New York, 1969, pp. 309–34.

7 See the *Discourses*, III, 19–23, especially 21; also *The Prince*, XVII.

8 V. I. Lenin, *One Step Forward, Two Steps Back*, Selected Works vol. 1, London, 1947, p. 346.

9 A. R. J. Turgot, *Oeuvres*, Paris, 1913, vol. 1, pp. 215–16 (translated by Walker Stephens, London, 1895, pp. 159–60).

10 *ibid.*, p. 202 (my translation).

11 Condorcet, *Outlines of an historical view of the Progress of the Human Mind*, translated London, 1795, p. 298.

12 *ibid.*, p. 366.

13 Andrei Amalrik, interview in the *Daily Telegraph*, 29 July 1970.

14 Beatrice Webb, *My Apprenticeship*, London, 1926, p. xiv.

15 Pascal, *Pensées*, II, 162.

16 This problem is particularly well discussed in Bertrand de Jouvenel's *The Art of Conjecture*, London and New York, 1967.

17 Aneurin Bevan, *In Place of Fear*, London, 1952/New York, 1953, p. 13.

ii. The Theatre of Embarrassment

1 *Sunday Times*, 10 October 1971.

2 Harold Macmillan, *The Blast of War*, London and New York, 1967, pp. 325–6.

3 Eldridge Cleaver, Essay in *The New Revolutionaries*, New York, 1968.

4 J. P. Plamenatz, *Consent, Freedom and Political Obligation*, Oxford, 1968, p. 11.

5 Bevan, *In Place of Fear*, p. 55.

6 *ibid.*

7 All quotations taken from a speech given by Papadopoulos in Thessaloniki on 28 August 1971.

8 *Cambridge Journal*, 1940.

9 Richard Heller, 'East Fulham Revisited', *Journal of Contemporary History*, vol. 6, no. 3, 1971.

10 R. D. Laing, *The Politics of Experience*, London and New York, 1967, pp. 12, 22.

11 Interview in *Gambit, International Theatre Review*, vol. 5, p. 17.

12 R. D. Laing and A. Esterson, *Sanity, Madness and the Family*, London and New York, 1970.

iii. The Political Actor

1 Disraeli, *Endymion*, London, 1880, ch. XCVIII.
2 F. S. Oliver, *The Endless Adventure*, London, 1930–5. The Introduction to this work was later published separately under the title *Politics and Politicians*, London, 1934.
3 W. S. Churchill, *The Gathering Storm*, London, 1948, p. 173.
4 Leo Amery, *My Political Life*, London, 1953, vol. 1, p. 271.
5 Oliver, *Politics and Politicians*, p. 75.
6 V. S. Naipaul, *The Mimic Men*, London, 1967, p. 228.
7 *ibid.*, p. 250.
8 Sigmund Freud and William C. Bullitt, *Thomas Woodrow Wilson: a psychological study*, London and New York, 1967.
9 Anthony Storr *et al.*, *Churchill: Four Faces and the Man*, London and New York, 1969.
10 W. S. Churchill, *Savrola*, London, 1900.
11 Martin Gilbert, *Winston S. Churchill*, London, 1971, vol. 3, p. 745.
12 Churchill, *The Gathering Storm*, pp. 526–7.
13 John Morley, *Life of William Ewart Gladstone*, London, 1903, vol. 2, p. 256.
14 Henry Fairlie, *The Life of Politics*, London and New York, 1968, p. 45.
15 Viscount Bolingbroke (Ed. A. Hassall), *Letters on the Spirit of Patriotism*, Oxford, 1926, pp. 19–20.
16 W. H. Auden, *The Dyer's Hand*, London and New York, 1963, p. 137.
17 Fénelon, *Directions pour la Conscience d'un roi*, Paris, 1748.
18 Bertrand de Jouvenel, *Pure Theory of Politics*, Cambridge, 1963, p. 9.
19 Jean-Jacques Rousseau (Ed. E. Barker), *Social Contract* (translated by Gerald Hopkins), London, 1947, vol. 2, p. 7.
20 Jouvenel, *Pure Theory of Politics*, p. 9.
21 Anthony Powell, *The Military Philosophers*, London and New York, 1968, pp. 53–4.
22 *ibid.*, pp. 183–4.
23 Stephen E. Ambrose, *The Supreme Commander: The War Years of General Dwight D. Eisenhower*, New York, 1970/London, 1971.
24 Murray Kempton, in *Esquire*, September 1967.
25 *ibid.*
26 Murray Kempton, in the *Spectator*, 11 April 1969.

27 Paul Foot, *The Rise of Enoch Powell*, London, 1969.
28 David Watt, in the *Financial Times*, 4 December 1969.
29 'A Conservative', in *The Times*, 2 April 1964.

iv. The High Comedy

  1 Tocqueville, *Recollections*, p. 67.
  2 Michael Oakeshott, *Rationalism in Politics*, London and New York, 1962, p. 127.
  3 Raymond Aron, *The Industrial Society*, New York, 1967/ London, 1968, p. 5.
  4 *ibid.*
  5 Adam Smith, quoted in F. S. Oliver, *Politics and Politicians*, p. 76.
  6 F. S. Oliver, *op. cit.*
  7 Ian Gilmour, *The Body Politic*, London, 1969.
  8 Molière, *Le Misanthrope* (translated by R. Wilbur), London, 1958, lines, 35–8.
  9 *ibid.*, 65–8.
 10 *ibid.*, 1553–68.
 11 *ibid.*, 146–66.
 12 *ibid.*, 1133–62.
 13 Rousseau, *Oeuvres*, Paris, 1821, vol. III, p. 50 (author's translation).
 14 Emile Faguet, *Rousseau contre Molière*, Paris, 1912.
 15 Edmund Burke, *Reflections on the French Revolution, Works*, vol. V, p. 158.
 16 Rousseau, *ibid.*, p. 53 (my translation).
 17 Fabre d'Eglantine, *op. cit.*
 18 Michael Oakeshott, *Rationalism in Politics*, London, 1962, p.23.
 19 Burke, *Reflections. . .*, p. 306.
 20 *ibid.*, p. 128.

ACT II

i. Novelty and Sentiment

  1 V. I. Lenin, *What Is to be Done?*, *Selected Works*, London, 1947, vol. 1, p. 170.
  2 *ibid.*, p. 174.
  3 *ibid.*, p. 126.
  4 *ibid.*, p. 229.

5 *ibid.*, p. 243.
6 *ibid.*
7 Georg Lukács, *History and Class Consciousness*, London, 1971.
8 *ibid.*, p. 51.
9 *ibid.*, p. 316.
10 *ibid.*, p. 320.
11 *ibid.*, p. 329.
12 Interview with Yvon Bourdet, 16 April 1971, in *L'homme et la société*, no. 20, Paris, 1971.
13 Herbert Marcuse, *Negations*, London and New York, 1968, p. 168.
14 A. Pozzolini, *Antonio Gramsci*, London, 1970, p. 29.
15 Joan Robinson, 'Problems of War and Peace' (1937), reprinted in *The Cambridge Mind*, London, 1970.
16 Douglas Jay, *The Socialist Case*, London, 1946, p. 258.
17 J. K. Galbraith, *The Affluent Society*, New York, 1961/London, 1962, p. 213.
18 Jo Grimond, 'Reassessing the Priorities of the Left', in *The Times*, 15 September 1971.
19 Edward Boyle, *The Politics of Education*, London, 1971, p. 89.
20 Popper, *The Open Society*, vol. 1, p. 4.
21 *ibid.*, p. 22.
22 *ibid.*, p. 23.
23 *ibid.*
24 *ibid.*, p. 24.
25 *ibid.*, p. 172.
26 *ibid.*
27 *ibid.*, p. 175 (my italics).
28 *ibid.*
29 *ibid.*, vol. 2, p. 24.
30 *ibid.*, p. 25, and see also note 61 to that chapter.
31 J. H. Plumb, *The Death of the Past*, London and New York, 1969, p. 59.
32 *ibid.*, p. 60.
33 *ibid.*
34 Popper, *The Open Society*, vol. 2, p. 60.
35 *ibid.*, vol. 1, p. 112.
36 *ibid.*, vol. 2, p. 136; Burke, *Thoughts and Details on Scarcity, Works*, vol. 7, p. 404; Marx, *Capital* (Everyman edition), p. 343 (note 1).

37 The *Spectator*, 5 May 1967.

38 Stuart Hampshire, *Modern Writers and Other Essays*, London, 1969, p. 165.

39 See in particular, Leo Strauss, *Natural Right and History*, Chicago, 1953; Peter J. Stanlis, *Edmund Burke and the Natural Law*, Ann Arbor, 1958; Francis Canavan, *The Political Reason of Law, Edmund Burke*, Durham (North Carolina), 1960; Burleigh Wilkins, *The Problem of Burke's Political Philosophy*, Oxford, 1967.

40 Canavan, *The Political Reason of Edmund Burke*, p. 19.

41 Harold Laski, *Political Thought from Locke to Bentham*, London and New York, 1920, pp. 236–7.

42 Alfred Cobban, *Edmund Burke and the Revolt Against the Eighteenth Century*, London, 1929.

43 Charles Parkin, *The Moral Basis of Burke's Political Thought*, Cambridge, 1956, p. 5.

44 Burke, Speech on the Reform of Representation in the House of Commons, 7 May 1782, *Works*, vol. 10, p. 99.

45 Burke, *Reflections. . .*, p. 438.

46 Russell Kirk, *The Conservative Mind*, London, 1954, p. 32.

47 Burke, *Reflections . . .*, p. 39.

48 This is perhaps best done by Charles Parkin in *The Moral Basis of Burke's Political Thought*.

49 Burke, *Reflections . . .*, pp. 124, 35–6.

50 *ibid.*, p. 168.

51 Plumb, *The Death of the Past*, p. 60.

52 Burke, *Reflections . . .*, p. 60

53 *ibid.*, p. 168.

54 *ibid.*, pp. 100, 352–3.

55 *ibid.*, p. 175.

56 *ibid.*, p. 339.

57 *ibid.*, p. 285.

58 *ibid.*, p. 306.

59 *ibid.*, p. 301.

60 *ibid.*, p. 259.

61 *ibid.*, p. 247.

62 *ibid.*, p. 284.

63 Burke, Letter to the Sheriffs of Bristol, *Works*, vol. 3, p. 183.

64 Isaiah Berlin, *Two Concepts of Liberty*, Oxford and New York, 1958, p. 103.

65 Burke, Speech on the Oeconomical Reform, *Works*, vol. 3, p. 344.
66 Burke, *Reflections* . . ., p. 196.
67 Popper, *The Open Society*, vol. 1, p. 112.
68 Burke, *Reflections* . . ., p. 184.
69 *ibid.*
70 *ibid.*, p. 122.
71 *ibid.*
72 *ibid.*, p. 123.
73 *ibid.*, p. 198.
74 *ibid.*, pp. 307–8.
75 As Canavan points out in *The Political Reason of Edmund Burke*, pp. 177–8.
76 Burke, *Reflections* . . ., p. 173.
77 Burke, Letter to William Smith, *Works*, vol. 9, p. 402.
78 Burke, *Reflections* . . ., p. 286.
79 See the Profile of Danny McGarvey by Helen Lawrenson in the *Sunday Times*, 17 October 1971.
80 Burke, *Reflections* . . ., pp. 166–7.
81 See above, pp. 69–70.
82 *The Times*, 6 September 1971.
83 F. S. L. Lyons, *Ireland Since the Famine*, London, 1971, p. 370.
84 W. B. Yeats, 'Easter 1916', *Collected Poems* (2nd ed.), London, 1950, p. 202.
85 *ibid.*
86 Thomas Pakenham, *The Year of Liberty*, London and New York, 1969, pp. 344–6.
87 *ibid.*, p. 386 (note 1).
88 Burke, *Reflections* . . ., p. 303.
89 William S. Rubin, *Dada and Surrealist Art* (quoting Tristan Tzara), New York, 1968/London 1969, p. 10.
90 Thomas Carlyle, *The French Revolution* (centenary edition), London 1937, vol. 2, p. 66.
91 Hugh Thomas, *Cuba, or the Pursuit of Freedom*, London and New York, 1971, p. 826.
92 *ibid.*, p. 256.
93 *ibid.*, p. 829.
94 *ibid.*, p. 848.
95 *ibid.*, p. 850.

96 30 December 1918, in *Rosa Luxemburg on the Spartacus Programme*, London (Merlin Press), 1971, passim.
97 *The Guardian*, 4 October 1971.
98 George Orwell, *Animal Farm* (Penguin edition), London, 1971, p. 36.
99 *ibid.*, p. 40.
100 Speech, 6 May 1924, published in *On England*, London, 1926.
101 Speech, 6 March 1925, in *On England*; see also the other speeches in this volume and in *Service of our Lives*, London, 1937.
102 Speech, 6 March 1925.
103 Charles de Gaulle, *The Army of the Future*, London, 1940.
104 *ibid.*, pp. 29–30.
105 *ibid.*, p. 20.
106 Elie Kedourie, *Nationalism*, London and New York, 1960.
107 Mazzini, *Ai giovani d'Italia* (new edition), Rome, 1887, p. 6.
108 Cobban, *Edmund Burke and the Revolt Against the Eighteenth Century*, p. 273.
109 Burke, *Reflections . . .*, pp. 24–5.
110 Tocqueville, *Recollections*, pp. 63–4.
111 Burke, *Reflections . . .*, p. 79.
112 *ibid.*, p. 131.
113 *ibid.*, p. 198.
114 *ibid.*, p. 309.
115 Burke, Fourth Letter on a Regicide Peace, *Works*, vol. 9, pp. 117–18.
116 Burke, Letter to a Member of the National Assembly, *Works*, vol. 6, pp. 34–5.
117 *ibid.*, p. 34.
118 Quoted in L. B. Namier, *Avenues of History*, London and New York, 1952, p. 49.
119 Stuart Hampshire, *Modern Writers and other Essays*, London, 1969, p. 165.
120 Burke, *Reflections . . .*, pp. 390–1.
121 *ibid.*, pp. 231–2.

ii. The Language of Change
1 Oakeshott, *Rationalism in Politics*, p. 127.
2 R. H. S. Crossman, *The Charm of Politics*, London, 1958, p. 138.
3 Oakeshott, *Rationalism in Politics*, pp. 125–6.
4 *ibid.*

5 Alexis de Tocqueville, *L'ancien régime et la Révolution* (translated by H. Reeve), London, 1856, p. 116.
6 I. L. Gower, *The Face Without a Frown*, London, 1944, p. 68.
7 Tocqueville, *L'ancien régime et la Révolution*, p. 270.
8 Harold Macmillan, *Reconstruction*, London, 1933.
9 Harold Macmillan, *The Middle Way*, London, 1938.
10 Macmillan, *Reconstruction*, p. 16.
11 *ibid.*, p. 21.
12 *ibid.*, p. 77.
13 Macmillan, *The Middle Way*, p. 37.
14 *ibid.*, p. 257.
15 Macmillan, *Reconstruction*, p. 8.
16 *ibid.*
17 Macmillan, *Reconstruction*, pp. 32–3.
18 N.E.C. Statement to Conference, Brighton, 1969.
19 *Sunday Mirror*, 2 November 1969.
20 Macmillan, *Reconstruction*, p. 3.
21 Macmillan, *The Middle Way*, p. 304.
22 *ibid.*, p. 310.
23 *ibid.*
24 *ibid.*
25 Samuel Brittan, *Steering the Economy* (originally entitled *The Treasury Under the Tories, 1951–64*, London, 1964), London, 1971, p. 14.
26 *ibid.*, pp. 15–16.
27 James Burnham, *The Managerial Revolution*, New York, 1941.
28 *Sunday Times*, 5 April 1964.
29 Tocqueville, *Recollections*, p. 170.
30 For the details of these events, see J. E. S. Hayward, 'Presidential Suicide by Plebiscite: De Gaulle's Exit, April 1969', in *Parliamentary Affairs*, 1969.
31 *The Sun*, 3 March 1971.
32 Enoch Powell, *Saving in a Free Society*, London, 1967, p. 132.
33 Speech at Bromsgrove, 6 July 1963, published in *A Nation Not Afraid*, London, 1970.

Finale
1 Samuel Beckett, *Proust*, London and New York, 1965, p. 28.
2 *ibid.*, p. 64.

Notes

3 Lionel Trilling, *The Liberal Imagination*, London (Peregrine edition), 1970, p. 11.

4 Interview with Henry Fairlie, 1963, quoted in *The Life of Politics*, p. 16.

5 Yeats, 'The Second Coming', *Collected Poems*, pp. 210–11.

6 John Raymond (Ed.), *The Baldwin Age*, London, 1960.

7 George Steiner, *In Bluebeard's Castle*, London and New York, 1971, p. 87.

8 *ibid.*

9 *ibid.* p. 94.

10 Collection Sir Edmund Bacon, exhibited in *The Shock of Recognition* at the Hague and the Tate Gallery, 1971.

11 Southey, *Colloquies*, London, 1829, vol. 7, p. 170 (quoted by Raymond Williams in *Culture and Society*, London, 1958).

12 Ephesians, ii, 12.

13 Disraeli, *Sybil*, vol. 2, ch. 5.

14 Communist Manifesto, London, Penguin edition, 1967, p. 78.

15 *ibid.*, pp. 120–1.

16 *What Does Spartacus Want?* reprinted in *Rosa Luxemburg on the Spartacus Programme*, London (Merlin Press) 1971, p. 37.

17 Communist Manifesto, 3, 1, a.

18 Alan Watkins, 'Mr Heath's Manager', *New Statesman*, 2 July 1971.

19 Disraeli, *Sybil*, vol. 4, ch. 14.

20 *Ibid.*, vol. 6, ch. 13.

21 George Steiner, *Language and Silence*, London and New York, 1967, p. 132.

22 *Ibid.*, pp. 73–4.

23 K. S. Karol, 'Conversations in Russia', *New Statesman*, 1 January 1971.

24 Noam Chomsky, *American Power and the New Mandarins*, London and New York, 1969.

25 27 February 1860.

26 Letter to Joshua Speed, 24 August 1855.

27 Letter to A. G. Hodges, 4 April 1864.

28 *Atlantic Monthly*, May 1865, quoted in *Lincoln's Letters and Speeches* (Ed. James Boyce), London 1894, pp. 231–2.

29 Disraeli's Maiden Speech to the House of Commons, 7 December 1837.

Index

268